The Reluctant Queen: The Story of Esther

Reluctant Queen is the rare plotline that not only matches but perhaps outshines the story of Esther in the scripture. Lin Wilder has proven to be an exceptionally skilled writer, able to handle both deep human connection and incredible action sequences around this sensitive matter, effectively imparting a heavily important message of humanity out into the world. She successfully captivates her readers with her expertise in both the scripture and the Jewish tradition and culture.

LONDON BOOK REVIEW

Wilder does an excellent job of fleshing out the society and finding a way to tie the famous story of the Persian Wars into the less well-known history of Purim as found in the Biblical *Book of Esther*. The highlight of the novel is Xerxes and his catastrophic descent into self-delusional madness thanks to his near limitless power. If the hand of God seems strong in the book, it's because the hand of God is believed to be strong in antiquity. There is nothing preachy and certainly nothing foreshadowing Christianity/Catholicism. Anyone, religious or secular, interested in reading about this period can enjoy this book.

CATHOLIC READS

plausible liars

plausible liars

A DR. LINDSEY McCALL MEDICAL MYSTERY

Lin Wilder

Plausible Liars

Lin Wilder

ISBN: 9798218297305
Library of Congress Control Number: 2023919320

Wilder Books

To Father Dan

The spirit distinctly says that in later times some will turn away from the faith and will heed deceitful spirits taught by demons through plausible liars.

—St. Paul, 1 Timothy

"But Lin, I thought that's what novelists *do*. They make the impossible, the incomprehensible, real. So readers can walk in the shoes of characters so far outside their own lived experience that they can get it."

That was my friend Paul's reply to my ten-minute whine about this new novel I was trying to write. Our conversation took place sometime during the summer of 2019. And for the next year, I flailed about, researching and working to create the story you're about to read. Finally, the following summer, I listened to my husband, John, who, after hearing a protracted version of that whine, advised, "Quit. This isn't your story. It's someone else who asked that you write it. Instead, write the book you would have written if Father Dan had never asked you to write this."

Being me, my first response to John was, "What? Quit?" But later that day, I was busily and, I might add, quite happily, working on *The Reluctant Queen: The Story of Esther.*

But *Plausible Liars* and its characters continued to lurk in the back of my mind. Joey/Zoey Carmichael and Dr. T. haunted me because these were the characters I needed to do a deep dive into. Enough that they could be felt, appreciated, even loved.

No matter how we euphemize it, this isn't a pleasant subject to think or read about. That dis-ease accounts for the absolutism of the defendants and practitioners of gender fluidity, the intransigence against any crack in the wall of certitude. And for those of us "on the other side," it's far more preferable to keep our heads down and refuse to accept that such beliefs are plausible. That is precisely what I was doing before my friend Father Dan's insistence that I write this story.

Four years ago, easily accessible information on transgenderism was scarce. Today, it's ubiquitous, with a vast selection of podcasts, books, and articles. With all the available information and opinions, it's tempting to think we understand how we got here, to trace its genesis back to the infamous sexual revolution, the rise of feminism, and the institutionalization of equality as a right. But those are merely consequences of the disorder unleashed on Creation and all creatures by our first parents.

Nothing I've ever written has been as brutally taxing as this story. There are hundreds of reasons for that, but I've come to understand that fear is the primary one.

I didn't come to fiction until I'd had decades of experience with writing and publishing non-fiction. The two are worlds apart. While writing is always taxing work, a never-ending search for clarity and coherence, nonfiction requires far less from the author than fiction. Fiction writers are responsible for creating characters: they must sit beside us as we read the story. If they aren't, we haven't done our job.

Therefore, writing about Dr. T.'s character forced me to plunge into places I had no interest in going. A person like her would not have come into this beautiful world looking for a kid to control, manipulate, or seduce. Something must have created massive wounds in her psyche.

Writing *Plausible Liars* has reintroduced me to the inescapable fact that delving deep into what we know is unnatural and indefensible forces a plunge into the problem of evil.

What is it?

Why does it exist?

Then we must look at it and name it.

If, after reading this novel, you're interested in learning more, I've added an abridged list of the sources I found most helpful.

Lindsey's breath of relief stuck in her throat. She felt pinned to the chair and tried to look everywhere but at that table, at those seven faces filled with pure, unadulterated malevolence.

What are the odds? A billion to one? Two indictments for murder in four years?

But her gaze was drawn like a magnet to the prosecution table. Zach Cunningham's interrogation had been easy; how could she have thought the worst was over?

Time seemed to slow as she watched Prosecutor Emilio Martinez push back his chair, gather some notes and rise. Only after he was standing did he look at her and smile. A wolfish grin stayed on his face as he walked to the witness stand where she sat.

As he sauntered over, Lindsey forced herself to study his shoes. They were Stacy Adams loafers. She was surprised to see them because they were her husband's favorite brand of shoes. She thought about that coincidence as she watched the shoes draw inexorably closer.

This is just a man, McCall. A man with great power over you and Kate, for sure, but just like Rich, he got up this morning, showered, shaved, and slipped into those loafers. He probably kissed his wife and kids goodbye. Then, he headed out the door, got into his car, and onto the freeway. Preparing to continue his battle of words. Words that were crafted to persuade twelve men and women of a conspiracy of hate.

Lindsey thought about the whiteboard with its lists of strengths and weaknesses, sitting in the great room of Kate's house. She also thought about the hours spent on that whiteboard. And finally, she recalled the two nights she and Kate spent in jail. They were frightening, terrifying even, but they'd survived.

Was this any different from the first cardiac catheterization she had done?

Or the last?

The terrible lesson was that she could do everything perfectly and make no mistakes; still, catastrophe could happen.

For the millionth time, Lindsey reflected on Nate Morrison, the oil executive who'd been persuaded by his internist to have a cardiac cath. Nate Morrison was a vigorous Houston oil exec who had been referred by his internist during his annual physical. He had no symptoms, but his doctor wanted it done to ensure his coronaries were clean. He had perfectly healthy coronaries but began to fibrillate just as they finished the procedure and could not return to normal sinus rhythm. He died at age fifty-three because of an overzealous internist who did not appreciate the risk of subjecting his patient to a cardiac cath. It was the last time she had set foot into a cath lab.

Lindsey took a deep breath and let her eyes travel up to Martinez's coffee-brown trousers, well-fitting jacket, and striped light blue shirt with a red striped tie. Then she locked onto his dark gaze. His eyes were almost entirely black.

"This isn't the first time you've been convicted of unintentionally murdering someone, is it, Dr. McCall?"

Of course, he would open with that; he'd be a fool not to.

Lindsey surprised herself with her calmness, but as she opened her mouth to reply, was stopped by a thunderous cry.

"Objection!"

CHAPTER ONE

October 16, one year earlier

Dear Diary,

I found you in the campus bookshop yesterday and was psyched at discovering your torn, scuffed-up cover underneath a bunch of half-price books. It felt like fate because I've been wondering how I can get my thoughts organized well enough to explain.

Ms. O'Brien has been talking all semester about the number of writers who recorded their innermost thoughts and fears in diaries or journals. Listening to her talk about Thoreau made me think about doing it, too, even though I misled Ms. O'Brien by quoting him last week in class.

Stupid, I know better than to talk in class, but I felt sorry for her because no one was paying attention to her. Most were either on their phones or staring out the window. So, when she said that Thoreau had lived on Walden Pond for three years, I didn't even think. I blurted out, "Actually, Ms. O'Brien, he lived on Walden Pond for two years and two months."

I could feel my face heat up when she spun around from the board and clapped her hands, "Why, Joey, you're quite right. Thank you." Her smile was so warm and genuine that

I kept talking. "I went to the woods because I wanted to live deliberately, to front only the essential facts of life and see if I could not learn what it had to teach, and not when it came time to die, to discover that I had not lived."

I was as surprised as Ms. O'Brien because I never talk in class. Ever. And now I've made her think I'm smart.

I feel kinda silly writing in a diary because boys aren't supposed to like doing this kind of stuff. But I need to practice telling my story, so my new friends can make sense of it. And maybe writing it will help me make sense of it, too.

So, here goes.

My name is Joey Carmichael. I was born in a tiny little northern California town called—if you can believe this—Strawberry. I have no idea who my father is, but my mom's name is Cassie, Cassie Carmichael. She likes the "CC," thinks it sounds like an actress. I bet I asked a trillion times about my father, but she refused to even utter his name, claiming that speaking his name would call down ruin upon our house. She would say that in a breathy hiss, just like the vampires and witches in the movies she loved to watch.

Mom could have been an actress, as she has told us kids a million times. She certainly has the looks. But she sacrificed that ambition to keep me and the rest of us off the streets. I believed her until—wait, I'm not going there! I am not!

When I was little, I looked exactly like Mom did at age three, then four, then five: freckles, curly red hair, and dimples. She showed me pictures to prove it. I've heard that some kids get stories read to them before bed. Not me. Just about every night, she would bring out that photo album and touch them and then me. "You're going to look just like me, Zoey, honey."

Oh no, Cassie Carmichael, I am not going to look just like you. In fact, by the time I'm done, we won't look like we're in the same genus. OK, diary that might be a slight exaggeration, but you'll see ....

"How dumb can I be? Switching from a physics major to pre-med?" LJ's bright green eyes shone in the light of her laptop. There was no response from her best friend, Morgan, who sat cross-legged, her own laptop open beside the huge physiology textbook she was studying. Morgan's expression was intense and focused. LJ groaned. Still nothing.

"Morgan, are you even here?" Both dogs jumped at LJ's shout.

"Of course I'm here. Where else would I be? You can see me, right?" Her brown eyes were lowered at the two dogs, now sitting at alert. "Max, baby, shhh, it's OK," she whispered. "Nothing to get upset about. It's just LJ's drama queen act. Gus, be still, boy. Everything is fine, just fine."

They were an unlikely pair, Max and Gus. Max was an eighty-five-pound pedigreed red Doberman, and Gus was a forty-one-pound mutt, a strange combination of pug and lab that somehow worked. Max had the purebred Doberman's beautiful, almost regal look: long legs, a lean, muscular torso, and expressive amber eyes. Gus was, well, the exact opposite.

LJ Grayson and Morgan Gardner were just as unlikely a pair. LJ was the biological daughter of Dr. Lindsey McCall. She'd gladly accepted Lindsey's offer to house her and fund her undergraduate education at California Polytechnic State University.

Morgan and LJ had become fast friends the year before while waiting in the mile-long registration line for freshmen who had not made the deadline for online registration.

"You're pretty," Morgan said. "I bet you had a bunch of boyfriends in high school, right?"

Before LJ could reply, Morgan continued. "I know, I'm getting personal way too fast, but I do that when I get nervous, and I'm very nervous right now. I have ASD." Noting LJ's puzzled expression, Morgan explained. "Autistic spectrum disorder … Asperger's, high-functioning autism, take your pick. If you'd prefer another, I have about ten more depending on which DSM the current psychologist uses."

Laughing in delight at Morgan's lack of guile, LJ extended her hand. "I'm Lindsey Grayson, but now I'm LJ for Lindsey Junior because my biological mom's name is also Lindsey. Her husband, Rich, decided that two Lindseys would be too confusing for everyone, most of all him. I live in Pismo Beach but am originally from Friendswood, Texas. Oh, and I'm an alcoholic." *And I'm babbling like a total idiot.*

The tall, awkward, geeky young woman and the short, shapely, lovely young woman grasped hands for support, then doubled over in hilarity, their sides heaving, unaware of the eye rolls around them. They were inseparable from that moment on.

Both dogs settled back down at the sound of Morgan's voice. Mirroring each other's splayed-out positions, the two now lay back-to-back, Max facing LJ and Gus's gaze fixed on Morgan.

After glancing at LJ to ensure she was focused on her studies, Morgan stared back at Gus. The happy little dog had taken to her when she met him. Morgan had never seen antics like Gus performed when greeting his family back home. First, his short legs carried his chunky body in a race down the stairs and across the deck. Then, upon reaching his person, he stopped and ran in tight circles before taking off again, the epitome of exuberance and joy.

But when Morgan and LJ studied, which was almost every night, Gus's preferred place was close to Morgan, like now. Staring into the dog's amber eyes, Morgan felt her unease subside. LJ had been right when she accused Morgan of being somewhere else. She had been acting like she was studying animal physiology, but her mind was that boy—girl-boy—Joey Carmichael. He was a transfer from Chico State, arriving halfway through the first semester, so everyone in her English lit noticed him. Something dark hovered around him. At first, Morgan tried to persuade herself that it was her imagination, but she could see it.

And it was growing.

CHAPTER THREE

November 2, 2019

Dear Diary,

I can't believe it's been over three weeks since I wrote to you. So much has happened. Some good and some not so good.

Here's the good part: Ms. O'Brien asked to see me after class the day I quoted Thoreau. I was super nervous because I was afraid she would ask me to do something I'd hate, like write a story about him or do a stupid talk for the class about why I loved "On Walden Pond."

But it was none of those things. Instead, she invited me to the GLSEN meeting on campus, which happened to be that night. I had no clue what she was talking about but I pretended I did.

Would I be free to attend?

Ha! Let me check my crammed social calendar. How about that? A free night for once! Sure, I can go. By then, I knew what it was: Gay, Lesbian and Straight Educational Network. Diary, that stopped me for a second or three. Am I gay? Can a girl who's decided to become a boy be a lesbian?

Cool stuff but I'm not about to say no at a chance to meet some other kids who might be weird like me.

She even bought me supper at 19 Metro before the meeting. And I was good. Instead of the hamburger and fries that I would have ordinarily stuffed down my throat, I ordered a salad, like her.

And here's the second piece of good news. I invited another student to come to the meeting, too. I hadn't planned to ask her, but she just happened to be standing outside the classroom, waiting for someone. So, I figured she was waiting for her beautiful friend, LJ. I see them together all the time.

So I introduced myself and began talking about stuff, intriguing stuff, even though she's odd. Funny I should call someone weird, right? But she is. I think she might be autistic because she doesn't say much, and she talks in a monotone voice when she does, as if she's reading a script. Now that I think about it, our conversation was pretty one sided. I talked nonstop, and I assumed she was pretending to listen. But Morgan really was listening because when I stopped to breathe, she said I was transgender. She didn't ask, she just said it in the same manner that anyone would say anything. Like "You're a Protestant" or "You're a Catholic," or "You're a Democrat."

No one has ever said anything like that to me. And she didn't back off when I stood there gaping at her like a fool. She didn't cover her mouth and say, "Gee, I didn't mean to notice that you bind your breasts and hack off your hair like a Marine recruit or have a body shaped like a block of wood—a very flabby wood, that is." She just stood there and looked at me as if I wasn't the weirdest person she had ever seen. As if zits and sparse red beards were a natural look.

So I blurted out, "Hey, Morgan, Ms. O'Brien invited me to come to the GLSEN meeting tonight. Would you like to come?"

When I walked into the meeting, Morgan was standing by herself, right by the door. Afterward, she told me about her friend, Dr. Lindsey McCall, head of the Animal Science Center. Morgan suggested that I go over there because Lindsey had twelve Dobermans there. They had heart problems, and Dr. McCall worked on nutritional methods to alleviate their symptoms. She said Dr. McCall was always looking for students to exercise the dogs. Would I like to help her?

Would I? Would I ever! I love dogs, all dogs, but especially Dobermans!

I meant to write a whole lot more—about the bad news, that is—but it's getting late, and I have to study.

Bye for now.

"Hi, Dr. McCall. I'm sorry. Looks like I interrupted your conversation just now. I can come back tomorrow if you like, I just had some free time between classes and wondered if I could walk any of the dogs for you."

Lindsey ended her call and then stood up to face Joey. "That's fine, Joey. My friend and I had to get back to work anyway. How much time do you have? They'd all like a walk before I close up for the day!"

Fourteen Dobermans were kenneled in pairs in the back of her lab, but Joey didn't care, he loved each of them. "Great!" he said, clapping his hands. "Let's get going then!" His broad, freckled face split into a wide grin as he did an about-face to leave her office.

As she followed the teen, Lindsey calculated that he was at least fifty pounds overweight. His skeletal frame was small, and he should weigh about 105 pounds—LJ's weight—not the 160 or 175 pounds it looked like he was carrying. She wondered about his hormone therapy. If he had received a cross-hormone treatment before the onset of puberty, he would not have experienced a growth spurt. Moreover, Joey's excessive weight gain indicated some dosage problems since testosterone should drop body fat, not increase it.

The dogs' frenzied barking put a stop to Lindsey's thoughts. By the time she arrived at the kennels, he already had the first two dogs, a red male named Cyber and a fawn-colored female named Lucky, leashed and was grabbing another two out of a second kennel.

"Joey! Hey, even two of these guys will be a handful! But

I was kidding; we don't have enough time to walk all of them before I close up at six." Lindsey tried to ignore the disappointment on the teen's face as she strode across the vast exercise area to close the kennel door.

Just then, she heard two sets of feet hurrying down the hallway toward the lab. The sound of footsteps was accompanied by her boss Jodi Tamarack's distinctive voice. "Hey, Lindsey, got a sec? I have a postdoc student who would like some time with you. I'll bet you have all kinds of neat trials she could dig into for the remainder of the semester."

Jodi's jeans-clad backside appeared through the hallway door before her tousled mass of curly brown hair and a red plaid flannel shirt. She was walking backward as she talked to the postdoc student behind her. Just as Jodi was about to back into a table loaded with a wide array of glass beakers and other breakables, she turned around.

"Well, that could have been a colossal mess," she said. "Sorry! Lindsey, meet our newest postdoc from UC Davis." Jodi was nearly out of breath. In fact, Dr. Jodi Tamarack, Department Head of the Animal Science Department at Cal Poly, was almost always out of breath, able to cram more words into a shorter space of time than anyone Lindsey had met, and yet she was still oddly calming.

"Dr. Christine Phillips, meet Dr. Lindsey McCall, former head of the cardiac Cath lab at Houston General in the Texas Medical Center and now our esteemed director of animal research."

"Dr. McCall, I'll just take these two outside for about ten minutes or so, OK?"

Somehow, Joey had kept the two leashed Dobermans calm, but with all the activity, they were getting twitchy.

Jodi noticed Joey for the first time. "Oh, please excuse my bad manners, but I didn't know you were here." Then she squinted at him. "Do I know you?" Jodi needed glasses to see any farther than a foot, but she hated wearing them.

Smiling at her clueless boss, Lindsey introduced Joey and then agreed to his ten-minute outing for the two fortunate dogs. "Joey is a sophomore in Animal Science. And no, you haven't met him before."

Jodi and Christine watched the odd-looking teen struggle with the dogs as he fought to get through the doorway. Joey's width with an eighty-plus-pound dog on either side required some juggling.

Jodi turned back to Lindsey, her lips parted as if to speak and her dark eyebrows drawn together in a frown. Cutting off Jodi's question before she could utter it, Lindsey smiled at the tall, thin, newly minted veterinarian. "Welcome, Christine. I can't tell you how delighted I am to meet you. Jodi's right: we have a long list of ongoing studies you can choose from."

She proceeded to deliver her elevator speech, which included a five-minute explanation of how an internationally known interventional cardiologist and researcher walked away to embrace animal research.

Lindsey trudged up the stairs to their Shell Beach home, still ruminating about Joey Carmichael, wondering for the hundredth time about her decision to help him. It had been nearly three months since he'd shown up at the lab just as she was unlocking the doors at 6:30 on a chilly Friday morning. Lindsey had invited him in for coffee and to meet all the dogs. From then on, Joey showed up three or four times a week. With each visit, the teen had divulged more about his life and the consequences of decisions he now regretted.

She was late getting home because Joey had walked back into her lab a little late, the two big dogs' tongues lolling as they panted happily. *He's running with them again!*

"Dr. McCall, I know I'm ten minutes late." Lindsey grinned, shrugged, and didn't mention that he was thirty minutes late. He was panting, too, and sweating like crazy; his shirt was wet and perspiration was dripping off his nose. Swiping his face with his long-sleeved shirt, Joey's face was wreathed in a huge smile, his warm brown eyes dancing. *For once, I don't see that awful sadness. This kid looks like a happy kid, albeit an obese one. The elixir of dogs and kids ....*

"Looks like you took them for a run, Joey. I'll bet they loved that! But, not to worry about the time. I have some data I'm behind on." Her smile grew at the glowing young person; Lindsey realized she loved this kid.

After she and Joey got the two happy Dobies settled in their kennels, Joey looked at her expectantly. Lindsey was momentarily puzzled, then said, "Oh yes, of course, Joey. Hold on for a sec." She half-jogged to her office, opened a drawer, and retrieved a small bottle of pills. Then returned to Joey and handed it to him. "Here you go, Joey."

Somehow she didn't mind being crushed in a sweaty hug as Joey mumbled a teary, "Thank you, Dr. McCall, thank you so much …."

In a long conversation shortly after Joey started coming to work with the dogs, her best friend, Julie Grayson, had explained several experiences she'd had with transgender students. Her advice was classic Julie: treat them like any other teenager. Just understand that these kids—at least the four or so female-to-males and three male-to-females that Julie had coached and taught calculus to—felt trapped in the wrong body. How they reached that perception was a whole other story, one "laden with many layers of rhetoric." Julie ended their conversation by saying that she'd had no experience with kids who had made the decision at Joey's age. "There's probably a lot going on with that kid he doesn't understand."

Although Julie's last comment concerned Lindsey, she had given Lindsey the confidence to continue with Joey as she had been doing and as she'd done when Morgan moved in. She was practical and, at the same time, profoundly wise. "Lindsey, she's a young girl with autism and in that order. Don't let the autism drive your relationship with her."

Lindsey's smile at the Morgan memories broadened when she opened the door and outraced Max and Gus, who nearly knocked her back down the stairs. Then, wagging their tails and wiggling their butts, the two dogs swept all thoughts of Joey Carmichael away.

So happy to see her, Gus began his mad circles on the stone porch, going around and around with dizzying speed. He was dangerously close to the steps but seemed to know how close he could cut it.

The red Doberman and lab/pug mix were an odd couple, just like LJ and Morgan, who stood at the top of the staircase on the main floor of the large home. One was tall, lanky, and subtly attractive, the other small, compact, and a knockout.

"Just in time, Madame," the two parroted. Morgan held a tray with a champagne glass full of something bubbly, while LJ held a plate with something that smelled delicious. "Dinner will be ready in about twenty minutes. Just enough time to enjoy this cocktail and hors d'oeuvres out on the terrace with your husband, eagerly awaiting you, tout de suite." She said all this with an impressive French accent.

Laughing, Lindsey looked up at the two faux French waitresses. "All of us home on a Wednesday night? And you girls preparing dinner? Did I miss a momentous occasion?" Then, taking the rest of the stairs two at a time, the weight from her day fell away.

CHAPTER SIX

December10

Dear Diary,

You'll never guess what happened at the last GLSEN meeting. Morgan was there again, and she saw me elected as president of the chapter!

Wowza!

I thought it was a joke when Michelle—a male-to-female trans junior—nominated me at the previous meeting. Before she entered my name into the running, she turned to wink at me, so I thought it was some kind of dumb initiation thing. But it turned out it was real. I'm now the president, so I get to plan the agenda for our meetings and most likely other stuff I don't know about yet.

Anyway, it's the first office I've ever held, and I'm kinda proud of myself, even though my guess is that everyone else who attends has probably done it before. There are only about fifteen of us, after all.

After the meeting, I had to do my first job as president: clean the room. That meant throwing away everyone's plastic water bottles and residue from the little party they threw for me. That took a while because there were cookie crumbs all over the floor, and I couldn't find a vacuum or a broom. I only found a dust-pan and brush after looking into empty closets and a bunch of cupboards. Annoying!

When I had finished, I was surprised to see Morgan sitting outside on the bench. Assuming she was waiting for LJ, I nodded to her as I walked by, but then she stood up.

"Joey, I was waiting for you because I thought you might like to grab a burger over at the Canyon Café," she said.

I stood there staring at her like a dork for what felt like forever. And Morgan just stared back—no expression on her face and apparently feeling no need to fill the silence with any words. Man, this girl is DIFFERENT.

"Why aren't you going home with LJ?" I asked.

"She's doing some extra work with a study group in organic chem," Morgan replied. "So they'll be at it for another hour and a half or so."

I couldn't believe Morgan was asking me for dinner a second time. I didn't want her to get the wrong idea, but I wasn't interested in dating her, and didn't know how to tell her because I didn't want to hurt the feelings of my only friend on campus.

She must have read my mind because she said, "Joey, this isn't a date. I'm not interested in you sexually. So, you can get rid of any worry about that score." Morgan's varicolored amber eyes bored into my head. I felt like she could see inside my brain and interpret thoughts I didn't know I had. Weird, I know, but maybe she's one of those savants. Like that autistic kid on a TV show I watched when I was a little kid.

After staring at me for another minute, Morgan said, "We are two people grabbing some food. We're friends. That's all."

I thought about her and her comment as we walked across the campus. "We're friends. That's all." Had anyone ever called me their friend? Then I thought about how weird she is. Maybe even more bizarre than me, if that's even possible, and I wondered why I felt so comfortable around her.

"Are you happy?"

I had just taken a big bite of my hamburger when Morgan asked that question. As usual, I didn't know what to say to her. So, I put up my hand and made a show of chewing and wiping my mouth. She had barely touched her food. That's why she's so skinny. She doesn't eat, unlike me, who eats continuously.

Finally, I emptied my mouth, but still didn't know how to answer. Are you happy? What kind of question is that to ask someone?

"Joey, it's a simple question. There are only two possible answers."

I picked up a French fry, but Morgan put her hand on mine and fixed me with those eyes that seemed to penetrate my soul.

"I don't know, Morgan. I don't have any idea what happiness is," I said. Then, right there in front of her and everyone else, I started to cry. But Morgan ignored my blubbering.

"A few weeks ago," she said, "I heard Michelle asking when you would get your top done. You said this month, in a week or so, is that right?"

I nodded. Her emotionless reaction was helping me get control of myself.

"Joey, is this your idea or someone else's?"

She can't know about him. I've never said anything to her—or to anyone else—about him!

"What do you mean?" I asked.

Morgan just sat there, studying me. She acted as if she could have waited for hours.

But as I sat there looking back at her, I smiled. "Can I tell you a secret, Morgan? Something I am happy about?"

Morgan looked surprised but nodded. I told her I was off the testosterone and had started taking estrogen, thanks to her friend, Dr. McCall.

Lindsey gazed out at the Pacific Ocean as she sipped her Prosecco and then looked back at her husband, Rich, who was absently caressing Max.

"It just doesn't get much better than this," he said. "Does it, Dr. McCall?"

They were sitting out on the deck that encircled the second level of the house, affording various ocean viewing areas outside each of the five bedrooms, the great room, and the gourmet kitchen. An overstuffed modular linen couch surrounded a steel fire pit in the eastern corner. In contrast, two oversized brown-and-white chairs with ottomans sat with their backs to the filigreed ocean, a glass table between them. Large area rugs with the same color scheme lay underneath the modular couch and at the entry onto the deck, completing the effect of a living room hovering over the sea.

"For a man over fifty, you're not half bad, Rich Jansen. A girl could do a lot worse than you." Her smile faded, and her expression softened as she regarded the man who had saved her life. "Have I told you lately how much I love you? How grateful I am that you persuaded me to buy this house? Its beauty envelops us, encases us in a splendid cocoon each time we come home to it."

Rich leaned in and kissed her, softly at first and then not so softly.

"None of that, you two. There are minors in the house, after all!" LJ said as she came out carrying a platter with four sizzling rib-eye steaks. Morgan followed with grilled asparagus and a Caesar salad. Setting down her trays, LJ looked at Rich with a raised dark eyebrow.

Smiling, he stood to his full six-foot-two-inch height, making LJ, at just over five feet tall, look like a dwarf. Then, hurrying over to the bar to wash his hands, Rich returned to test each steak by pressing on them with his index finger. "Perfect, LJ!"

Morgan and Lindsey stood to shout. "Bravo!"

Rich was a gourmet cook. During the months when he was recovering from the effects of a shootout in Houston that almost cost him his life, he had taken up cooking. And had become a bit of a snob about it. So, like everything else he had done, Rich decided to become an expert. He devoured cooking books and television shows. In the process, he learned the fundamentals of gourmet cooking and the trivial details that, Rich believed, made the difference between mediocrity and excellence.

Lindsey and Morgan had enjoyed watching LJ's persistent attempts to grill a perfect steak to please the master. Even after at least six attempts that did not pass Rich's standards, she didn't give up. Instead, LJ listened carefully to the long list of apparently insignificant details of grilling a perfect steak, and tonight, it seemed, she had done it.

While the girls carefully placed the sizzling plates and silverware around the glass table, Rich stood next to the firepit, coaxing it to light, fighting the sudden breeze from the Pacific. Then, with a whoosh, it did. Almost instantly, the heat began to push back the chill of the evening ocean air.

They sat, said grace, and dug in. After her first piece of steak, Lindsey cried, "Bravo indeed, LJ. This steak is perfect!" The only sounds for the next twenty minutes were oohs and aahs about the perfectly grilled medium rare steaks, grilled garlic asparagus, and restaurant-quality Caesar salad.

Rich stopped LJ and Morgan from cleaning the table with, "You two did all the work; I'll clean all this up in the morning. I don't have to go into the office."

"Do you guys have to study, or can we continue the party?" Lindsey hoped to prolong the pleasant evening but understood their schedules' rigor. Both girls had heavy course loads in the second semester of their sophomore year. LJ had switched majors twice the previous year but had finally decided on pre-med. Much of Lindsey and Julie's lengthy conversation the week before had centered on LJ's surprising decision to go into medicine. At least, it was a jolt to Lindsey, who had stammered an off-the-cuff reply when Julie asked why she was surprised that her daughter wanted to follow in her footsteps. Lindsey had mumbled something about the focus and determination required in the rigorous pre-med science courses. Julie laughed and asked if she had ever noticed anything *but* persistence and intensity in LJ.

Lindsey's thoughts were cut off by the girls' answer to her suggestion to stay and talk. Her grin was as wide as theirs in response to their unanimous reply that they'd love to, and yes, they could take the night off.

"Just one rule," Lindsey said. "No talking about school!"

"But what else can we talk about? School's our entire life!" LJ cried. Then she slapped herself on the cheek. "Yikes! I hate it when I whine!"

Rich chuckled. "I've lost count of all the movies you two have managed to cram into your tight schedules. How about telling Lindsey and me about some of your favorite films?"

Morgan leaned forward, eager to give her opinion. "He's right, LJ. I bet we've seen at least ten in the last couple of months. *JoJo Rabbit* had it all: satire, dark history, and pathos.

That was the best of them all."

LJ's eyes widened. "You've got to be kidding! What a nutty movie it was. A little kid playing at being a Nazi brownshirt with Adolph Hitler living in his head. And then finding a Jewish girl hiding in the closet? Stupid."

"LJ, it was a *satire* on World War II and Hitler's xenophobic, antisemitic brainwashing of the German people," Morgan muttered.

"*Men in Black: International* was the best of them all," LJ continued, ignoring Morgan. "Tessa Thompson was awesome!"

Noting Morgan's audible accompaniment to her eye roll, Rich looked at Lindsey. "What's the last movie we saw, Linds?"

Lindsey wrinkled her nose. "That weird movie with Matt Damon and practically no one else. *The Martian.* That's the last one we saw."

Lindsey shivered despite the fire's heat. Without missing a beat, Rich got up. He grabbed her a heavy sweater they had brought out in anticipation of getting colder and brought it over to her.

"Mmmm, thanks, babe." Lindsey took the heavy sweater and drew it around her. She glanced at LJ and Morgan, who were mesmerized by the flames in the pit. "Do you two need something warmer, or are you back to worrying about school?"

"Good idea," LJ said. "I'll go in and grab a couple of sweaters. Be right back." She jumped up and hurried toward the door to the great room. Then she stopped and looked back. "Tonight, for once, I'm not worrying about school. Morgan helped me with advanced calculus last night."

Rich and Lindsey turned to Morgan for a response. When Morgan merely returned their scrutiny, Rich smiled. "How did you help LJ last night, Morgan?"

Her thin shoulders shrugged. "I just told her to stop expecting it to make sense. It'll never make sense. There's no logic or reason to quadratic equations, and they can't be applied to reality. Still, they serve as an excellent aid to memory." She grinned. "One of the few advantages of being autistic is you quickly accept that most things, including people, make no sense."

After thinking about her words, Lindsey nodded. "I wish someone had told me that a million years ago when I was in pre-med."

Morgan nodded in agreement, her eyes remaining on the flames. Then she looked up. "Lindsey, you know Joey Carmichael? He's been coming to see you and the dogs, right?"

"Yes, almost every day lately. I was later getting home than planned tonight because he took a couple of the older dogs for a longer-than-expected walk. But I didn't have the heart to get upset with him. They, and certainly Joey, needed the exercise."

LJ returned with the sweaters, and she and Morgan snuggled into them.

"Joey Carmichael. That's a name I haven't heard before," Rich said. "Who is he?"

Lindsey's gaze diverted to the fire's dancing light, and Morgan and LJ exchanged an odd expression. As the seconds ticked by, Rich waited … and wondered why the hair on his neck bristled.

"Joey goes to school with LJ and me," Morgan replied. "He transferred to Cal Poly from Chico State five months ago. He's majoring in animal science, too, so we're in many of the same classes." She hesitated but did not divert her gaze from Rich. While Lindsey continued to stare at the fire, LJ was hanging on her every word. "Joey was born Zoey, a girl, but somewhere around age eight, Zoey decided she didn't want to be female. So, Zoey became Joey and has been on testosterone for years. I've attended a few GLSEN chapter meetings at Cal Poly with Joey."

Seeing Rich's look of confusion, Morgan explained the term. "GLSEN stands for Gay, Lesbian, and Straight Educational Network. But after attending a few meetings, I think the 'and straight' part was added just to *look* inclusive. The conversation at the last meeting concerned gender ideology, identity, and the merits of being non-binary. We also discussed the details of nullification surgery because Chad wants to be Carol and has decided the best way to do that is genital confirmation surgery." Morgan smiled. "The vocabulary is quite intriguing."

Although LJ and Morgan had been best friends for over a year and a half, periodically, she jolted LJ. This was one of those times.

"You've gone to those meetings with Joey?" LJ asked. "And you find this stuff *intriguing*? Are you ..." Sputtering, bewildered, and fearful, LJ searched for the right word. Morgan had not mentioned her friendship with Joey or her attendance at the meetings.

"A lesbian? Non-binary? Thinking of becoming a male? Deciding if I want to be Joey's girlfriend?" Morgan shook her head. "No, none of the above. But I'm concerned enough about Joey to find out what this is all about."

"And have you?" Lindsey asked. She was as fascinated as Rich by the raw, painful honesty of this young woman who had plunged into their lives. Not just honesty but a preternatural insight. Lindsey wanted Morgan's take on this troubled teen who was crawling into her heart and making himself at home.

"Have I what?"

"Figured it all out," LJ said. "Have you?" LJ wondered at her own reaction. Was she jealous that Morgan had this friend? No, she decided, just really surprised that she'd not said anything about Joey. Or had Morgan mentioned it, and LJ just hadn't listened? That was indeed likely.

Either overlooking or not noticing the confusion behind LJ's question, Morgan shrugged. "Yes and no." She paused to stare into the flames. "For some reason—Zoey's mom is the most likely candidate—years ago, Zoey decided she didn't want to be female or become a woman. And obviously, somebody has helped her get the drugs for transitioning. They're pretty expensive. But the drugs haven't worked out all that well because Joey binds his breasts." She paused, thinking, "And I don't think he menstruates. The testosterone would have prevented that from ever happening."

She regarded Lindsey, "Why wouldn't the testosterone have stopped Joey's breasts from growing?"

"He told me he didn't like how the Leuprolide made him feel, so he stopped taking it six or eight months ago. Usually, both drugs are essential to completely stop puberty." Lindsey thought, *A year ago, I didn't even know puberty suppression was a thing. And now …* Her thought was cut off by Morgan's following remark to Rich.

"In one way, I get the attraction of female to male transition. Sex is way more complicated for us than you guys. Guys can walk away from one-night stands." Then she glanced at LJ and back at Lindsey, whose serene but wry smile reflected the truth of Morgan's unfinished observation.

"Having your body changed so drastically is weird. Puberty changes you in every way—emotionally, physically, and psychologically—none of which can be controlled—without drugs, that is. One day your chest is nice and flat, and suddenly these two things appear and grow. You have to wear different underwear to support them, and boys look at you differently. In fact, often they don't look at you at all. They stare. At *them.* So the breast binders stop all that nonsense … excuse the non sequitur." Morgan took a deep breath, then let it out as a whoosh. Her eyes glistened wetly in the reflected light of the fire.

"I don't think Joey has any interest in being a guy. He doesn't affect masculine behaviors or language like other trans guys. He's sweet. And naïve and innocent." Morgan grimaced as a couple of tears escaped and rolled down her cheeks. Thinking of the secret Joey had told her, Morgan said, "Joey's presence in your life was my idea. Maybe not such a good one, but Joey and I had dinner together shortly after he transferred from Chico State. I overheard a conversation between him and some others about Joey's upcoming surgery."

Lindsey frowned. She was surprised because Joey was so happy to get off the testosterone and maybe get back to being a girl again. "Surgery? Don't tell me he's considering a double mastectomy?" Lindsey asked in horror.

"It's not called a mastectomy. It's called a 'top job,'" Morgan said. "He's scheduled to have it sometime this month. But I don't think it's his idea. I think it's someone else's."

Lindsey thought, *Well, that would explain why he appreciates my help. There's someone else in this picture.* The foreboding that Lindsey had been feeling grew.

"OK, a top job," Lindsey said, her mind racing. "Has Joey said anything about anyone helping him? Like, who is paying for this and his medications?" A double mastectomy probably costs at least $40,000, even more, if a male nipple was constructed. And testosterone injections were pricey as well, running anywhere from $100 to $300 per shot.

Morgan studied Lindsey as if she were looking to her for the answer. But Lindsey suspected Morgan wasn't seeing her face. Instead, she was accessing some kind of inner knowledge or vision. Lindsey and Rich had experienced the power of Morgan's extraordinary abilities the previous year. In addition to clairvoyance, she was also an empath, able to read emotional and psychic landscapes like a book. But ironically, Morgan's autism precluded her from revealing her own emotions.

"There *is* someone," she said. "Joey refers to him as 'he'—no name. When I was pushing Joey to promise to wait for the surgery until meeting you, his hesitation was due to that person. He always tells Joey how much money he has spent on him. Joey was concerned about postponing the surgery because of this person's reaction. He may be on the faculty because Joey sees him often." Morgan's frown deepened. "I think Joey might be afraid of this person."

She did not tell Lindsey and Rich about the blackness she saw surrounding Joey. It wasn't that she was keeping it a secret; she just didn't know how to describe it. Plus, it might disappear if she didn't speak about it.

"I'm sorry for getting you into this, Lindsey," Morgan said, "but I didn't know how else to help Joey." Her voice cracked with emotion.

"Morgan, I'm glad you did," Lindsey said, putting her hand on her shoulder. "Don't ever apologize for risking helping someone in desperate need, even if the help you offer is mine."

Rich regarded Morgan, realizing she was no longer the gawky, unattractive young lady who had moved in with them the previous year. Lindsey and LJ's offer to take her to a spa when life returned to normal last Christmas had wrought miracles. Shorter hair, stylish glasses, and subtle makeup accentuated her varicolored amber eyes and long lashes, producing a lovely young woman. She was most likely a savant, among the most gifted people he had ever known.

He reached over and grabbed his wife's hand, filled with love and pride at the psychic barriers that had collapsed due to the presence of these girls. But the hairs on the back of his neck still bristled.

CHAPTER EIGHT

"Linds?"

Her head popped out of the bathroom, her mouth filled with toothpaste suds. She pointed to her ears and nodded, indicating she could hear him.

Rich smiled at his wife's antics. "I'll wait until you're free of toothpaste."

A few minutes later, Lindsey reappeared. With her wet blonde hair tied in a ponytail, her face scrubbed free of makeup, and her long, toned legs emerging from her shapeless T-shirt, she looked more like one of her students than her actual age of forty-three. She stood at the end of the bed and Rich gave her a quizzical look as he patted the bed beside where he was stretched out. She climbed into bed beside him. "You're worried about Joey. About my getting involved with something that may suck me into a pit."

Rich looked gravely at his wife. "How did you guess?" The sarcasm was intended to mitigate his growing anxiety. Rich was concerned. He doubted if Lindsey was aware, or even cared, about the powerful transgender advocacy groups protecting children's rights considering changing their gender. He and his law partner had refused to represent several of them during the last few years. Her response served as a surprise and an affirmation.

"So am I." She frowned, reached back to grab the hank of wet hair, and pulled it over her right shoulder, toying with it. "This kid doesn't have anyone, Rich. His mother is a druggie and probably a prostitute. He had all the side effects of testosterone overdose and wants help, but his 'friends' tell him this is normal. They claim he'll 'grow into his rightful maleness.' He just needs to give it time." Her lips thinned out in a grimace.

Rich caught the past tense in Lindsey's remark, "he had all the side effects of testosterone overdose," but said nothing.

"Given what Morgan just told us, the clock is ticking. That surgery must be scheduled sometime in the next couple of weeks. Some adult invests extensive time and money in him to make matters even more interesting. But to what end? And who? Another transgender woman who is Joey's mentor and is on faculty?"

Lindsey swallowed. Hard. "Joey begged me to help wean him from the testosterone." She took a deep breath and stared at Rich. "So I did. And I gave him a low-dose estrogen prescription before I left the office." Now, she avoided looking at Rich and stared at her fingers, which were clasped together, working one another.

"He's mentioned me to some of his friends because I have a meeting with the college president tomorrow afternoon, and I doubt she wants a report on my animal research. She blew out a long breath and regarded Rich. "I checked out the GLESN club that Morgan mentioned at dinner. This is not an organization that welcomes dissent in any form. I see why Morgan said she thought the inclusion of 'straight' in the acronym was purely perfunctory. What do you think I should do, my husband and lawyer?" There was no sarcasm or levity in her expression.

Rich did not hesitate. "Go to the meeting. Listen carefully to what the president has to say. She has no interest in antagonizing you, a woman who single-handedly financed the Animal Science Research Laboratories. Plus, even PETA writes positive stuff about your research with the dogs. So, don't go in there thinking she's your enemy.

"If she asks you direct questions about your actions, try to avoid answering. But don't lie." Rich pondered his remark and said," Linds, I'd be surprised if she does. I'd guess your boss will just tiptoe around this thing. You're an asset to the university."

He took both thumbs and forced a worried frown from her eyebrows, eliciting a chuckle as he did so. "You did what you felt was right. If this comes back to bite us, so be it."

Rich leaned closer, about to kiss her parted lips, then stopped himself. "And honey, as soon as possible, get in touch with Father John." Rich was thinking of what Morgan had said about the mysterious "he" whom Joey feared. He knew she could have said more but had chosen not to, and Rich thought he might have some insight into why. "There is no better heart, mind, and soul to help us than Father John."

Lindsey bumped fists with her husband, grinning in relief at his practical, even-handed advice. "I am so glad you are on my side, Rich Jansen! Calling Father John for some counsel is sheer genius!" Their friend, Father John Tobin, held doctorates in philosophy and clinical psychology and had been a spiritual director for both of them.

Two hours later, Lindsey lay listening to Rich's even breathing, wondering about the meeting tomorrow. *Why do I feel like a kid called to the principal's office? Can she fire me for getting involved with this kid? Yes, of course she can.*

"Lindsey! What a delightful surprise to hear from you on this Thursday morning."

Lindsey did not need any technological aid to picture the priest, which was good because Father John's tolerance of twenty-first-century technology stopped at his cell phone. Since she could hear him chewing, she imagined him in the vast kitchen shared by four priests, an archbishop, and the cardinal of the Co-Cathedral of the Sacred Heart in downtown Houston.

"Sorry, Lindsey, just finishing a bit of breakfast."

"Do you need me to call back in an hour or so, Father? I hate to interrupt your breakfast."

Father John was an ascetic; Lindsey had guessed this during their initial meetings when she began studying Catholicism. His cleric's collar and black pants were a loose fit, and the planes of his long, angular face were prominent, almost gaunt. Last year, when he came out to the coast for their housewarming party, he had cropped his gray hair so close that Rich had jibed him about joining the Marine Corps.

"No, I need to get out to Beaumont by noon. So, let me grab this last bite, and I'm all yours."

Smiling with happiness just to hear his voice, Lindsey pictured herself seated across from him at one of the small tables in the corner by a window facing Jefferson Street as he ate his simple but outstanding bacon, lettuce, and tomato sandwich for breakfast.

"How are you all doing on the central coast, Lindsey? A few of those ocean breezes would come in handy here." Houston, Texas, had lots of aspects going for it, but its climate was not among them. Even in winter, the temperatures were frequently in the high eighties, along with oppressive humidity. "But I am guessing you're not calling for a weather report, are you?"

"I'm not sure where to start, Father."

"At the beginning might be nice," he quipped.

"It's a long and complicated story."

"Of course, it is."

Lindsey chuckled at the man's acerbic style. There were no affectations with Father John, nothing superfluous in his body or speech. He had been brought up as a Catholic, had stopped attending church in his undergraduate years at Berkeley, and had not entered seminary until he was thirty-eight. John had observed that his age was one of the Lord's first methods to teach him humility. He described a few humorous classroom experiences in the seminary; he was thirty-eight among forty-three other seminarians aged twenty-four or younger.

As he listened to Lindsey's story, the priest smiled and nodded. *Once again, Lord, there are no coincidences with you, are there?* Father John had acted as consultant and advisor to their mutual friend, Kate Townsend, for the last few months, first about the content and then the explosive public reaction to a series Kate had published in the *Houston Tribune* on transgenderism.

He asked no questions during Lindsey's condensed narrative, only emitting audible exhalations at specific points, such as in response to Joey's deep sadness, history of iatrogenic fractures, and repeated requests that Lindsey help him "get back to being the girl I used to be."

Only when Lindsey said that she'd guided the teen in reducing, then stopping, the testosterone injections so that Joey could take low-dose estrogen did he comment. But she missed it the first time.

"I met with the president of Cal Poly yesterday afternoon," Lindsey continued, wrapping up what she knew about Joey. "After a few minutes of somewhat gratuitous compliments about our work at the animal research center, Dr. Peterson got to the reason for the meeting, asking if I had any issues with the university's commitment to diversity or the importance of supporting each student, regardless of race, gender, or sexual preferences. She listed the various clubs and organizations on campus to support non-binary students or students searching for alternatives. Although she didn't mention Joey specifically, her message was loud and clear."

Lindsey thought back to her impressions of the meeting. Dr. Alexandra Peterson was the quintessential female executive. Lindsey guessed that the light white wool suit that clung tastefully to her well-exercised body was an Altuzarra, and her four-inch alligator pumps were Manolo Blahnik. All in all, the outfit would have cost around twenty thousand dollars. As she reflected on Peterson's ensemble, Lindsey realized that her disdain for management had reared its ugly head.

She had met with Dr. Peterson only one other time, about six months before, after Reverend Blaise Roderick, S. J., her former boss, had been persuaded to retire. Dr. Peterson had shocked Lindsey when she offered his department head position to her. Not thinking, Lindsey had blurted out an adamant refusal. She protested that Jodie Tamarack, a veterinarian with far more experience in animal science than Lindsey, should replace Father Blaise. The expression on Dr. Peterson's face mirrored that of Dr. Christine Stewart's, Chair of Internal Medicine at the University of Houston Medical School, when Lindsey had refused her offer of an endowed chair of cardiovascular research so that she could instead take the medical director job at Huntsville Prison Hospitals. It was a curious combination of repugnance and fascination as if asking, "What is this creature?"

Lindsey suspected her decision to wear scrubs and running shoes to work that day and to the meeting was a not-so-subtle statement to Dr. Peterson. She smiled ruefully, remembering Jodie's barbed comment about dressing up for the meeting with the boss. She was so absorbed in the memory of that meeting that she missed Father John's first question.

"I asked if you're willing to incur risks like loss of your job, or worse, to rescue Joey," he said once she asked him to repeat it.

All Lindsey could do was blink in surprise.

"After seventy-plus years on this planet," Father John said, speaking into the silence, "I've learned that it is best to first understand the consequences when seeking to rescue another person."

Yes, I guess that is what I'm doing here, a rescue, Lindsey realized with an inaudible sigh.

"For Joey to have gotten all this medical treatment for transitioning from female to male, he would need support. It sounds as if his mother is impoverished financially and maybe intellectually. But somewhere along the way, this young person has attracted the attention of someone with the incentive and means to direct and pay for the therapy. Regardless of this person's motives, he or she has much at stake in this youngster. Given your boss's warning, I'd guess she—or more likely he—has influence at the university."

As she listened to Father John, Lindsey's mind churned. So many of his observations mirrored her own. Joey could not be paying for all of this.

Father John suggested another probable and disturbing dimension of Joey's mysterious benefactor. Although Lindsey knew of the Department of Women's, Gender, and Queer Studies at Cal Poly, she had not considered the possibility that Joey had a mentor on the faculty at Cal Poly, maybe even a department head. If true, that could explain Peterson's "warning." Lindsey had flinched at Father John's use of the word, but that was precisely what it was: a veiled warning. Faculty connections would also explain how Joey, a transfer from Chico State, had quickly become president of the club Morgan mentioned at dinner. She was trying to recall the acronym for the group when Father John spoke again.

"I had several young patients who were profoundly affected by Monique Wittig's dramatic entry into American academia. She spent her first year in the US teaching at the gender studies program at Berkeley."

Lindsey knew Father John had been a successful psychotherapist in Southern California with a thriving practice until he could no longer say no to the "hound of heaven." But she could not recall him ever mentioning his life before the priesthood.

"All six of these young women were Berkeley undergraduates in their late teens and were referred to me by colleagues who were aware of my interest in anorexia. These women refused to eat because they had decided they were no longer female. Their self-imposed starvation rid them of female attributes they no longer wanted, including breasts and menstruation. Each carried a copy of Wittig's The Lesbian Body and could quote liberally from it. For example, 'Women and men are economic and political categories, not eternal ones' and 'Woman does not exist; it is an imaginary formulation, a tool of oppression.'"

The memories of these disturbed young people impelled Father John to stand up and pace in the Sacred Heart Co-Cathedral kitchen. "Monique Wittig had a tortured brilliance with a charismatic presence that could set her audience on fire. So, after my first patient died of starvation, I drove to Berkeley to hear her speak. Think Karl Marx and Simone de Beauvoir packaged in a beautiful French woman, and you have Monique Wittig. Her talks were standing room only."

Lindsey heard what sounded like a muffled sob as the priest continued speaking. "All but one of the six managed to starve themselves to death."

Stunned, Lindsey's mouth opened, but no words came out. What could she say about such a thing? She couldn't think of anything,

Once again, Father John's voice cut off her wandering thoughts. "After Katherine died, I tried psychoanalysis on Cindy and Bridget and a combination of Harry Stack Sullivan and Anna Freud on Annie and Paula." His voice had dropped to a whisper. "Then I finally realized I had *nothing*." The word was close to a hiss.

"Desperate, I got on my knees for the first time in years and begged God to show me how to save this girl. Of course, he did. That was when I stopped ignoring that still, small voice. I sold my practice and enrolled in the seminary." He forced a chuckle. "I couldn't help anyone, but I knew who could.

"Lindsey, I'm sorry, but we're flat out of time. I needed to leave for Beaumont ten minutes ago. We need to talk more, a lot more. I don't think you know what you're up against here. About seven o'clock your time?"

While Father John walked to his car, he dialed another number. "Kate, I just talked with Lindsey. I'd like your OK to share some of our discussions because she's getting involved with a female-to-male transgender teen." He paused to listen to her response and then laughed. "Yes, you're right. It's a strange coincidence if you think such things exist."

"Hi, Lindsey. Sorry to cut off yesterday's conversation so abruptly. Have you thought about what we discussed?"

Lindsey had been at her lab for the last hour. She had lain awake for most of the night and finally got up at 3:30 a.m. Rich had not noticed her preoccupation at dinner because he was preparing for a trial. He had been sleepless all week because it was his first high-profile case on the central coast and a doozie. A well-connected senior at Cal Poly with wealthy Boston parents had been indicted for raping a freshman Hispanic teen from local Santa Maria. All that week, Rich had been on the phone with his partner, Zach Cunningham, long into the night. Lindsey knew Rich thought his young client, Blake Cameron, had raped the young woman, but Cameron claimed he was innocent. It was a classic case of "he said, she said." Upon getting the call from their son, Cameron's parents had flown to the coast, where they had hired Rich and Zach to defend Blake.

Exhausted, Rich had gone to bed at nine, and Lindsey had no interest in waking him up when she gave up hope for sleep and crept out of bed. Both dogs opened their eyes to see what she was doing, but neither moved from their bed.

"Father John," Lindsey smirked, "I haven't given our conversation a single thought!"

The priest's answering chuckle to her sarcasm was forced. Then he cleared his throat. "Every once in a while, Providence speaks loudly enough that even deaf priests can hear him. I doubt you've heard about 'Creating Chemical Eunuchs: Corrupting America's Children,' but given the conversation I just had with Kate Townsend, I suggest you read it, Lindsey, as soon as you can."

"Kate Townsend?" Lindsey exclaimed. *Why would Kate be talking to Father John about her writing?*

"The last of her three-piece series was published in the Houston Tribune last week. Since her point of view is telegraphed clearly by the title, you can guess how it has been received by Houston's large LGBTQ community. The protests outside of the Trib remind me of Berkley in the late sixties. Kate's turned down multiple offers to appear on Good Morning America and an impressive array of radio and television talk shows. The Tribune has hired three people to handle the volume of mail, social media posts, and offers for speaking engagements. Several lawsuits have so far come to naught. Still, Eleanor told me last week the Trib's team of attorneys has received letters from the ACLU, the Southern Poverty Law Center, and a dizzying array of LGBTQ advocacy groups."

Lindsey closed her eyes. *Eleanor, dear Eleanor, and Marguerite. This has been such a trying year, and it sounds as if the forecast is for continued stormy weather.* Eleanor and Marguerite Philbin were brilliant businesswomen from an old Houston oil family. Their grandfather had started the *Houston Tribune* around the turn of the last century as a local paper for merchants. Under their tutelage, the newspaper's circulation had rivaled the *Washington Post* and the *New York Times* in the years before social media. Although Eleanor was in her mid-late eighties and Marguerite was several years older, their energy levels seemed inexhaustible. But Lindsey was concerned about the two women who had become her dear friends.

"Kate called me last night because she and Steve have decided to become Catholic Christians," Father John said.

"They want their children to be baptized in the Church."

Lindsey knew Kate and Steve had talked with Father John about baptizing their son, JH, shortly after his birth, but they couldn't make the commitment back then. She wondered what had changed in their lives when Father John's comment stopped her cold.

"Kate's hoping to fast track joining the Church for numerous reasons. Uppermost among them are the diabolical threats she's received. The paper has inactivated Kate's Facebook and Twitter accounts because of the nature of some of the curses."

"Curses?" Lindsey said. "Surely you don't mean *curses* as in some kind of Satanic malevolence, do you?"

Father John's lips were compressed into a thin line. "Yes, Lindsey, I mean precisely that." *This is one of the times I wonder at the ignorance of the smartest of us,* he thought. *This woman is, without a doubt, one of the most accomplished people I've ever met. But her skills, intellect, and sheer willpower are no help when faced with the blatant evil surrounding her. Our unwillingness to accept the reality of Satan and his minions astounds me.* But clearly, Lindsey was already frightened, and he had no desire to intensify her fear.

"Look, Lindsey, you can easily access Kate's articles online. But I wonder if it might not be a better idea for you to collaborate in person. Is there any way you could get away from your job and family to see her? Since you also came to faith in midlife, your perspective would be useful to her. As a quid pro quo, Kate's in-depth investigation into transgenderism can clarify your decisions about young Joey. Maybe a win-win?"

Lindsey mused about spending some time with Kate. She had liked the investigative journalist almost from the first time she met her close to five years earlier. In fact, another series of

Kate's had galvanized Rich, chief warden of Huntsville Prison, to risk his job by investigating Lindsey's indictment and conviction of murder. If Kate had never written her Pulitzer Prize-winning series, *Murder in the Texas Medical Center*, Lindsey might still be in prison. *But we learn to take miracles for granted,* Lindsey thought. *Time dulls even the most profound gratitude. How easily I have forgotten what might have been had two extraordinary people—Rich Jansen and Kate Townsend—not met and collaborated.*

"Lest you think I'm abandoning you and the conundrum of your young friend, Joey," Father John said, "I'm planning to get out there soon to baptize the children and bring Kate and Steve into the flock." He chuckled. "Who knows? Maybe we can fast-track their entrance into the faith, the whole family will receive the sacraments together, and I'll still have enough time to spend a long weekend with you, Rich, and the girls. Maybe I can even meet Joey if he would like that."

Lindsey felt as if her face would split in two. Rich had convinced her to drive his vintage Mercedes 380 SL convertible the 250 miles from Pismo to Palo Alto. Her face felt chapped from the wind, but she had not felt so exhilarated and alive for months.

He hadn't hesitated when she related her conversation with Father John. They were getting ready for bed the night before when she described the priest's persuasive nudge to get away and spend a few days with Kate and her husband, Steve Cooper.

"Linds, that is a fantastic idea!" he said. With ease, Rich deflected her objections about her work and concerns about leaving him with the dogs and the girls for three days. "By my count, our last vacation was over a year ago. If you categorize nearly getting killed in four countries as a holiday, that is." He was referring to a nearly perfect plan to extinguish most of humanity that had embroiled the Swiss Federal Intelligence Service, him, and Lindsey. And, in the process, revealed Morgan's extraordinary abilities.

Rich let out a long sigh. "Besides, I can focus on my options in this rape case without you here to distract me. There are few to none, but if I withdraw from this case, I need to do it, like yesterday."

Lindsey looked up from her packing in shock; her hands were stilled on the folded clothes as if keeping them in place. Rich's face was drawn and tense as he looked out their bedroom window toward the crashing Pacific Ocean, which they could hear but not see. *Withdraw from the case? Can he even do that?* But from the look on Rich's face, he was planning to do just that. Grim, his jaw tight and his teeth clenched, she knew that expression well. She realized he was convinced that the wealthy "all-American" college senior had raped the young, poor Hispanic Cal Poly freshman girl. Therefore, he could not defend him. No wonder he wanted time alone. Lindsey knew Rich would not even consider doing such a thing without discussing it with Zach. That must have been the reason behind all the late-night calls with his partner, trying to find another solution. *What a colossal mess, Rich.*

Rich turned back to Lindsey and forced a smile. "Don't worry about me, Linds. Zach and Toni are flying in today from Mustang. Can you believe I'm looking forward to seeing our wild and bellicose investigator? Who knows what rabbit she might pull out of the hat?" He shook his head at the irony of his change of heart toward Toni Martinez, an aggressive private investigator for whom the law was malleable. A fact that was particularly frightening to a former homicide cop. Although he'd practiced criminal defense law following graduation from Harvard Law, Rich could stomach it for only a few months. So, he enlisted in the Marines. Following four years in the Corps, he applied to the Police Academy. Within just a few years, Rich became a homicide detective.

"Father John's right. You and Kate can help each other immensely and have a bit of fun while you're at it." He let out another long sigh as he walked into the bathroom, muttering. "Satanic curses? Why am I not surprised that Kate Townsend is getting cursed?"

Lindsey didn't bother mentioning the number of organizations protesting Kate, the *Houston Tribune,* and its owners, Eleanor and Marguerite Philbin, for publishing the series. Rich had enough on his mind with what he faced over the next few days.

Leaving home before 5:00 a.m. made the 250-mile drive north a breeze. Lindsey pulled into Kate and Steve's driveway at precisely 8:30.

Just as she reached into the convertible's back seat to grab her bag, the door to the house flew open, and a dark-haired little boy raced out. Kate followed, holding her sleepy one-year-old.

"JH? Holy cow, you've grown! You weren't much bigger than your little brother the last time I saw you."

Four-year-old JH came to a screeching stop and stared up at Lindsey with huge, warm brown eyes. "You look just like your Daddy, JH!" Lindsey and Steve Cooper had been close friends while working as cardiologists at the Houston Medical Center. Steve's little boy was a miniature replica of his father, right down to the errant cowlick in his thick dark-brown hair and the deep cleft in his chin.

JH smiled shyly and waved at Lindsey. Kate took him by the hand and walked back up the flagstone path to the sprawling adobe home. "Welcome, Lindsey!" she said over her shoulder. "I have a fresh pot of coffee with some reading material at the kitchen table. Help yourself to the best blueberry scones you have ever tasted. In addition to being an Oxford dropout, Lucinda is a fantastic cook! I'll be a few minutes settling everyone down, and then I'll join you."

Lindsey smiled as she watched her friend hold her squirming infant in one arm and tow her little boy with the other. Somehow, she still managed to point right to the patio door where Lindsey was to enjoy her coffee.

There is nowhere else I'd rather be right now. Thank you for this, Father John and Rich. I can feel my soul expanding!

Lindsey stepped through the patio doors into the cool morning sunshine, then sat on one of the green, blue, and white paisley overstuffed wicker chairs. She grabbed a steaming cup of coffee and looked around the beautifully landscaped yard, which was filled with different hibiscus plants with blooms ranging from bright red to a muted, pale peach amid roses, gardenias, and daylilies in artfully arranged islands of various shapes and sizes. There were also colorful blue and varicolored flowering plants she recognized but could not name. The overall effect was a profusion of color in a natural, unmanicured English garden style.

Lindsey sipped the coffee and then took a generous second gulp. It was delicious. Then she picked up Kate's articles and began to read.

"I'll sue you for negligence, Jansen!" Blake's father, Peter Cameron, yelled. "Blake's trial is supposed to start in thirteen days. You can't withdraw from this case! You will *not* destroy Blake's life, you son of a bitch, not on my watch! I won't permit it!" Peter's face was beet red, and the massive wooden conference table shook with each word as he pounded it with his fist.

Fella, that fist will ache like crazy as soon as you calm down, Rich thought. *You might even break something while you're at it.* Now that the decision had been made, Rich felt extraordinary relief. Zach was sitting at the end of the long, heavy oak table, looking like he needed a couple of phone books to elevate him. Dressed in one of his trademark custom-tailored Armani suits, a soft light gray with a light blue striped shirt and mahogany and light gray- and blue-striped tie, Zach's face was expressionless, as if explosive outbursts by men outweighing him by two hundred pounds were everyday occurrences.

Glancing over at Zach, Rich thought for at least the hundredth time how fortunate he was to have him as a partner and a friend.

Next to Peter Cameron sat his wife, Maureen, a reed-thin, dark-haired woman whose mouth was pursed into a thin line as if to bite off any words that threatened to escape and annoy her husband even further. To her left sat Blake, a carbon copy of his father at six-foot-four, with a blonde military-style haircut and his dad's tight-end shoulders and chest minus his ninety pounds of excess fat.

Peter wasn't done, yet again pounding his meaty and now very red fist on the table. "This is all because she's a poor Mexican immigrant, and Blake's a rich white kid. I'm sick of this bullshit reverse racism, sick to death of feeling like I should apologize for building the number-one construction business in Massachusetts."

"Mr. Cameron, you need to hear why we are withdrawing—"

At the sound of Zach's peculiarly deep, gravelly baritone, Peter pushed back his chair so abruptly that it fell over as he stood.

In one fluid motion, Zach stood up, broadcasting his diminutive stature. At just five-foot-six inches tall and 145 pounds, Peter could have easily crushed him like a bug.

"Pick up that chair and sit down, Mr. Cameron. *Now.*" The long scar that started in the middle of Zach's left cheek and extended almost a third of his mouth was starkly white against his ebony skin. Although he had not raised his voice, the authority emanating from his thin, wiry body was sufficient to compel the oversized man to pick up his chair and sit. Maureen's eyes widened as he did so, and her mouth parted in shock. Apparently, such a reaction from her husband was rare. Zach looked over at Rich and nodded, his countenance one of calm command.

Rich stood up and walked out to the foyer outside the conference room where Toni Martinez, an investigator for the law firm, sat holding a pair of red bikini panties in a plastic bag. Rich's smile at Toni came out more like a grimace. He could only pray this would work.

Still young enough to pass for a college student, Toni had spent the last couple of days at the campus. By checking out Blake's social media posts, she found a talkative former girl-friend, Amelia Simmons, who broke up with Blake because he decided to join a fraternity rumored to require proof of sexual conquests from its recruits. Amelia's tears belied her anger at her former boyfriend as she talked with Toni and walked her to Blake's locker.

"Blake's in the top five percent of our class and captain of the football team," the pretty dark-haired girl told Toni. "Why would he jeopardize his whole life for this stupid fraternity?"

Amelia's third guess at the combination for the locker opened it. And there she found the panties. Now sobbing, Amelia stammered, "They must have made him take something to do this." The girl gasped for breath and said, "Blake doesn't even *do* drugs!" Amelia swiped her eyes hard, smearing her mascara across her cheeks. She looked at Toni and said, "If I write him a note, can you take it to him?" Without waiting for Toni's nod, Amelia scribbled a note. *Blake, I know you did it. But Thad talked you into it. Please tell them the truth.*

When Rich and Toni stepped back into the conference room, the silence was thick and oppressive, like a living, breathing thing. No one looked up as they entered. Peter was sitting with his head down. Maureen stared through the plate-glass window at the historic Mission Catholic Church in downtown San Luis Obispo. Zach was paging through some documents.

When Toni pushed—accidentally, she insisted later—Blake Cameron's chair as she walked by, the college senior startled and looked up at her. His gaze surveyed her heavyset body and colorful sleeve tattoos, then rose to meet her dark, almost black-eyed gaze. Blinking a few times, the kid finally tore his eyes away, his gaze resting on the red panties in the plastic bag. And Amelia's note was taped to the bag. His bright blue eyes widened, and his mouth dropped open. Tears sprang to his eyes as he read her words.

Blake turned to his father. "Dad, I did it. I *did* rape her. The girl was not lying."

The story of the dare came out in a chaotic tumble of sobs mixed with words. Blake had agreed to come on to a freshman girl, which was easy for a handsome senior, to appease the new macho leader of the Pi Kappa Xi fraternity, Thad Coppinger. He was to put a roofie into her beer, take her to bed, and keep her panties in his locker as proof of the deed.

"I'm so sorry," Blake said, sobbing. "I'm so sorry ...."

Rich glanced over at Zach, who nodded. Rich realized it was time to get the district attorney, Cody McManus.

While Rich was walking out the door to get McManus, Zach turned to Blake. "You were high on something when you did this, weren't you, Blake?"

Rich thought about Toni's conversation with Blake's ex-girlfriend and wondered if Cody would be willing to go after Thad Coppinger, the jerk who'd come up with this wicked challenge. *The girlfriend's right. This kid needed drugs and alcohol to do this. Blake's had a 4.0 GPA for all four years and awards for all kinds of athletic competitions. Coppinger got to him with a dare he couldn't walk away from. Maybe Cody and I can at least stop this from happening again.*

Blake nodded, his face a picture of misery. "Yes, I drank a six-pack, then snorted some coke before ...."

CHAPTER TWELVE

April 3

Dear Diary,

Dr. T. is coming to get me tomorrow. I'm to meet him when I get out of organic chemistry, and I'm scared. Tomorrow is National Coming Out Day. That's when he's taking me to CHLA's Adolescent Health Department for Transgendered Youth for my top job. Isn't that a terrific way to describe cutting off breasts?

I'm not just scared, though; I'm terrified because this means scars and male nipples. I can't stop looking at my breasts because suddenly I don't hate these things. How weird is that?

I guess one good thing is that I won't need that awful binder anymore. Actually, it's the only good thing because everything else about this sucks.

He called last night to tell me it's a done deal.

"We're all set," he said. "Your mom signed the forms for me to have medical power of attorney."

But of course Cassie signed all the documents, I thought. You probably gave her enough oxy to last a year.

He was gushing, so he didn't notice my lack of enthusiasm.

I want to stop this. I keep thinking about my friend, Morgan, her friend, LJ, and Dr. Lindsey. They are female and have adapted to being in a woman's body. Why can't I do that? Morgan's right; it's not a "top job." It's a double mastectomy! Major surgery. What am I doing to myself here?

I feel better being off the testosterone. Way better. And I've lost ten pounds; I think the weight loss might be because of the estrogen. And of course, the almost daily runs with Dr. McCall's dogs.

But how do I tell him? He's been planning this for months. So, how do I tell him I don't want to be a guy anymore, that this has all been an awful mistake?

CHAPTER THIRTEEN

"Creating Chemical Eunuchs: Corrupting America's Children: Introduction"

Learning firsthand about the pernicious ideological attack by radicals on our children has changed my life. So absolute has been the change that my husband and I will be Catholic Christians in a few months. We're doing this because we understand our world is at war.

But the battle is not with people. As St. Paul explains, "For we wrestle not against flesh and blood, but against principalities, against powers, against the rulers of the darkness of this world, against spiritual wickedness in high places. Wherefore take unto you the whole armor of God, that ye may be able to withstand in the evil day." To us, the armor of God is made tangible in the sacraments of the Catholic Church.

I am the mother of two boys: a four-year-old and a nine-month-old. About seven months ago, I experienced the vastness of a conspiracy to destroy the identity of our children and the terrifying intransigence with which any disagreement is received.

Initially, I searched for someone, or an institution, to blame. The most vulnerable among us—our children—are being seduced into a corruption of unimaginable proportions. To American educators, physicians, and professional organizations, "gender affirmation" is the fitting response when their two- or three-year-old boy stutters out a desire to have a doll like his little girlfriend or change his name to a girl's name. These practitioners base their actions on widely circulated but controvertible data revealing the significant risk of suicide in gender-dysphoric children.

Confused and frightened families are referred to one of many gender clinics nationwide. There, children meet other boys and girls who are encouraged to dress and act like the opposite gender. By age seven or eight, these youngsters are given puberty blockers—chemicals that block the release of GnRH or gonadotropin-releasing hormone from the pituitary gland in the brain—thus suppressing the production of the hormones testosterone or estrogen, which are necessary to form adult men and women.

Drugs like Lupron Depot, Norethindrone, and Depo-Provera were initially created to treat prostate cancer in men and endometriosis in women. One of these drugs or a variant is "prescribed" to transgender children for lifelong consumption, thus ensuring sterilization by the end of their second decade. The second article in this series details a long list of widely varying side effects.

Initially, I was baffled when interviewing more than twenty physicians with credentials from the top medical schools specializing in transgender cases among children. I was bewildered for several reasons, but primarily, it was the almost uniform manner in which the doctors answered my questions. For example, when I asked, "How can you justify the removal of healthy breast tissue?" Whether in San Francisco or Boston, the physicians replied: "Tissue is not healthy if the patient hates it." To my logical follow-up question, "Would you amputate an arm or a leg if the patient decided she hated the limb?" Again, the answers scarcely varied: "Of course not! That indicates pathological thinking, a delusion." It was almost as if the doctors were reading from a script.

Over the last five years, three ostensible watchdogs of medicine, the American Academy of Pediatricians, the American Psychiatric Society, and the American Psychological Association, have endorsed "parental affirmation" regardless of the child's age. This response to the whimsical fantasies of toddlers mystified and enraged me. That rage became a profound fear because it was evident that something different was operating here, something formerly hidden.

Since "evil" is a word I have never considered either in my thoughts or writing, I turned to a Catholic priest I met a few years ago while writing another series. The priest, who I will refer to as Father Dan Cavendish in this series, is a trained psychoanalyst with doctorates in philosophy, psychology, and theology. He seemed uniquely qualified for my purposes.

After listening to my emotionally laden tirades, Father Dan asked what I was looking for. I recall staring at him for what felt like hours, but which was only seconds, as his question echoed in my head. What *was* I looking for? Sifting through and rejecting a hundred iterations of "I want to finish this story," I voiced a question that sounded remarkably like my four-year-old son: "How did we get here?"

Surprised that I said "we," I blinked at his face on the computer screen as I elaborated on my initial question: "How did a civilized, technologically advanced culture like ours degenerate to this … abyss of evil?" Although tears streamed down my face, I felt oddly calmer and cleaner.

Father Cavendish's reply both attracted and shocked me. "The entire story of humanity is contained in Genesis," he said. "Everything is explained there. Read the first three chapters, then read them again and again." As he spoke, his expression softened, and his piercing gray eyes seemed to drill into my heart. "A former pope, Saint John Paul the Second, speaks of the 'Great Heart' that we hear beating behind these words in Genesis. I think you're ready to hear his heartbeats, Kate."

After searching through countless boxes of books I had not glanced at in years, I found my mother's Bible, took a deep breath, and opened it. Aware that something momentous was happening, I did as Father Dan advised. This agnostic journalist read and reread the first three chapters of Genesis countless times, growing awareness with each reading of the telling's beauty, enormity, and majesty. "And the Lord God formed man from the dust of the earth and breathed into his nostrils a breath of life, and man became a living being … It is not good for man to be alone. I will make a helper suited to him … The man gave names to all the tame animals, all the birds of the air, and all the wild animals, but none proved to be a helper suited to the man. So the Lord cast a deep sleep on the man … and built the rib he had taken from the man into a woman … That is why a man leaves his father and mother and clings to his wife, and the two of them become one body."

He made Adam first in the image and likeness of God. Then came a helper *suited* for him, intended to unite, complement, and complete him. Humanity was created as the union of males and females. Then, the woman was deceived. From the beginning, the most cunning of all creatures knew to approach *her*, the woman. Not Adam, but her. Unthinking, dizzy with the forbidden fruit, she persuaded her husband, "bone of my bone and flesh of my flesh," to disobey the God who sought and walked with them in the breezy time of each day. Only then did the subjugation of females to males, the pain of childbirth, and hard labor begin.

All this hideous *stuff*—sexual politics, gender identity, gender dysphoria, war, hatred, genocide—began there with that first lie in paradise. She believed, and then she told her husband.

For the first time in my life, I have a glimmer of understanding about the natures we were initially given by that Great Heart of God and the colossal cost to Creation when we listened to the father of lies collectively and individually.

Mesmerized, Lindsey completed Kate's introduction and absorbed each subsequent article.

Starting with the enlightenment of the eighteenth century and progressing forward, Kate elucidated not just the Marxist but the anti-theist foundation of secularism. Kate mainly relied on three philosophers: Friedrich Nietzsche, Auguste Comte, and Henri Lubac. Nietzsche famously argued, "God is dead; we have killed him." Therefore, humanity was beyond good and evil. In God's absence, moral absolutes did not exist, leaving mankind to assert its will to power. Obsessed with power, Nietzsche wrote that humanity's only hope lay in becoming the strong man: an "Übermensch" or Superman.

A devout follower of Nietzsche was Comte, the "father of logical positivism," a philosophy arguing that only meaningful philosophical problems can be solved through empirical observation and logical analysis. Lindsey vaguely recalled her best friend and college classmate Julie Grayson talking about this idea while undergraduates at Rice. Back then, Lindsey was focused only on the coursework required for med school.

Using Catholic language and principles, Comte claimed that science was the *true* God, rightly enthroning humanity as master of the universe. Catholicism's goal was the Kingdom of Heaven, while the goal of positivists was establishing humanity's kingdom on Earth.

Since all religions require priests, the positivists' priesthood was the scientists. However, only a particular type of scientist with an encyclopedic mind could envision mastery of biological, social, and psychic phenomena. People would be subjected to their reasoning and understanding through social engineering aimed at improving humanity. Personal instincts would be subjugated to the good of the social collective.

Furthermore, Comte predicted that biological engineering would produce humans worthy of entering the "Great Being." Only selected, genetically superior people would be approved to breed, thus creating superior beings. These "supermen" would shed their individual personalities and embrace the collective through the purification of the objective life. Armed with these tools, humanity would create its own destiny.

What a neat way to justify everything: abortion, genocide, eugenics, man's deification, Lindsey mused.

A couple of Henri Lubac's one-hundred-year-old observations slammed home to Lindsey. For instance his remark that it wasn't true, that people needed God to organize the world but that "what is true is that, without God, [humans] can ultimately only organize it against man." He also wrote, "Christ came into the world not to bring peace but a sword." First and foremost, Lubac declared Christ is "the great disturber."

Only briefly did Kate discuss queer theory and its ubiquitous presence at American colleges and universities. Then, she correlated the approach with its antitheist predecessors.

The second article reviewed the use of puberty blockers in young children. Kate's discussion of the side effects was saved from a pure clinical review by personal anecdotes from three adults. Their reasons for detransitioning were written in their own words, each more horrifying than the last.

The final article described the catalyst for the series. Kate's experience with a teacher in the California preschool program where her four-year-old had been enrolled was shocking. If Lindsey had not known Kate so well, she would have thought the tale was written by a conspiracy nut. It seemed so unbelievable. Kate's objective style of relating precise descriptions of places, people, and their conversations chilled the morning air as Lindsey read the piece.

Kate's statement that until the "Great Divorce," there was "just one sacrament: the union of man and woman" brought tears to Lindsey's eyes. It was a short synopsis of St. John Paul II's *Theology of the Body.* It provided a compelling, incisive, and strangely haunting end to the series.

How many books did you read for this, Kate? Lindsey wondered. *At least seven or eight, and knowing Father John at least another five or six on Catholicism once he learned you wanted to convert.*

Startled by a loud cry from a bird on one of the many trees in Kate's backyard, Lindsey looked up. She'd been so absorbed in her reading that Lindsey had forgotten where she was. The clarity of the morning air and the profusion of glorious flowers provided a welcome contrast to the newspaper material. The beauty around her pushed back the malicious darkness of social engineering and the insanity of a world led by people who deified humanity while wholly unconscious of consequences. And like countless times before, Lindsey considered the years when science had been *her* god. In a real sense, she, too, had deified humanity until her entire world collapsed. She reflected on her conversations with Father John about those decades in which she ignored everything but her research. The contrition about her mother and sister at times was suffocating.

Lindsey collated the articles into a pile and considered the shocking personal nature of Kate's writing. Not to mention the considerable research Kate had done for the series and her astounding correlation between the first three chapters of Genesis and religion with science. She mused that many priests, ministers, and Christians considered those early chapters in the Bible as fiction or allegory. Reading these words in a newspaper was more than startling—an audible "Wake up!"

Of course, Kate's introduction prepared readers for something very different, even unique. Kate was an excellent journalist, but this series was almost otherworldly. God's hand was all over this.

Lindsey understood the firestorm that the newspaper was weathering. Like San Francisco and many large cities, Houston's LGBTQ community was well represented in government and institutions. *What a gutsy move, Eleanor and Marguerite. He says he wants to set the earth on fire. Well, by golly, you've done it.*

Smiling as she thought of the Philbin sisters who owned the *Houston Tribune*, she was suddenly thrown back in time.

It was the third year of Lindsey's cardiology fellowship. She and the chief surgical resident, Matt Chambers, had been working on a trauma case. A thirty-two-year-old mother of twin infant girls had been broadsided by a semi on I-45. Remarkably, the babies were untouched, but the mom was a mess. It had taken the Life Flight crew almost two hours to get her out of the smashed car. While Matt repaired her lacerated liver, fractured pelvis, and broken femur, Lindsey monitored and treated her heart. The young mother had sustained severe myocardial damage when she slammed into her car's steering wheel and incurred dangerous arrhythmias during surgery. After five hours, the grueling operation was finally done, and she was stable. They rolled their patient into the ICU and high-fived each other, astounded that they had cheated death. Too many other times, they had lost the battle. It was 10:00 p.m., and their shift had ended four hours earlier, so they could turn their pagers off, a rare privilege.

"I'll buy the first round!" Matt's grin was infectious. He had asked her out during their parallel residencies at least ten times. Both had achieved the distinction of chief resident—Matt in surgery and Lindsey in cardiology.

This time, when Matt asked, she thought, *Why not?* Thirty minutes later, they sat at a small table at the iconic blue door of Marfreless in River Oaks. One drink led to another and then … Lindsey was on the pill, but her hours were so erratic that she was not surprised when that one-night stand resulted in pregnancy. On-call five out of seven days for two years, Lindsey hardly knew day from night. So, remembering to take that tiny blue pill was a joke.

Believing she had no choice when she learned she was pregnant, Lindsey made an appointment at the Southwest

Planned Parenthood Center. Although politically liberal and pro-choice, she'd studied embryology and knew this "fetus" was no mere amorphous mass of cells. After a sleepless night before her scheduled abortion, Lindsey gave in to inspiration and called her best friend and devout Catholic, Julie Grayson, newly married and completing her master's in theology. Julie persuaded Lindsey to meet her for coffee before her appointment.

Sitting there on Kate's patio, Lindsey shuddered for the thousandth time at the precariousness of her daughter's existence. This vibrant and beautiful teen whom she had come to love so dearly. LJ wouldn't be alive had it not been for Julie, and now this remarkable person wanted to walk in *Lindsey's* shoes and become a doctor? Lindsey shook her head in amazed humility at the thought.

Just then, Kate burst through the kitchen door and onto the patio. "I'm sorry to leave you for so long, Linds, but JH and Nicholas were giving Lucinda a harder time than usual."

Lindsey stared up at Kate, her eyes still wet with tears in response to her reflections. "You look lovely, by the way."

Kate flushed, putting her hands on her hips. "Right, twenty extra pounds that are happily broadening my butt and have no interest in going away anytime soon." She nodded to the plate of scones, which were untouched. "I'd consider it an act of mercy if you would eat at least one of those scones, Lindsey. Clearly, you don't have my problem. You look even thinner than you did the last time we saw each other."

"OK, Kate, twisted my arm." Lindsey admired her friend's vibrant, lively expression and tousled dark, glossy hair. "But I'm telling you, you look … ravishing. I know my comment sounds like Cary Grant in a forties movie, but I've never seen you look so great! And I'll bet Steve tells you that every night!" She wiggled her eyebrows in a reasonably good imitation of lasciviousness.

Cheeks flaming, Kate chuckled. "Eat, woman! You're in my house, so eat!" She sank into one of the patio chairs. "Seriously, though, Lindsey, when Father John told me that he thought you were coming for a long weekend, I was ecstatic. So was Steve. He's just sorry that Rich couldn't come with you."

Kate was intentionally distracting Lindsey from what she'd just read. She was surprised at her nervousness; while eager to hear Lindsey's reaction, she dreaded hearing it. If asked, she wouldn't have been able to explain why she felt this way. Kate loved and admired Lindsey, maybe more than any other woman she'd met, but in some ways, Lindsey intimidated Kate. And this series wasn't just personal; she'd put her heart and soul on display for all to see.

Not noticing Kate's discomfort, Lindsey was just now absorbing the reality of feeling "off." She'd taken Kate's suggestion and eaten the first scone while Kate was talking, delighting in the simple joys of being with a trusted friend, eating delicious food, and, at least for the next couple of days, having no deadlines to meet. It felt glorious. And reading Kate's articles cemented her own conflicting emotions about Joey. She was doing the right thing.

Lindsey finished the last bite of her scone. "You're right! These are magnificent! You've been very busy since I last saw you. You've had a second child, and I didn't even know you were pregnant! And once again, intrepid reporter, it looks like the Tribune has had to hire half the city of Houston to keep up with your mail. Rich's sole comment last night was wondering why he wasn't surprised to hear that you are being cursed with an actual curse.

"Your articles are superb. Provocative, informative, and disturbing. And the preschool teacher? You've got to tell me the entire story, Kate."

Kate's expression finally caught Lindsey's attention. She leaned closer to her friend. "What's wrong?"

Kate wiped away the fallen tears in response to Lindsey's warmth and concern, blinking several times to clear her vision. "Nothing's wrong, Lindsey. I wasn't sure how you'd react to this series. You're the first person to read it in front of me. That is, more or less in front of me. And you liked it."

"*Liked* it?" Lindsey scoffed. "Kate, you're good, very good. Remember, even the New York elite has judged you and found you worthy of a Pulitzer." It wasn't necessary to mention that Lindsey's incarceration had prompted the series that catapulted Kate into the national scene. "But this? There's just one word for writing like this: inspired. So, of course, it's hated." She waved her hand impatiently. "The story, tell me the whole story."

Kate smiled and wiped away her remaining tears. "Because three-year-old Danny Sugarman decided he no longer wanted to be called Danny but Susan, Addison Meeks, the preschool teacher, bought Danny/Susan a chocolate cake with the name 'Susan Sugarman' written on it. Then Addison took all the kids outside to circle Danny and sing, 'Susan, come out.' Danny removed his pants and put on a skirt Addison had purchased. Since I was getting JH early for once, I got to see and hear the entire bizarre party.

"After I parked, I sat and watched because it looked odd. The kids were outside, and Danny Sugarman was in the middle of their circle, looking at a cake. Curious, I got out of the car and walked up the driveway. When I got there, Danny began crying hysterically, screaming that he didn't want to be Mia, over and over. The other kids, including JH, started to cry, too. So, I asked Addison if I could help. When she said I could, I picked up Danny, swapped the skirt for his trousers, and he stopped crying instantly. Addison didn't care for that. She asked me what I was doing and why.

"Instead of answering her, I suggested we get all the children back inside the kindergarten. I hoped the situation could be managed before the other moms and nannies arrived. So, I had JH take Danny and two girls inside the kindergarten without waiting for Addison to say anything. Meanwhile, Addison asked me again why I'd changed Danny back into the trousers he'd been wearing before he 'came out.'

"'Addison, you heard Danny screaming because he didn't want to be like his older sister, Mia, right? And now he's no longer screaming. You see this, correct? In fact, he's acting like any other three-year-old little boy, chasing after JH and the others.'"

Although it had been months, Kate shook her head, still trying to process what seemed like wholly irrational behavior on the part of the young teacher.

"Addison nodded as if she agreed and started to say something, but I cut her off and asked her why she would treat a three-year-old child as mature enough to decide that he wanted to be a girl and then to treat him as if he were a transgender male to female, even ceremonially changing his name and clothing. Why would she do such a thing? Then I asked if Danny's parents had told her it would be OK with them."

Listening to Kate's objective and straightforward story, Lindsey was impressed with how she'd handled herself. She had covered all the angles, even the unlikely possibility that Danny's parents would approve of him transitioning to a girl.

"Acting huffy, Addison said that she'd studied under Dr. Matt Heathcock, one of the theorists who brought the diagnosis of gender dysphoria into the twenty-first century. He also wrote and passed the transgender education legislation pioneered in California." Kate smiled sardonically. "Another step forward for humanity from Sacramento."

Lindsey shook her head, impressed by this gutsy, level-headed woman.

"According to Addison, Danny has the right to decide his gender," Kate continued. "Since Danny had been calling himself a girl for the last couple of afternoons, Addison felt obligated as his teacher to 'affirm' his gender identity. She said that, unfortunately, parents are frequently too 'emotionally involved' to help their children become who they are meant to be.

"Once we got the detritus of the cake cleaned up and all twelve of the kids back inside, Addison thanked me for my help. For a moment, I thought she was having second thoughts about what had happened. So, I asked Addison if she planned to speak with Danny's parents about the party and what had happened. Then you'll never guess what this twenty-something-year-old child did. She smiled at me and said, 'Kate, you mean *Susan's* parents, not Danny's, right?'"

Lindsey studied Kate.

"What? You're looking at me as if I've developed a third eye or something, Lindsey!"

"I'm just flabbergasted at this story." She picked up the second scone and broke off a piece. Without picking it up, Lindsey said, "And I can't express how very proud I am to be your friend." Toying with the piece of scone, Lindsey popped it into her mouth, swallowed, and said, "So many of us would have just grabbed our kid and walked away. And tried to forget what had happened. Even pretend it *didn't* happen."

"Don't touch anything, LJ," Rich said into his phone. "I'm less than five minutes away. I'm leaving now."

Rich had spoken quietly, but Zach raised an eyebrow to recognize the sound of a new problem. He nodded at Rich, indicating that he and Toni could finish up. Then, just as Rich was about to leave the room, his cell phone buzzed again.

"Call 911 now," he said, louder this time.

The chaos had subsided somewhat because the DA himself had arrived and was talking with the distraught Cameron family. Even Peter had sat down and was quiet. Cody McManus had been the DA of San Luis Obispo County for twelve years. Like Rich, McManus had practiced on both sides of the law, beginning in criminal defense and then switching to prosecution. He exuded competence and confidence.

At Rich's cry, Cody stood and spoke softly to his assistant, Terri Bannister. Then he caught up with Rich as he hurried out the conference room door.

"Just your average Friday morning, huh, Counselor?" Cody smiled grimly. "Could you use some help?"

"Lindsey's daughter and Morgan found one of their classmates unconscious in one of the Cal Poly pastures. They thought she … they thought *he* was dead, but apparently, the student is still breathing."

Cody caught the pronoun confusion; he didn't miss much. "How about I take you over there? We can put the siren on and be there in a few minutes."

True to Cody's word, his truck arrived just as the EMTs

were hoisting a stocky teen into the ambulance. Within seconds, LJ sobbed in Rich's arms, but Morgan walked along with the techs carrying the litter as if she were standing guard. Her eyes never left the unconscious teen's face. Clasping LJ around her waist, Rich half-walked and half-carried the sobbing girl.

"What did you see first, Morgan?"

Reluctantly, Morgan's gaze switched to Rich. "We thought he was dead."

As Rich waited for her to say more, LJ's sobs quieted to hiccups and then heavy sighs. She started talking but stopped when Rich squeezed her waist, indicating he wanted to hear from Morgan first.

"And we touched nothing," Morgan continued. "LJ knew right away that it was a crime scene. But those guys," she nodded at the EMTs who were now in the ambulance, "they made a mess of everything."

Morgan noticed Cody for the first time and stared at him.

"Hi, Morgan," Cody said. "I'm Cody McManus, the DA here." He glanced at Rich as if to say, "You got this, right?"

Rich saw the look but didn't answer; he didn't want to distract Morgan.

"Joey was face down, still, and with his head turned this way." Morgan turned her head to the left to demonstrate. "But while LJ was calling you, I saw the dirt move next to his lips and realized he was breathing."

Morgan's eyes scanned the three of them. As if in answer, they all nodded.

"He was supposed to have the top job yesterday," she continued, "but he didn't want to do it. Either he got a hold of something and overdosed on purpose, or the man ..." Morgan paused, thinking. "I'm not certain it's a man. I only know that

Joey referred to a 'him' and a 'he.' But that person might have done something to Joey because I know Joey is afraid of this person." She said all of this matter-of-factly but with a frown. For Morgan, a frown was the equivalent of LJ's sobs.

The four stood in the dust of the ambulance as it tore off for French Hospital.

"Morgan." Cody's voice was muted but forceful. Surprised, she looked at the DA but didn't say anything. "You seem to know Joey well. Can you take the detectives who'll be here in a few minutes to see Joey's room?" Cody turned to Rich. "Assuming that's OK with you."

"But I'd like to be with Joey when he wakes up," Morgan said, her frown deepening.

"Of course," Cody said. "But I'd guess the doctors will work on him for a couple of hours, so you'll need to wait until they figure out what happened. Do you know where Joey lives on campus?"

Morgan nodded as a nondescript gray sedan pulled up.

"Well, let's take these guys over there," Cody said, then explained to the two detectives what was happening.

Morgan watched them get out of the car. "Actually, it's one guy and a woman, Cody, but OK, we can go to his dorm." Then she looked at LJ. "Are you coming with us?"

CHAPTER FIFTEEN

As he entered the Sierra Madre residential quarters at Cal Poly, where Joey lived, Rich couldn't help but wonder how a poor kid from a tiny northern California town could afford such plush accommodations.

He thought someone was paying a bucketload for this kid's education. But who and why?

Gaping at the double bed, large desk, freshly painted light gold walls, and large picture window overlooking the tree-lined campus, he shook his head. There was no comparison with the dorm room he'd shared with three other guys at Harvard, which had just enough space for two bunk beds and two small closets.

The colorful bedspread accented the walls and matching window coverings. It was no guy's space. Instead, it was a pretty, feminine room, reminiscent of LJ and Morgan's rooms at home.

A framed photo stood on the nightstand. Rich and LJ, who was with him, saw it simultaneously. It featured Lindsey and three of the Dobermans at her clinic.

LJ's eyes were sad as she looked at the picture and its prominence in the room. There was no other picture.

Morgan was looking through the neat stacks of books on the desk, but she glanced at the photo when she heard Rich and LJ's comments about it. She shrugged, wondering what the big deal was.

The two detectives, Cindy Ralston, and her partner, Stan Kingsbury, hovered by the door, whispering with Cody McManus. Rich heard snippets of the conversation about the evidence techs. They'd found little at the scene and wondered why they'd been asked to come to the dorm.

"Joey calls him Dr. T."

In seconds, Cody, the two detectives, Rich and LJ, were huddled around Morgan as she read from a tattered coffee-au-lait-colored leather journal.

Where did she find that? Rich wondered.

She glanced up at the group, then continued reading. "Here's the last entry in his diary, where Joey says Dr. T. was coming today to take him for the top job." She looked at Rich. "We need to go see him now." Then, she handed the journal to Cody.

"Don't you think you should call Lindsey and tell her about this?" LJ had composed herself and now seemed like a clone of her biological mother. Rich stared at her. *No, not a clone,* he thought. Their body types and coloring were almost opposite. While Lindsey was tall, blonde, and lanky, LJ was barely five feet, with dark hair that was almost black and a voluptuous build. *It's their eyes,* Rich thought for the hundredth time. The intensity of LJ's emerald-green gaze was made even more dramatic by her coloring.

While Morgan had hesitated when they got to the ICU where Joey was being monitored, LJ strode in as if to examine him until a nurse kindly but firmly asked her to step away from the bed while she adjusted some gadgets.

Rich sighed. He hated to disturb Lindsey, but the girl was right.

CHAPTER SIXTEEN

"Well, that's good news then."

"But I can't do anything until I have the consent signed."

Rich had left the ICU to speak with the hospitalist, Dr. Amanda Dyson. She'd explained that there wasn't any evidence of drugs in Joey's blood. The problem, she and the consulting neurologist believed, was a clot in one of the arteries in his brain. The good news was the embolus was positioned where it could be dissolved with a new drug, obviating the need for a craniotomy or a burr hole.

"That's a problem," Rich said. "We found a diary where Joey wrote that Dr. T. had secured medical power of attorney from his mother. But we have no idea who this Dr. T. is."

Rich was impressed with the woman. He'd told her only the brief facts he knew about the teen and that morning's events, and she couldn't have been more forthcoming. But they were still stuck.

"Why couldn't your friend, Cody McManus, get an emergency waiver signed by a judge, so Joey can get the treatment he needs?" Morgan asked.

Rich had not seen her approach, so he didn't know how long she'd been standing there. He decided to let Dr. Dyson answer.

"You're the young woman who found his diary?" Dr. Dyson asked, to which Morgan nodded in response. The physician looked at her with admiration and gratitude. "Thank you. You're right. In California, the state can act as guardian for a minor in extremis."

Rich dialed Cody and then handed Dr. Dyson his phone.

Smiling, she nodded to Rich and Morgan as she explained the situation to the DA.

"Lindsey, I don't think you can do much here. According to the hospitalist, Joey's coma isn't drug-induced. At least there are no signs of drugs in his system, and we're getting Cody to get a judge to sign emergency consent to their use of … three or four syllables beginning with T."

"Tenecteplase."

"Yep, that's it."

"He flipped a blood clot to the middle cerebral or basilar artery." She felt terrible. *If I'd begun the estrogen earlier, could this have been prevented?* Lindsey squinted into the California sunshine, thinking about her long discussions with Joey. She'd explained to the teen that there were no data to even guess at the effects of stopping long-term testosterone and then re-initiating the estrogen that had been suppressed. Since Joey had stopped taking the puberty-suppressing drug months before, the kid reasonably hoped that the masculinizing effects of long-term testosterone could be mitigated.

She'd called two endocrinologists she knew and affirmed what she'd guessed. There wasn't any way to predict what the response of the body would be in this case.

"What, Linds? I couldn't hear what you just said." An ambulance with a blaring siren had rolled past, drowning out every sound.

"Joey was off the testosterone injections and had started a low dose of estrogen that I prescribed for him. The embolus could have formed because of the hormones.

"But Tenecteplase is a good drug from what I read about it." She paused for a second to think. "Hey, Rich, think there's any chance I could speak with the doc?"

"I don't know. Let me head back there and see if she's still around."

Rich saw the back of Dr. Dyson's salt-and-pepper-haired head and long white lab coat. "Hold on, Lindsey," he jogged down the hall to catch up to her.

Curious at the sound and pace of Rich's leather-soled loafers on the hospital corridor, she stopped and turned around. "Yes, Mr. Jansen?" There was a flicker of annoyance in her voice, but Dyson put on her game face as she waited for him to catch up.

"Please forgive me for the interruption, Dr. Dyson, but a colleague of yours would like to speak with you." He doubted the woman would know Lindsey, but he figured it was worth trying.

Frowning but curious, Dr. Dyson took the proffered cell phone. "Yes? This is Dr. Dyson."

Moments later, barely suppressing a grin, Dyson returned the phone to him. "Mr. Jansen, 'my colleague,' your wife, would like to speak with you. She and I are eager to hear how you knew we were in the same medical school class."

Lindsey was laughing when he brought the phone to his ear. "Rich Jansen, you're a natural—cop, warden, defense attorney. Whatever you do, you pull it off."

"Were you and she really med students in Houston together?"

"Yes! And we both knew it was a shot in the dark!" The chuckle faded quickly. "Amanda's good, and she's got this. I couldn't do as well as she's done in diagnosing and treating Joey. You're right. There's no reason for me to leave Kate and Steve's when Joey's getting all that can be done. What happened with your case? Did you have to withdraw?"

She shook her head as Rich related the events leading up to Blake confessing he had raped the girl.

"So, this twenty-year-old athlete with a 4.0 GPA now faces at least ten, maybe twenty years in prison because of a stupid fraternity?" she asked.

After the call, Lindsey rejoined Kate and Steve. "I hope you two can figure out how to keep your boys away from drugs, girls, and fraternities until they're forty-five?" After explaining what had happened with Rich and Zach's client, Steve and Kate merely looked at her, saddened by the story of a ruined life.

After a moment, Kate asked, "So, you don't need to leave, Lindsey?"

"Nope. You've got me until Sunday morning if I can get to Mass here in Palo Alto before heading home."

CHAPTER SEVENTEEN

"I think I know who Dr. T. is."

Rich, LJ, and Morgan were waiting in the ICU waiting room to hear the results of the clot-busting drug intervention. Rich had been dozing, exhausted due to several sleepless nights. Pulling himself out of the semi-fetal position he'd adopted, he looked at Morgan and waited for her to continue. She was fiddling with her phone as LJ looked on. Both girls seemed as tired as Rich felt.

"Did you find Dr. T.'s name spelled out in the diary?" Rich asked.

She shook her head, still focused on the phone. "Joey told me."

His eyebrows shot up in surprise. He was just about to ask, "What the hell are you talking about?" when LJ caught his eye and shook her head.

Rich nodded, taking a deep, steadying breath as he considered Morgan's words. Her senses were different from most people's. Somehow, Joey, who'd been in a deep coma for the last six hours, had told Morgan who the mysterious benefactor/mentor was. He glanced at LJ, who was smiling at him and returned the gesture.

Morgan did not exaggerate, nor was she prone to fantasy. Instead, her speech reflected the realities of her world, a world with extraordinary psychic insight and clairvoyance. Last year, Morgan's extrasensory perceptions had been startling—and lifesaving—for all of them, yet it was a year that Rich preferred not to dwell on.

"Joey told me," had to mean precisely that, Rich decided.

Somehow, Morgan's unique set of keen senses had gotten through. He recalled an article about a neuroscientist who'd figured out how to use MRI scanning to communicate with people in a vegetative state, determining that 20 percent of such people could be reached.

As the stark reality of her statement set in, he looked at Morgan, who appeared to have found what she was looking for. He knew better than to call her a human MRI machine, but it wasn't a bad analogy.

"Meet Dr. Adam Turner," she said, extending her phone to them. It featured a picture of a bespectacled person in their late thirties or early forties. The web page said Dr. Turner was chair of the Department of Gender, Queer, and Women's Studies at Cal Poly. With short curly hair, a narrow face with small features, and close-set eyes, Dr. Turner could be either a man or a woman, which Rich surmised was the objective.

Scrolling down the page, he read a long list of academic credentials, awards, and publications in science and technology, feminist theory, and engineering. It also said Dr. Turner's pronouns were "his" and "theirs."

So, Dr. Turner, he thought. *What's your interest in Joey?*

Just then, Cody entered the waiting room. He looked over Rich's shoulder at the face on the phone. Then he nodded hello to LJ and Morgan.

"Is this a person of interest in this evolving mystery?" Cody asked.

"Yes," Morgan replied, nodding.

Cody turned to Rich. "I'll call you when we pick up Dr. Turner. Do you want to be there when we question him?"

"Yes," Rich and Morgan replied in unison.

"Lemme get this straight," Steve said. "Kate writes an explosive series on the transgender craze. At the same time, you get drawn into the saga of a transgender female-to-male whom you're helping detransition. Now he's suddenly comatose, possibly due to an estrogen or testosterone-induced clot, and awaiting thrombolytic therapy. Neither of you knew what the other was doing until you spoke with Father John."

Lindsey raised her wine glass—her third—in a mock salute. "Leave it to Dr. Steve Cooper to compress at least thirty pages of complicated events into three sentences!"

Steve chuckled. "Well, did I omit anything?" He frowned in response to Kate and Lindsey's shared, wry look. "Cliff Notes, ladies, remember them?" That prompted a laugh from both women.

"They think they have the name of the person who's financially backing this kid," Lindsey said.

"Don't tell me it's someone from the college faculty." Kate's large brown eyes were moist in the dancing light of the gas candles.

"Unfortunately, it is." Lindsey gave no details, and Kate and Steve were smart enough not to ask for them.

The three were silent for several moments. Finally, Lindsey spoke. "Steve, will you survive the effects of Kate's investigative series at Stanford?" She'd been thinking about Father John's premonitory words about her involvement with Joey. Lindsey suspected that with this latest development, Dr. Peterson would ask for her resignation. Although Peterson hadn't mentioned a name, someone on the faculty had complained about her intervention with Joey. It's the only way she could have known. Now, that complaint would grow legs.

All too familiar with the politics of academic medical centers, Lindsey figured that Stanford would react to the actions of the chief of cardiology's wife.

Kate and Steve looked at each other and came to a silent agreement. Then Steve turned to Lindsey. "I've accepted UT San Antonio's offer for chairman of cardiology. We've got the house on the market. Kate and I are flying out next weekend to look for a place.

"Lucinda, God bless her, is eager to leave California," Kate added, "so she'll move with us to Texas."

Lindsey nodded thoughtfully. "A&M has called me a few times over the last several months, but until last week, I ignored their calls. But thanks, you two, for helping me see the wisdom of returning home to Texas. Monday, I'll talk with the Dean of Veterinary Medicine." She was surprised at herself for a couple of reasons. First, Lindsey never spoke about changing jobs before it happened. She was almost superstitious about it. Second, the thought of leaving their stunning Pacific-view home in Pismo didn't disturb her. Not in the least. She had loved living in that house, but Rich's early description of the place as a "McMansion" had stuck. Furthermore, there was a connection among the four of them, Steve and Kate and Rich and Lindsey. It was far more than mere friendship and the prospect of returning to Texas ....

"I get that Rich would love to return to Texas—and Zach won't object since San Antonio's a whole lot closer to Mustang, Oklahoma," Steve cut into Lindsey's thoughts. "But what about LJ and Morgan? They're sophomores at Cal Poly, right?"

Lindsey nodded. "Rich and I dropped a couple of hints

last week. Then last Wednesday night at dinner, we did it again. Morgan blew through our subtlety and said, 'So, you're considering moving to Texas? If you do that, can I come with you? I'd love to go to A&M. Of course, if you'll have me.' Morgan looked at LJ for a response. She just shrugged and said, 'Their animal science and pre-med programs are as good as Cal Poly, maybe better.'"

Lindsey regarded Kate. "But are you happy about going back to Texas? Is it my imagination, or did you dislike our Texas xenophobia?"

For a minute, Kate didn't reply; she just looked back at Lindsey with a smile. And then the smile broke into a grin. "No, you're right, Linds. My first year in Houston was jam-packed with West Coast prejudice—and you've gotta admit, Lindsey, neither the city nor the weather can come close to this." She extended her arms as if to envelop the cool, dry evening air.

"But now, quite honestly? I can't wait to get back to Texas xenophobes!!"

Rich left Morgan and LJ to await Joey's return from the declotting procedure, which would hopefully bring him out of the coma. It took some persuasion to convince Morgan to stay away from the session with Turner.

"You're right, Morgan. You'd figure out Dr. T.'s motives in a flash."

They'd been at it for a good ten minutes. Rich's last comment caused Morgan's eyes to narrow. "I'm waiting for the 'but.'"

Rich shook his head and then nodded. *What a handful you're growing up to be, Morgan Gardner.*

"Three people will question Dr. T. Morgan, all law enforcement. I might be able to slip in unnoticed, but there's no way you could."

She studied him and then agreed. "Yes, I understand, Rich."

"Do you have a sense of this person, Morgan? An idea of why Dr. T. is supporting Joey's transition to becoming male?"

Most of Morgan's vast psychic and empathic abilities were a pure mystery to Rich. Still, he'd learned she usually didn't speak about her insights or visions. He and Lindsey surmised that the teen unconsciously feared she could speak things into existence and, therefore, guarded such premonitions carefully. But if questioned directly, Morgan usually replied.

"From the beginning, I saw a blackness surrounding Joey … like a cloak. At first, I thought it emanated from him. But as I spent more time with him, I realized it was riding him."

Her gaze still fixed on Rich; she waited for a response.

"Riding, huh?" Despite himself, Rich shuddered. "You mean *riding* like … a horse." His voice dropped to a whisper as he thought about the image. "Like a demon?"

"Yes, like that." Morgan was still looking at Rich, but he didn't think she saw him. Instead, she was pondering this strange dyad. "Joey's afraid of Dr. T., but I don't think it's because he feared Dr. T. killing him. I think Joey's scared of the power Dr. T. holds over him."

Although Rich heard every word, he couldn't rid himself of the devil-rider picture. "Morgan, have you seen this before on other people?"

"You mean the blackness?" She shrugged. "Sure, all the time." Noting Rich's shocked expression, she grinned, an uncommon expression for her. "Don't worry. You don't have any or anyone else at thirty-six Bluff Drive."

On the drive to McManus's downtown San Luis Obispo office, Rich was puzzled over how they should approach Dr. Turner and even if they should.

Too late for second thoughts, Jansen, he thought. *They're well into it now.*

McManus's assistant showed him into the conference room. Detective Cindy Ralston was sitting at the end of a long glass conference table, McManus at the other end. On opposite sides were Stan Kingsbury and the alleged "Dr. T.," a.k.a. Dr. Adam Turner.

Cody acknowledged Rich when he entered the room, nodding toward an empty chair beside Turner. Turner was so focused on Ralston that he didn't even notice Rich as he sat down.

"So then, you've known Joey Carmichael since he was a small child?" Ralston asked.

Rich was impressed by the detective's composure. She was exceptionally pretty but tried to mute her beauty by tightly pulling back her coppery-brown hair in a ponytail and hiding her startling blue eyes under huge, black-rimmed glasses. It didn't work; it just made her look smart and beautiful.

"I've known Joey since he was six. I taught him in kindergarten and then again in second grade." Turner's emphasis on the name and pronoun was courteous but distinct.

Ralston nodded and looked down at a legal pad filled with cursive. Then she looked up. "Your partner, Dr. Nancy Demitres, is the surgeon at UCLA who had planned to do Joey's 'top job' before he lost consciousness. Is that correct?"

If Turner was thrown by Ralston's sudden switch, there was no sign of it. "Dr. Demitres is my wife and heads up the gender-affirmation team at UCLA." Once again, the correction of "partner" to "wife" was subtly emphasized. Turner couldn't staunch the slight smile of pride that escaped his mouth, which seemed unaccustomed to smiling.

Ralston nodded, pinning Turner with her disconcerting blue gaze. "The boy's mother has transferred medical power of attorney to you, Dr. Turner." She glanced back down at the legal pad. "Ms. Carmichael did so just two weeks ago. She did this so you could sign the surgical consent forms for the double mastectomy, correct?" She tapped the legal pad with her index finger.

Turner shifted in his chair and looked away from Ralston. Then he looked at Rich, blinking owlishly through his rimless glasses. "Who are you?"

Rich opened his mouth to answer, but before he could, Ralston spoke, retaining command of the interrogation. "His name is Rich Jansen. He's the father of the two Cal Poly sophomore women who found Joey." Rich didn't correct the detective; he enjoyed watching her technique and didn't want to risk putting Dr. Turner in charge.

Waiting for a beat, Ralston twisted the knife a bit. "His daughter, Morgan, told me they initially thought Joey was dead. Imagine if the girls hadn't happened upon him near the pastures?"

Rich had seen many interrogations and conducted countless such sessions independently. But neither he nor anyone he'd ever watched came close to Ralston. She was a natural.

Turner had no choice but to return his attention to Ralston. Clearing his throat, Turner stiffened his posture. "Detective Ralston, am I being charged with somehow causing Joey's coma?" Looking around the room, Turner's gaze lingered on Rich, then returned to Ralston as if waiting for an answer. Then he shrugged. "I think we're done here, Detective."

As Turner pushed back his chair, Kingsbury spoke for the first time. "Dr. Turner, we have an unconscious teen whom you've mentored for nearly ten years, yet you seem unconcerned. Were you unaware of the embolic risks of long-term testosterone injections?"

"You must not have heard me, Detective. I'm through answering these questions." Dr. Turner stood up, bent down to pick up a leather briefcase, then headed toward the door.

McManus also stood, towering over Turner. "Please stay in the area, Dr. Turner. We'll need to speak with you again."

"Of course. Perhaps you'll be willing to listen precisely to what I saved Zoey Carmichael from."

As Turner left the room, McManus closed the door and eyed Ralston. "Sorry, I was late. Did Dr. Turner explain what he was doing with this kid and why?"

The two detectives shook their heads. "Cody, we could barely get Turner to tell us his name," Ralston said.

Rich said, "But you heard that last comment, right?"

"What do you mean?"

"You just asked Turner not to leave the area. And he answered, 'Of course. Perhaps then you'll be willing to listen to precisely what I saved Zoey Carmichael from.' Why wouldn't Turner explain what he was doing and why while he was here? Why make it seem as if no one would listen to him?"

The DA and the two detectives studied Rich. Ralston spoke first. "Playing games with us?"

"Maybe," Rich replied. And thought about the unusual person who had just left. "Or with himself."

CHAPTER TWENTY

Lindsey smiled at her friends. "Congratulations, Steve. Have you got a lot of loose ends to finish up in the department or …?"

"The dean of medicine was more than happy to bid me farewell today." His eyes narrowed as he looked at Kate, shifting uncomfortably in the rocker. Grabbing his wife's hand, he continued. "Naturally, this isn't how I'd expected to leave Stanford, but we went into our intrepid girl reporter's latest project with eyes wide open." He paused, noting Kate's wry expression. "Actually, I kind of pushed you into doing this, didn't I?"

"Kind of? As I recall, dear husband, after I told you about the fiasco at the kindergarten, your words were, 'And what are you going to do about this?'" Kate looked across the patio at Lindsey. "I was a mess when Steve returned from China."

"China?" Lindsey blurted.

Steve and Kate looked at each other. Then Kate nodded. "You first."

Steve grimaced. "About six months ago, a senior Chinese official contacted Stanford. He'd had a cath, was told he needed surgery, and wanted a second opinion. From a Stanford cardiologist."

Lindsey burst out laughing. "Of course, Pickering couldn't resist an invitation like that!"

Stanford's chief of medicine was an aggressive risk taker, and pulling off a cooperative effort between Beijing and Stanford would be a coup. At best, the new affiliation between Stanford University Medical School and the Peking University People's Hospital had been tenuous. The surprising request could make or break the fragile relationship.

Nevertheless, Steve's boss, Ross Pickering, believed Steve was an ideal choice to deal with the machinations of medicine in the People's Party. Steve had disliked travel even before the pandemic. Sitting masked in an airplane for nearly twenty hours and then playing the role of the humble American consultant wasn't a task one would wish on anyone. But he had no choice except to grin and bear it.

Still smiling, Lindsey shook her head as she regarded her friend and colleague from her days as head of the cath lab at Houston General. "Pickering couldn't have made a better choice, Steve. If anyone could navigate that tightrope, it's you." Then she stopped, one eyebrow raised. "Was it as politically sticky as I'd imagine?" Requests for second opinions were notoriously dicey. Few egos were as massive as physicians, especially those without the academic credentials of their teaching hospital colleagues. Add the cross-cultural challenges, and the enormity of the task could be overwhelming.

Steve rolled his eyes and groaned. "Let's just say I wouldn't wish a week like that on my worst enemy. But yeah, when I returned to Palo Alto, I was the golden boy of Stanford Medical School until a board member's brother in Houston called to tell her about an intriguing series called 'Creating Chemical Eunuchs' written by the Stanford chief of cardiology's journalist wife. Said board member's sister is the first graduate of Cleveland Clinic's Transgender Surgery and Medicine Program."

"Oops," Lindsey said, then looked at Kate. "Your turn."

Kate hadn't heard about the board member and was starting to feel guilty until she remembered whose idea this was. "Once I told Steve about what happened with Addison Meeks and three-year-old Danny Sugarman at the kindergarten, he asked me what I planned to do about it." Kate sighed and pointed at the monitor through which they could hear their sleeping boys' occasional stirring and sighs. "I told Steve he'd forgotten about them, but of course he hadn't." She put her hand on Steve's thigh. "You had it all worked out in your head. It just took me time to catch up with you. The notion of a British nanny felt …."

"Posh?" Lindsey suggested. "Elitist? Pretentious? Too white bread? Like a McMansion in Pismo Beach?"

Startled, Kate stared at her, and then both doubled over with laughter.

"Yes! Yes, exactly!" Kate said. "But the truth is none of those things." Kate took a fortifying sip of wine. "I was scared. For almost five years, I've been a mom and been scarily content with caring for these two amazing human beings."

For a few moments, no one spoke. The only sounds were the occasional deep breaths from one of the boys and the rustle of palm trees in the gentle night breeze.

"But …."

Kate laughed. "Right, Lindsey, 'behold the underlying truth.' Once I got into the research, the high of the chase was on. But my first three or four iterations ended up getting dumped."

"Really?" Steve said. He knew she'd had trouble, but not that much.

Kate nodded. "Yeah, I danced around it."

"Danced around?" Lindsey asked.

"Yes. I kept losing myself in the details of what *could* be done to these kids medically, surgically, and hormonally. It was as if I were teaching someone how to transition from a boy to a girl or the opposite. I just didn't want to take the covers off. After dumping at least twenty thousand words, I remembered what I saw at that kindergarten and what I heard from that teacher: sheer evil. So, I called Father John Tobin."

Transfixed, Lindsey leaned forward, shaking her head and chuckling. Noting Kate's puzzled look, Lindsey referred to the name Kate had used in her series for Father John, "Also known as Father Dan Cavendish, Father John's the reason I'm here, Kate! I don't watch the news; I had no clue you'd written your articles until I called Father John for advice about Joey. After he'd listened to my long saga, he told me about your series. Father John also told me you guys were about to join the Catholic church. Since we're all converts, he strongly recommended that I come in person instead of reading your articles online." Lindsey's eyes glittered. "Is it possible to think any of this is a coincidence?"

Dr. Turner stepped out of the SLO County building, shaking his head in dismay. *How could these people not understand that everything I did was for Joey? To save him from turning into his mother?* Turner shuddered at the thought of Joey mimicking his mother's destructive, nightmarish life. Her alcohol and drug addiction, the prostitution that paid for her habits, and the resulting never-ending stream of men. Turner knew it was only a matter of time before one of those dirtbags would turn from Cassie to her child.

Dr. Turner pictured that small, gorgeous little girl as he walked into his second-grade classroom. She seemed lonely. Something clicked between Dr. Turner and the adorable child, so he began to spend extra time with Zoey after school. Of course, he'd not been Dr. Adam Turner then but Amanda Bernstein. Turner's mother never called him anything but Mandy, even now.

The countless times he'd asked herself, "Why this kid?" the answers had been rote and not genuine.

Zoey was the child he'd always wanted. Finally, a stunning little girl that Turner could safeguard from the horror of being female.

Of course, Dr. T. wanted to protect the kid from men who preferred the tight, tiny bodies of little girls. More importantly, Cassie reminded Dr. Turner of his own mother: narcissistic and a master manipulator.

Those reasons were valid, but none was Turner's motivation. It wasn't until he finished his dissertation in clinical psychology that Turner figured it out. Of course, by then, it no longer mattered.

There was plenty of tutoring time for the little girl and young teacher because Cassie was always late. At least an hour, sometimes two. Instead of tattling on Cassie to the principal, Turner used the extra time to tutor Zoey. Within a few months, Zoey was reading at a sixth-grade level and had conquered her fear of math. In addition, she was a quick learner with an excellent memory. After a few days, when Cassie forgot to pick up her daughter, Turner offered to drive Zoey home on his way to his job teaching night classes.

Cassie gladly accepted the offer, and Turner was treated to a firsthand look at Zoey's pitiful surroundings: a double-wide trailer that hadn't been cleaned in decades, chickens running around in the dirt, and Cassie, partially clothed with a drink in one hand and a cigarette in the other. It was Providence, Turner believed. He'd been led to the tiny town in the middle of nowhere, northern California, to save Zoey.

Near the end of his dying relationship with Paula, a former girlfriend, Turner agreed to take five days off, rent an RV, and camp over the long July 4th weekend at Strawberry Campground. Immersed in the turquoise water of the Sky River and hiking in the Plumas National Forest almost brought Paula and Turner back to the reasons they'd initially committed to one another—almost.

In a way, Turner understood Paula's complaints. Turner had spent every waking moment completing his Ph.D. in psychology at the University of San Francisco. The coursework and clinical internship had been grueling, and Paula had stuck it out by Turner's side for three years. So when the two women finally broke it off during the camping trip, Turner decided that staying in the remote town of Strawberry, California, was the key to healing a broken heart. Strawberry Elementary School had been eager to accept Turner's application.

When the school year ended, Dr. T. suggested he take Zoey for a long weekend in that Plumas Forest he'd fallen in love with. Cassie loved the five-day break because she was a foster parent to three other girls, and eight-year-old Zoey wouldn't be missed. On that vacation, Turner asked Zoey if she wanted to grow up to be like her mom.

They'd been roasting marshmallows, and there was blackened detritus around Zoey's mouth when she'd asked, "What do you mean, 'grow up to be like Cassie?' No, I don't want to be a druggie or drunk like her." The child stared into the fire and said, "If there were a way I could avoid growing up to be a woman, I'd take it in a second."

Turner studied the girl, said nothing, and waited.

"What?" Zoey stared at him and said, "You mean there's a way *not* to grow up to be a woman?"

Rich didn't know what he'd expected, but it surely wasn't this. Joey was back from the procedure, but nothing seemed any different. The teen looked the same. There were intravenous lines in both arms, monitor screens flashing his heart and respiratory rates, a catheter, and a half-filled urinary collection bag. Joey lay motionless, his eyes closed.

When LJ saw Rich, she jumped off the chair she'd been perched on, eager to escape. Morgan, however, was sitting as close to the bedside as possible. She seemed to be studying Joey's face.

"Wait. We're not going to leave Morgan here," Rich said to LJ, who was almost pushing him out into the hall.

"She's not leaving, Rich. She says Joey can't be alone, that he needs her here."

Shaking his head, Rich walked around the side of the bed. Morgan didn't move.

"We're leaving now, Morgan."

She raised her eyes and looked at Rich.

Rich locked eyes with her and then nodded firmly. He ignored the expression of exquisite sadness on the girl's face and leaned down to help her stand. As she did, tears coursed down her face, and she began to mutter. Rich couldn't understand what she was saying and didn't want to. Whatever was happening to Joey, it wasn't good. Either the doctors were too late to get to the clot, or they had failed to access the artery.

He couldn't believe that he and Toni had been displaying a pair of red bikini underpants just nine hours earlier. It felt like a lifetime ago.

LJ had come back into the room when she saw Morgan crying. Wisely, she said nothing, just held out her hand and waited. Morgan took it, and the two young women left with Rich following them.

So, who's supposed to tell this kid's mother what's happened? Rich wondered. *And given that I'm elected, what in the blazes should I say to the woman?*

"Dr. T., it's gotta be him. There's no one else."

LJ stopped. "What did you say, Rich?"

Not realizing he'd spoken aloud, Rich slowed and looked at her. "Someone's got to tell Joey's mother about his condition, and Dr. T. is the only one who can do that since he has power of attorney."

He pulled out his cell phone and called Cody McManus. He heard other voices in the background at the other end of the line. "Hey, Cody, we just left Joey's bedside. He looks no different from before the procedure. There wasn't any doc around to ask, but I think the treatment didn't work. He's still unresponsive. Can one of your people contact that prof and ask him to call Joey's mother or get her information so that someone can call her?" He listened for a moment. "OK, great. Thanks."

As he disconnected the call, Morgan turned to him. "I think the drug worked fine." Her tears were gone, and Morgan was back to her detached self. Startled, Rich stopped in the middle of the hospital foyer and stared at her.

"Hey, guys, we need to get home. The dogs …" LJ stopped talking when she noticed Rich's attention was fixed on Morgan. He asked, "Is Joey communicating with you, Morgan?"

Tears welled up in Morgan's eyes as she nodded. "He doesn't want to live. Joey's hoping he can die. He hates himself and his life."

After consuming another of Lucinda's fantastic gourmet dinners, the three moved outside onto the patio. They talked about the day's fun and the simple pleasure of being together.

They had spent Saturday wandering around Union Square, enjoying cappuccino and biscotti in an Italian restaurant. After that, at Kate's suggestion, they did some window shopping in Chinatown and then caught the Saturday Vigil Mass at the stunning St. Peter and Paul Catholic Church across from Washington Square.

"Then you can take your time heading home tomorrow morning, Lindsey," Kate had said. "You'll already have gone to Mass."

Lindsey was entranced by the beautiful neo-Gothic twin bell towers and the stone-washed white simplicity of the exterior building. But her jaw dropped when she entered the church. It was one of the most beautiful churches Lindsey had ever been in. She couldn't stop staring at the enormous painting of the risen Christ on the ceiling. Evidently, Kate and Steve were regulars because a couple of ushers called Steve by name.

Watching the couple at Mass, Lindsey could see their knowledge of the liturgy and the sincerity of their prayer during the service. Not yet received into the Church, however, Steve and Kate could not receive Christ's Body and Blood.

Later, they sat outside on the patio at Kate and Steve's after dinner. Lindsey stated the obvious. "So, you guys are joining the Catholic Church." Lindsey thought it odd that neither had discussed such a big decision at dinner the night before.

"Um, yeah, the elephant on the table." Steve's chuckle was forced.

"Why now, Steve?" Lindsey asked. For some reason, she thought Steve had backed off from joining the church after their first child, JH, was born. She knew Kate and Steve had spoken with Father John about their responsibilities if JH were baptized in the Catholic Church. "Is it because of Kate's articles, the threats to her, or …."

This time, there was no chuckle, not even a smile; this was serious. From the corner of her eye, Lindsey saw Kate lean closer toward her husband on the double swing they were sitting on and placed her hand on Steve's thigh.

Steve's warm brown eyes narrowed. "I bet you understand why there's no easy answer to why now, right?" Then he lifted an eyebrow at Kate.

Lindsey, also a Catholic convert, smiled and nodded at him but said nothing, waiting for more. She was startled when Kate spoke. "Steve wanted to join the church four years ago, Lindsey. I'm the one who wanted to wait. I can't explain why, but I couldn't make the leap from non-practicing Episcopalian to Catholic. Maybe it was all the mostly misunderstood papal infallibility or the far more rigorous demands on Catholics: obligation for weekly Mass, in-person confession, distinguishing between mortal and venial sins." Kate paused and then smiled ruefully. "Or maybe it was just what Steve said more than once: laziness."

Lindsey knew what she meant. Kate was the last person in the world whom anyone would call lazy, but spiritual laziness was something else entirely. Only when someone peels back the layers of their soul do they understand the seven sins that the Church calls cardinal. Sloth was a thing Lindsey had never heard of, but once she began to study, pray, and ask Father John about it, she began to understand.

"In my introduction to the article series, Linds, my statements about evil were vastly truncated. All the other pieces I did—the one on you and your wrongful conviction, Gabe McAllister's wrongful conviction, and the series I did on the homeless in San Francisco—were written out of certainty that *people* cause the world's horrors, for money, power, fame, whatever.

"But Allison Meeks introduced me to something very different. This *child* parrots insane theories without question." Kate's voice cracked. "That was the beginning. The demonstrations, threats, and curses cemented what I knew. This isn't the work of people." She ignored the tears pouring down her face. "But of course, none of this is new. It just looks that way, especially to people like me who have been so blind." Absently, Kate took both hands and brushed her cheeks dry. Her smile was sad. "There's so much I don't understand, probably will *never* understand about God and the Catholic faith. But finally, segueing back to your question, 'Why now?'

"Because I'm a huge part of the darkness taking over our world. For most of my adult life, I've ignored the commandments. I used God's name as an adjective and thought sleeping around was fine so long as no one got hurt. But of course, they do, don't they? Those birth control pills we take mindlessly are abortifacients. They kill human embryos." She sighed. "Making a god of my career. Offending God without even thinking about it. *Sin.*" Kate paused. Searching for the right words, only to discover there weren't any.

"I'm with Peter. 'Where else can we go, Lord? You have the words to eternal life.'"

Lindsey thought of Kate's phrase in one of her articles, "institutional cowardice," concerning her meeting with her boss, Dr. Peterson, the week before. Thinking about what Peterson had said, she suddenly realized the woman had indeed *warned*—not threatened—her. Someone from the faculty who knew Joey had complained. So, Joey must have told someone that she was helping him detransition. Maybe someone from the GLESN meeting? The group that had elected him president.

Lindsey's animosity against her boss, Alexandra Peterson, rolled away as she sat in the quiet evening with her friends. She thought *I'd be no different in her shoes—is it cowardice? Not if you've not taken the time to figure out what you believe about all this. But isn't there something immoral about determinedly staying on the surface? Remaining intentionally ignorant? That is precisely where I was before Joey Carmichael tumbled into my life.*

Lindsey was grateful for the upcoming meeting with A&M because whoever had complained about her to the college president surely knew about Joey's coma—and, she thought, could easily blame her. They needed to leave California.

Finally home, Rich watched LJ and Morgan with the dogs. The two-legged and four-legged creatures were racing and dancing, pent-up energy taking all four of them throughout the house.

"Hey, why don't you two take Max and Gus for a run?" Rich said. "It'll be light for another hour, and it'll take me—"

The door slammed before Rich could complete his thought. "About that long to get dinner ready." Shocked by the sudden silence, Rich breathed more deeply than he had in days. At least that's how it felt. He wandered through the kitchen to the walk-in pantry and thought about comfort food. That was what they needed. After grabbing two different kinds of pasta, olive oil, and the ingredients for marinara sauce, he got some diced garlic from the refrigerator and a large frying pan. Five minutes later, the house was suffused with the fragrance of garlic.

While waiting for the water to boil for the pasta, Rich pondered Morgan's last statement about Joey. *Of course, he'd rather stay in a coma ... or die. The kid lives in a body that's been treated like a lab rat.*

Although Rich had been immersed in Blake Cameron's tragically stupid rape case, he'd listened to Lindsey when she'd talked about Joey. The joy he'd felt with the Dobermans was something Rich understood. The summer after his wife had been killed and he'd nearly died from a shootout in northern Houston, there were plenty of days when Rich yearned for death. But Max, that astounding red Dobie boy, hadn't let him. Rich smiled at the memory of the dog sitting beside his bed, patiently but persistently insisting he get up, get dressed, then walk, jog, and run.

His phone pinged. When he saw it was Cody, Rich picked up and said, "Hey Cody, what's up?"

"Ralston, Kingsbury, and I are talking about them driving up to Strawberry tomorrow morning to talk to the mother in person. Maybe we can get some information from her about Turner if we tell her about the boy's condition in person. Or something else that could help us figure out what's going on with this kid. Ralston wants to know if you'd like to tag along." Rich could hear her talking in the background but couldn't understand what she was saying.

Rich thought of the framed picture of Lindsey with the dogs in Joey's dorm room. *Was it just this morning when we saw that picture?*

Wham!

Rich winced at the downstairs door slamming into the foyer wall. Why hadn't he inserted that doorstopper he'd thought about a million times?

"Hey Cody, I'm just about to put dinner on the table. Can I let you know in an hour or so?"

When they appeared, he bowed before the panting girls and dogs. "Your dinners are served."

"No. I need to get back there, Rich. He's all alone!"

Setting his fork beside his empty plate, Rich looked at Morgan, then down at her plate, which was still mostly filled with aioli pasta. "It's after nine at night, and we can't see him, Morgan. It's too late. Besides, you haven't eaten anything today. Can you please try to eat some of your dinner?"

Morgan began to speak but was interrupted by LJ. "He's right, Morgan. It's delicious. Rich made it because it's one of your favorite meals."

Surprised, Morgan turned to Rich. "I'm sorry. I barely noticed what was on my plate. That was rude and thankless of me." She picked up her fork, took a small bite, and then another. Soon, she'd finished and shyly asked for more.

Once the meal was over and the dishes cleared, Rich addressed the girls. "I'm driving up north to Strawberry tomorrow with Detectives Ralston and Kingsbury to meet with Joey's mother." It felt like a small thing he could do for this teen. And for Morgan. And the detectives were right. You could get much more information when looking at someone face to face than on the phone.

"I know you'd like to go, Morgan, but you two should get back to your classes." When Morgan said nothing in reply, he continued. "Is there anything specific you'd like me to speak with her about other than his obvious condition?"

"I think it's good that I stay away from Joey's mother," Morgan replied shakily, her coppery eyes flashing angrily. "I could fill books with what I'd like to talk to her about." Then she calmed down and regarded Rich steadily. "Thank you, Rich. Your name suits you. He's given you many gifts and made you truly rich."

Rich felt his cheeks warm. "Thank you," he said, avoiding Morgan's gaze. The young woman had lived with them for close to two years now. She'd bowed her head during grace before their meals and attended Sunday Mass with them. Still, she had never mentioned religion, God, or faith until that moment.

"Whaddayuh want?"

If her eyes weren't bloodshot with huge purplish bags under them, her blonde hair a frizzy, unkempt mess, and her lips etched into a sneer, Cassie Carmichael might have been an attractive woman.

Rich and the two detectives had driven to Strawberry in under four hours. However, finding Cassie's double-wide trailer was dicey since the things dotted the tiny town and weren't well-numbered.

"Ma'am, are you Ms. Cassie Carmichael?" Detective Kingsbury stepped back slightly as a bearded man appeared behind Cassie.

Rich saw Ralston's right-hand drop to the holster beneath her black blazer in his peripheral vision.

"Augie, it's OK," Cassie said. "They probably need something signed for Zoey." Giggling, she corrected herself. "I mean Joey. I can't get that kid's names straight."

Even eight feet away from her, the stench of alcohol on her breath was overpowering. Or maybe it was Augie who was billowing cheap whiskey and wine.

"Yes, I'm Cassie Carmichael," she said. She peered up at Kingsbury, who was over six feet tall. "You are here about Joey, right?" Before the detective could answer, Cassie turned to Augie, whose shadow was hovering behind her. "Would you be a good fella and grab my robe, please? This wind is blowin' good and cold."

She was right. When they'd left the central coast, it had been sunny with temperatures in the low eighties. But with the rise in elevation northward into the mountains, the temperature had plummeted, and the gray skies signaled the potential arrival of a late spring storm. The clouds looked ominous.

Taking advantage of the interruption, Rich stepped forward and said, "Ms. Carmichael, you're right. It's quite cold out here, and we didn't dress for it. Can we come in and speak with you about Joey, please?"

Startled, Cassie stepped back just as her boyfriend appeared with a sweater. Rich and the detectives stepped into the trailer, rubbing their hands together dramatically.

Rich glanced at Ralston, who moved forward, extended her hand, and said, "Hello, Ms. Carmichael; my name is Cindy Ralston. I'm a detective with the San Luis Obispo police. And yes, we are here to speak with you about Joey."

Cassie stood staring at her, but Cindy kept her hand out until she took it. And mumbled, "Hello."

Looking at a cluttered dining table with four chairs, Cindy said, "Okay if we sit here for just a few minutes?"

Before Cassie could reply, both detectives took a seat. Cindy gestured to Cassie to sit across from her. "Thank you for letting us interrupt your Saturday morning." Very briefly, she glanced at Rich as she began to talk about Joey. In a low voice and at a measured pace, Cindy explained what had happened and what was being done for him.

Augie had stuck his head out of what must have been the bedroom, but when he saw Cassie seated with the detectives, he went back into the room and shut the door. He overlooked Rich, who was in the room behind Cassie, looking at an open laptop showing the first of Kate's newspaper articles. This lady didn't seem to be a person who would surf the net for news. Someone had alerted her to the newspaper series, and Rich wondered who and why. And then he spied a card next to the laptop. He looked around the room to ensure no one was watching him and grabbed his phone to take a picture of the card. "Rachel Stawarski, JD, Transgender Law Center, Oakland, California." Staring at the card, Rich thought, *Transgender Law Center; I've never heard of it but bet I'm about to learn plenty.*

Rich's thoughts were cut short when Cassie suddenly shouted. "Something went wrong with that surgery, didn't it?"

Cindy leaned forward and very gently touched Cassie's arm. Clearly, the woman hadn't heard a word the detective had been saying.

"No, he's in a coma. He didn't have the surgery."

"Then what happened?" Her voice was lower now. "I signed the consent that Dr. T. brought so he could have that top surgery." She looked more confused than angry.

Cindy looked at Rich, who had just taken the last seat at the table.

He nodded and explained. "Ms. Carmichael, I'm Rich Jansen." Deciding it was simpler to keep Detective Ralston's version of his relationship with Morgan and LJ, he said, "My daughters are friends of Joey; they are in Joey's class at Cal Poly. Joey collapsed in one of the pastures on campus the morning he was supposed to have the surgery. My daughters found him and called 911.

"The doctors believe he has a clot in his brain. They've given him medicine to break it up and hope he'll wake up, but he hasn't yet."

Cassie had been staring at Rich, concentrating on what he was saying. Without diverting her gaze, she attempted to smile and said, "Thank you. I'm glad Joey has friends." Then, she asked, "Do you think my boy will wake up?"

And looked almost grateful when Rich answered, "We don't know, we can only hope and pray."

Once outside and back in the car, Ralston shook her head. "Thanks, Rich; I'm glad you came with us. I guess I wasn't speaking English." She looked in the rear-view mirror at Rich in the back seat. "Did you find anything on that open laptop?"

"She was reading a series of articles about transgenderism written by a friend, Kate …."

"Townsend, Kate Townsend." Kingsbury gushed. "You know her? My wife and I are looking for private schools for our kids because of her articles."

While the detective continued his enthusiastic rant about Kate's articles, Rich wondered why he'd not told the detectives about finding the lawyer's card from the Transgender Law Center.

CHAPTER TWENTY-SIX

"Cassie …."

Dr. Turner had been able to utter only that one word for the last fifteen minutes, saying it repeatedly.

Exasperated, Turner's wife, Dr. Nancy Demitres, a plastic surgeon, strode across their expansive parfait floor, plucked the phone out of Turner's hands, and ended the call, ignoring Turner's incredulous and annoyed expression. "Adam, the woman won't listen to anything you have to say. Cassie Carmichael has never been willing to hear any other voice but her own. No matter how long you remained on the phone listening to her incoherent babble, you'd never have been able to say anything."

After pocketing the phone, Nancy lowered her voice. "And if you had been able to speak to her, what would you say? What could anyone say? Embolic phenomena are a well-known complication of testosterone therapy, especially over an extended period. Joey's been on it for six years, right?"

"Eight and a half years." Turner's voice was a cracked whisper. Then, his face crumpled with sadness, but there were no tears. Turner hadn't cried since he was a young child. Nancy had long ago intuited that Turner had been "taught" not to cry by his insane mother.

Putting her hands on Adam's thin shoulders, Nancy guided him out of the foyer and then into the great room of their 4,500-square-foot home. She pushed Adam down on the leather recliner, which looked out onto the massive rock in Pismo Bay.

"Stay." The canine command elicited a soft giggle from Turner.

Nancy pivoted back across the room to the bar and prepared a double bourbon and water. Nancy watched Adam in the mirrored wall behind the bar as she made the drink. He was huddled in the recliner, taking up less than a third of the oversized chair.

You are such a tiny, fragile human, trying painfully hard to keep that shell around your heart, Nancy thought. *Maybe you fool your students, Dr. Turner, and even those cops, but not me.*

They had met while Nancy was completing her plastic surgery residency. Nancy had been reeling after her divorce from a Marine helicopter pilot. She'd expected to stay married to Scott until death. But med school and her extensive residencies had demanded supernatural patience and support. Scott had stuck with her throughout her general surgery residency, but when she added another two years of plastic residency, Scott had had enough.

On a lark, she went to a gay bar and met Adam there. Even after living with and marrying Adam Turner, Nancy didn't consider herself a lesbian. She couldn't explain their attachment in words, not even to herself, but she knew it was more of a friendship than any erotic love that kept her with Adam.

Sighing as she poured herself a scotch on the rocks, Nancy shook her head. *Erotic love's been out of the question for Adam since he was young.* The mutilation of Adam's genitalia was worse than that of orthodox Muslim females.

Nancy had begged Adam to let her operate and mitigate some of the damage, but Adam had gotten so angry at the suggestion that he'd not spoken to her for a week.

Evidently, the woman who had given birth to Adam had

devised countless torture methods for her little girl's tiny body. Among the most obvious were cigarette burns. They were all over Adam's body, especially his breasts. Adam's mother had also used several cutting methods, including razors, scissors, and knives. They had been used on the vulva, clitoris, and perineum. Her mother had so mutilated Adam that two surgeries were required to repair the damage to his urethra. That happened when Child Protective Services took Adam away from his mother. Adam was eleven at the time.

Nancy had learned all this through friends in the social services department. Adam refused to talk about his mother, family, or upbringing.

Nancy momentarily left the drinks on the bar and returned to the kitchen to prepare a few appetizers: a little pub cheese, crackers, smoked salmon, and olives. She placed them all on a tray with forks, plates, and napkins and put them on the table beside Tuner's chair. Then she picked up the drinks and handed Turner his bourbon and water.

"Don't say a word until you've consumed half of that drink. And then you can talk about what you want to do about Cassie and Joey." She smiled, "Doctor's orders."

Kate raised her martini glass and held it up to study its simple elegance. Steve smiled after a good thirty seconds of watching her stare at the drink. "So, you ordered that drink just to look at?"

"Well, Dr. Cooper, you must admit that few cocktails are more elegant than a vodka martini with olives. Neat. And shaken, not stirred, in the classic Bond version. I think it's been five years since I've had one of these, husband of mine." She blinked at Steve. "I've either been pregnant or breastfeeding for five years."

Steve grinned at his wife, delighted to see her so excited and vibrant.

"So, I'm warning you. Be ready for some serious s—"

"Sleep," Steve said, completing her sentence for her.

Nodding vigorously as she suppressed her laughter, Kate took a sip, then another, and then a third. "My goodness, Steve, I'd forgotten how wonderful these things were!"

Their trip had been flawless. Some dear person at the University of Texas Medical Center in San Antonio had booked a first-class flight the morning before yesterday for all five of them. JH and Nicholas had behaved perfectly on the four-hour flight. And the three-bedroom suite at the Sonder at the medical center was spacious and comfortable.

Steve met with the medical school's chairman and several medical department heads that day, after which he was named the new UT San Antonio chief of cardiology.

Their server arrived with two sizzling New York strip steaks. "Can you both check your steaks to ensure they're cooked how you want?" Dressed in a black shirt with a bolo tie and black jeans, their waitress, Barbie, was as cute as her name.

Once she left, Kate and Steve focused on Perry Steakhouse and Grille's signature steak and grilled asparagus.

"How about some dessert?" Barbie asked when she returned to their table and saw they were nearly finished.

Steve's "Sure thing" overrode Kate's "No," and soon they shared a crème Brulé.

"I'm stuffed! I cannot believe I ate all this. That five pounds I lost are now back and brought friends." Kate sighed and said, "I'm whining—forgive me, I hate it when I complain, especially about a dinner like this. She looked at her lanky husband and said, "Thank you for bringing us back to Texas."

Smiling, Steve said, "Nothing to forgive. Plus, you'll walk it all off. Remember, we're going to buy a house tomorrow."

"Let's start with the basics: how many bedrooms? One floor or two? Are there things you do or don't want in a general layout?" Their realtor, John Smith, smiled in response to their puzzled expressions. "Carpet, wood floors, wine cellar? Stuff like that. Also, would you like a private space for your au pair, like a guest house? Are there things about the property itself that you want? Like a lawn for the kids and dog if you have one?" He waited for their reply as he stood before a computer display that showed a map of San Antonio studded with hundreds of real estate offerings.

While still in California, Kate had been referred to John and his wife, Michele, by a friend. During their initial conversation, Michele suggested they bring the boys and Lucinda with them since their office conference room had plenty of room. They also had toys for kids to play with. But even Lucinda couldn't get Nicholas to settle down despite all the distractions. After what felt like thirty but was probably only five or ten minutes, Lucinda stood up from the large white conference table with Nicholas in her arms, now quiet and staring curiously around.

"It's been lovely meeting you both, and thank you very much for all your trouble accommodating us," Lucinda said, "but I think it best if the boys and I take a short walk around the neighborhood." She started outside with the boys and then stopped. "Kate and Steve, I'm OK with whatever layout you choose. If the house you're drawn to has a guesthouse, wonderful. If not, fine." She walked out the door, Nicholas cradled in one arm and JH holding her other hand.

John grinned and shook his head as he watched her go. Then he turned to Kate and Steve. "Do you ever get accustomed to that Oxford accent? Everything she says sounds so …."

"Educated, refined, intellectual?" Michele said.

Kate and Steve smiled at each other as they sat together at the opposite end of the large conference table from John's computer display. "No, you never get used to the accent," Steve said. "And you're right, Michele. Lucinda makes the most ordinary conversation sound literary." He turned back to Kate. "Kate, you barely had time to even think about our California house. I made all those decisions for us. So, go for it."

Kate leaned forward, looked at John, and said, "Okay, here are the essentials. At least four bedrooms, a large yard with lots of trees, super big kitchen for our nanny/gourmet chef." She thought for a minute, "Single level is better but not essential. A guest house for her is important." She looked at Steve. "Don't you think?"

He nodded and said, "Yes, I think that is an essential—if

not a house, at least private space."

The realtors were listening attentively. Michele was tapping on her phone, looked up, and said, "What about the commute time to the medical center? There are some stunning restored homes less than ten minutes away."

"With the freeways, aren't the newer homes in the north a thirty-minute drive or less?" Steve looked at Kate and said, "San Antonio's a lot different from Houston in almost every way, including traffic."

John and Michele looked at one another. Then John said, "Let's show you homes that meet your requirements in several San Antonio neighborhoods. And Steve, you're right; the new construction on the edge of the Hill Country is within thirty minutes of the medical center. And, what are you guys thinking for your price range?"

Kate said, "We're getting more than we asked for the Palo Alto house, so how about a 1.2 to 1.5 million ceiling." She turned to Steve, who said, "Sounds good."

Dr. Turner stared at the carefully prepared breakfast of a beautiful omelet and bacon cooked exactly as he liked it, burned. After failing even an approximation of a smile in appreciation for Nancy, he pushed his chair back and raced into the bathroom. He vomited what little he had in his stomach, then waited for the dry heaves to end. Finally, washing out his mouth, Turner stared into the mirror.

Cassie Carmichael's drunken, stoned rant had been irrational, as usual, but a few of her shouts kept circling in Turner's brain.

Who's gonna take care of Zoey/Joey now that he's a vegetable?

Are you footing all these hospital bills?

Where's Joey going to go once the hospital's done with him?

Staring into the mirror, Turner asked himself, "So, precisely what are you planning to do, *Mandy*?"

Turner's use of the name he abhorred transformed the image staring back at him into his mother. The long black hair, long-lashed, almost black almond-shaped eyes, and full, sensuous lips of Miss Georgia 1983 stared back.

Turner closed his eyes. When he opened them again, he regarded his own face.

"You know what you need to do. Go get it done."

When Turner left the bathroom, Nancy stood by the table holding two plates of perfectly prepared omelets, both untouched. Her blue eyes followed Adam as he entered the foyer and grabbed his briefcase. Nancy had taken the week off from work because she wanted to be there for Adam. She'd offered to drive him to the hospital that morning, but Adam had refused.

At times like these, Turner couldn't understand why Nancy stayed with him. He'd withdrawn from Nancy and was almost wholly uncommunicative. Turner had also isolated himself to the point of sleeping in the guest room to ensure no undesirable affection could thaw his resolve.

Turner could feel Nancy's gaze on his back as he walked down the path and got into his car. After starting the engine, he hesitated.

What are you going to do?

Mandy, what are you going to do?

The traffic was light on the 101, so he got to the hospital in less than twenty minutes. He found the ICU and spied Joey in the cubicle on his immediate right in the circle that composed the critical care unit. Conveniently, the tech at the monitors at the nursing station didn't see him, and it looked like no one was in there with Joey.

"Good morning, Dr. T.," someone said, causing Turner to nearly jump out of his skin.

Lindsey was late. She'd been taken aback when Dr. Tom Parker, Dean of Veterinary Science at Texas A&M, returned her call early that morning with unbridled enthusiasm.

"Dr. McCall, I'm delighted to finally speak with you." He continued in classic Texan style, welcoming and disarming. But he startled her when he said the deans of Medicine and Public Health wanted to meet her. Would she consider a triple faculty appointment in medicine, public health, and veterinary science?

Would I consider it? You've got to be kidding me! I nearly had to beg for an interview at Cal Poly two years ago. Texas, I sure have missed you!

"Of course, I'd consider three appointments. That's unbelievably generous of y'all." Lindsey chuckled as she heard her native Texanese creep back into her language. "When would you like me to come for an interview?" The pause was so long that Lindsey thought the connection had been dropped.

"Is there any way to get here tomorrow?" he asked. His question was followed by another long pause, this time from Lindsey. "I'm sorry, Dr. McCall. I—"

"Please call me Lindsey."

"OK, Lindsey, and I'm Tom."

"Yes, Tom, I can rearrange my schedule to get there tomorrow. Thank you for your invitation. I must confess I'm excited at the thought of returning to Texas. Three faculty appointments are more than I could have hoped for."

Just then her boss, Jodi Tamarack, walked into her office. Once Lindsey disconnected, Jodi's large brown eyes widened. "Three faculty appointments? Was that A&M?" Jodi had graduated from the A&M School of Veterinary Medicine and had loved every minute of those four years.

"Yes! Can you believe it?" Lindsey gave her a quick hug. "But I'm so sorry, Jodi, I need to run. Can you save me time for lunch when I get back? And can you assign Christine some time here in the lab to take care of the dogs? I probably won't be back until Friday 'cause I might as well take a few days to look at houses while I'm there."

Lindsey's flight to College Station, Texas, left in less than an hour. She was cramming a suit, running gear, and a pair of jeans into her carry-on bag when she felt eyes on her. Pivoting to look behind her, she saw Rich standing with one arm around Morgan and the other around LJ, tears running down the girls' cheeks. Max and Gus sat like sentinels in front of the trio.

Lindsey hurried across the room, shaking her head. "Oh, girls, I'm so sorry, so very, very sorry. Joey's dead, isn't he?"

At that, their quiet tears became sobs. Rich hugged the girls even tighter. "Dr. Dyson apologizes for not waiting to speak to you, but there was a multi-car crash on the 101. They were expecting an onslaught of patients, and she had to get to the emergency room. She thinks he flipped another clot, this time to his main coronary artery. They coded him for over twenty minutes but couldn't bring him back." He handed Lindsey a slip of paper with Dr. Dyson's cell number on it. "She said you could call her from the airport."

Lindsey felt the pressure of tears building and opened her mouth to say she'd cancel her trip, but Rich shook his head, anticipating her response. "You need to get going, Dr. McCall. We'd all like to know if we're moving back to Texas—and when."

Morgan lifted her head. "Lindsey, this is what he wanted. Joey knew he couldn't go back to being a healthy human. Even with your help getting him off the testosterone and on estrogen, he'd be neither a man nor a woman but somewhere in between. A kind of wasteland. He couldn't face the rest of his life like that."

Looking at the young woman while she spoke, Lindsey realized Morgan was consoling *her*. In that strange and remarkable autistic brain that prohibited typical human emotions' facial and verbal cues was a reservoir of exquisite sensitivity that almost brought Lindsey to her knees.

She didn't doubt that Morgan was repeating things she knew about Joey. Lindsey had no clue how the two had communicated while he was ostensibly comatose, but her scientific mind didn't seek evidence in this case.

Then, as only Morgan could, she switched off her sorrow and began describing the classes that A&M offered in animal science that Cal Poly lacked.

By then, LJ had caught Morgan's excitement about possibly switching from Cal Poly to Texas A&M pre-med. "We think we may graduate six months earlier at A&M if what we've learned online bears out," LJ said, the tears still drying on her cheeks. Then she batted her eyelashes at Lindsey. "Just think, I could be in med school and Morgan in vet school by January next year."

Picking up on the changed atmosphere, Max and Gus began to dance.

"Rich, are you sure?" Lindsey asked. "It feels like all I've done lately is drop in for a visit and then take off again."

Her husband began to hum, then sway with the girls from side to side, and then the three of them began to sing the following song.

I've seen a lot of places
I've been around the world
I've seen some pretty faces
Been with some beautiful girls
But after all I've witnessed one thing still amazes me
Just like a miracle you have to see to believe
'Cause God blessed Texas with his own hand
Brought down angels from the promised land
Gave 'em a place where they could dance
If you wanna see heaven, brother, here's your chance
I've been sent to spread the message
God blessed Texas
First he lit sunshine
Then he made the waters deep
Then he gave us moonlight
For all the world to see
Well everybody knows that the Lord works in mysterious ways
He took a rest then on the very next day
God blessed Texas with his own hand ….

CHAPTER THIRTY

"Kate, sorry to bother you. Are you somewhere you can talk?"

"Sure, Jeff, just give me a few minutes. Can I call you back in five?"

Kate's editor, Jeff Simmons, sounded very different from the cheery man she'd talked to two days earlier when he welcomed her back to Texas.

It was only 7:00 p.m., but Lucinda and the boys were already down for the night, and Kate didn't want to wake them with her conversation. At Kate's enthusiastic agreement, Steve had accepted an invitation to dinner with the dean of the medical school and a few other chairs of medical departments. They had narrowed the list of potential houses to three—two if Steve nixed one after sleeping on it—and planned to return to Palo Alto on Sunday morning after placing an offer.

Kate was pleased with their progress but was tired. None of them slept well because of the almost constant sirens of ambulances and police around the medical center. Furthermore, although the three-bedroom suite had felt spacious when they arrived, it felt cramped for the five of them after nearly a week. Even JH, who was usually phlegmatic, was getting irritable.

Kate pocketed her key and walked outside into the warm evening.

"Hi, Jeff, what's up? You sound—"

"Worried? The wolves are circling, Kate. Jaworski's using all of his leverage to keep you out of the local Texas media circuses. And mostly, he's managing to hold them off. But he's heard rumors that the Northern California Federal Court impaneled a grand jury to indict you and Lindsey McCall on a conspiracy to commit a federal hate crime against the American transgendered community and unintentionally murdering a teen named Joey Carmichael. Jaworski's worried. He doesn't hold any heft with the US Justice Department.

"I'd guess you know about Lindsey's involvement with detransitioning a transgender female-to-male teen at Cal Poly. He's dead. Because of your articles about Lindsey's wrongful conviction for her mother's death four years ago, they think they have enough to indict both of you for conspiracy."

John Jaworski was a senior partner of Fulbright and Jaworski, one of the leading law firms in Texas. He was also President of the Board of Trustees for the Houston Tribune, wielding enormous power in the state.

Jeff said, "Someone at the Transgender Law Center has the Attorney General's ear."

Kate's mind reeled. She thought *That poor kid died? Lindsey's being accused of causing it? This is happening so fast!*

But she said, "I'll need to look up the definition of a federal hate crime."

Jeff had worked with Kate for fifteen years and thought he knew her well. However, she occasionally managed to stop him short with her unflappability, like now. Kate didn't even sound surprised.

Shaking his head at her calm reply, Jeff said, "I've got it right here. Are you ready?

"Fire away."

"'In violation of 18 USC 249: prohibiting willfully causing bodily injury to another because of actual or perceived race, color, religion, national origin, gender, sexual orientation, gender identity, or disability.' Co-Prosecutors are from the

Transgender Law Center, the ACLU, and the Southern Poverty Law Center. Jaworski's source says there may be more because this isn't just hot, it's sizzling."

Kate eyed her sleeping husband with envy. And she thought, *I sure wish I could sleep on planes. But if Steve couldn't sleep on a rock, he'd have never made it through residency or his fellowship.*

She glanced across the aisle at Lucinda, who had JH on one side and Nicholas on the other. All three were sound asleep. Everyone was exhausted after five days of driving all over San Antonio and comparing the layouts and properties of close to thirty homes.

She sipped at her cup of tomato juice, happy to simply sit and not have to look at another house.

640 Rattler Pass. Can we get more Texan than that? Despite herself, Kate was excited about the ten-acre property. It was in the Texas Hill Country but only a twenty-minute drive to the medical center for Steve. Lucinda didn't even try to hide her delight at her new home. The guest house was twice the size of the one in California, with quaint Texas furnishings, including lamps with horseshoes adhered to their wooden bases and metallic shades with Texas stars. The furniture was brown leather, and it seemed to Kate it was all furnished according to a masculine taste, but Lucinda loved everything about it.

The Smiths thought the owners would like their offer and figured closing would occur in about thirty days. That would work well, Kate thought, because it looked like they had a serious buyer for their Palo Alto house.

When they returned to California, Kate assumed the subpoena would be at the Palo Alto house. No, they had to deliver it in person. Or wait, that was for being a witness. She's no witness but the guy on trial. They'd come to the house to arrest her. For a few minutes, Kate began to panic at the thought of her boys watching their mother arrested. But suddenly, like a descending cloud, it disappeared.

They will put me in jail for twelve years if I'm found guilty. Yes, true. But nothing can disturb the peace they'd all been given.

Acting on a hunch, Kate had called Father John before leaving for Texas. He picked up the phone on the first ring, chuckling. "I think I know what you're about to tell me, but please say it because I've been wrong before."

Kate's eyebrows furrowed, curious at the priest's reaction. "Steve's been offered the chair of cardiology at UT San Antonio, so we're leaving on Friday for him to do a meet-and-greet, sign papers, and look for a house."

"Ah, Gracious God." Father John's voice was filled with what Kate could only describe as awe. "I'll be in San Antonio next week as well, Kate. An OMI priest friend has asked me to do a few lectures at the Oblate School of Theology. Father Greg and I were in seminary together back in California. He heads up the doctoral program in spirituality there and is extremely interested in meeting you. Greg read your series and raves about it each time we talk. In fact, he sent it to oblate priests world-wide."

He paused, waiting for questions. When Kate said nothing, he continued. "Greg's a smart guy, an exorcist, and quite aware of the attacks you must receive from every direction. I told him you and your family are ready to join the church, and we're just trying to coordinate schedules. When we spoke yesterday afternoon, he brought you up again. Greg said he dreamed of you and Steve coming to San Antonio."

He paused again, awaiting a response, but heard nothing. "You still with me, Kate?"

"Yes, right here, Father John."

"Greg wants us both to concelebrate the rites of bringing you, Steve, and the boys into full Communion with the Church at the Oblate Chapel," he said. "I'll text you the times when we can do it."

Sipping on her tomato juice, Kate reflected on the majesty and solemnity of the sacraments they had celebrated yesterday afternoon. The baptism of the boys came first. There were tears in Lucinda's eyes when she repeated the promises of a godmother. Then Father John heard Steve's confession, and Father Greg, hers.

Although Father Greg was delightful, his unbridled praise of Kate's articles was embarrassing. In response to her repeated deflection of any skill on her part, that it had been Father John's direction to the reading of Genesis, Father Greg had said in his Polish-accented melodious voice, "Never deny the goodness of the gifts God has given you, Kate. That's false humility."

He was right; she knew the instant he said the words. And felt eager for this "stranger" to hear her first confession. Following confession, they were back in the Oblate Chapel. She and Steve stood before the simple altar of the Oblate Chapel with the sun streaming down through the stained-glass windows as if in benediction, where together, Fathers John and Greg conducted the ancient, magnificent cleanse of human souls and entry into the Roman Catholic Church.

Do you reject Satan?

I do.

Do you believe in Jesus Christ, his only Son, our Lord, who was born of the Virgin Mary was crucified, died, and was buried, rose from the dead, and is now seated at the right hand of the Father?

I do.

Do you believe in the Holy Spirit, the holy Catholic church, the communion of saints, the forgiveness of sins, the resurrection of the body, and life everlasting?
I do.

God, the all-powerful Father of our Lord Jesus Christ has given us a new birth by water and the Holy Spirit, and forgiven all our sins. May he also keep us faithful to our Lord Jesus Christ for ever and ever.

CHAPTER THIRTY-TWO

Max took off like a shot, with Gus following surprisingly close to the Doberman and Rich following at a slow jog. Running no longer came as easily as it once did, at least not during the first mile, and he knew that being over fifty and way out of shape meant that he needed to take it slowly.

When was the last time I went running? Man, everything hurts. I feel like I did right after the shooting. Man up, Jansen.

Shaking off the self-disgust at his poor conditioning, Rich forced himself to breathe slowly and deeply, focusing on the fact that they were back home in Texas. Not until he returned and saw the Texas plates did Rich realize how much he'd missed it. California was beautiful, and their former Pismo Beach home was splendid, but it didn't come close to Texas.

Eventually, his muscles loosened. Although he could feel the pull around the three bullet wounds in his abdomen and torso, they were just a reminder of old trauma. Max and Gus suddenly appeared, racing around the corner of the forest path, tongues lolling to make sure that Rich was where he should be. Rich grinned at his dogs. "I'm coming, guys. You'll just have to give me a few minutes."

Assured that Rich was OK, the dogs took off. Rich had been somewhat concerned about Gus. He didn't have the Doberman's endurance and agility; he'd been a city dog. Still, the little guy kept up with Max seemingly without effort.

We all need this, the dogs, me, and Lindsey.

He doubted she'd had time to explore the forest around the house.

Ten minutes later, Rich had loosened up sufficiently to get

close to his average speed. He and the dogs padded together along the forest path carpeted with pine needles. The trees were packed together, permitting only filtered sunlight and protecting Rich and the dogs from the day's rising heat.

"I feel like my left arm's about to be amputated!"

LJ stared at Morgan, who waited for her friend to calm down.

Stamping her foot, LJ glared at Morgan. "I don't *want* to go back to Friendswood. Been there; done that in high school! I want to finish my undergrad with you!" Then, her anger evaporated, and she dissolved into tears.

"Then don't."

"What do you mean?" LJ asked. "We're back in Texas. Mom will expect me to—"

Just then, the front door opened, and in raced Gus and Max. Rich wiped his perspiration-slick face with the bottom of his T-shirt a few seconds behind the two dogs. "Mom will what, LJ?"

"You heard all that?" LJ asked, her cheeks burning.

Rich shook his head and chuckled. "LJ, the neighbors could hear you, and they're almost ten miles away! So, what will your mom expect of you?"

After nearly a six-mile run in the woods abutting the College Station home they'd moved into last week, Rich felt nothing could dissipate his mellow glow. Bending down to untie his running shoes and kick them off, he regarded LJ from the corner of his eye.

She's bordering on hysteria. LJ's into drama, but she always maintains control. So, what on earth could have prompted this?

LJ's adoptive mother, Julie Grayson, wouldn't have

"expectations" of LJ other than wanting her to become who God had in mind when he thought her into being. In Rich's eyes, Julie was the quintessence of selflessness toward her adoptive daughter. Moreover, he and Lindsey had had enough discussions with LJ about her "two moms" for Rich to think LJ meant what she was saying.

Standing up, he met Morgan's intense gaze that looked like she was telegraphing something to him. Rich walked through the great room to get the dogs fresh water, then stopped so abruptly that Gus ran into the back of his legs as he got it. *LJ was afraid to get back to the crowd, who were her alcoholic buddies in high school. At least one or two would likely be at U of H. Got it. Thanks, Morgan.*

"Sorry, bud." He bent down to scratch the little dog under his chin. Then he turned to Max, who was waiting patiently. "Good boy." He turned to look at LJ. Feeling his glance, she was startled out of her crying jag and wiped her eyes with her hands, leaving mascara trails as she did. Then she stood up straighter and pasted on a wobbly smile. She was embarrassed at her breakdown and surprised that Rich had heard her outside.

"Morgan's right, LJ. Don't go to U of H and live with your mom and dad. Stay here with us. We'll get the course transfer stuff at A&M worked out. In fact, I think Lindsey's made some headway with somebody about three of those Cal Poly classes."

The front door opened, and the entire Grayson family tumbled in, followed by Lindsey. Pure reflex drove LJ into Julie Grayson's arms. Within seconds, the girl was stammering through a blast of explanation, apology, and tears that boiled down to "I've changed my mind. Do you guys mind if I stay here with Morgan, Lindsey, and Rich to finish undergrad?"

Julie Grayson and her husband Theo embraced their

adopted daughter and said, "Honey, of course, we don't mind if you stay here! A&M's a better place for you; we get it." They looked at Rich and Lindsey, laughed, and said, "So you guys get to be parents for another few years!"

Their eight-year-old son Charlie looked up from the floor where he was wrestling with Max and Gus and said, "Any chance we can eat sometime soon? I'm starving!"

CHAPTER THIRTY-THREE

"Have I told you how much I love this house, Linds?" Rich asked.

"Yes, about a million times, but you can keep saying it all you want. It's kind of miraculous the way everything fell into place. That week of interviews should have been stressful, but I don't think I've ever had so much fun!" Lindsey's face glowed. "After two hours of meeting with the Public Health, Medicine, and Veterinary Medicine chairs, I asked them when they would start interviewing me. As if on cue, Sam Epstein, President of the Health Science Center at A&M, walked in and said, 'Dr. McCall, we've been trying to get you to A&M for months. If you think we're trying to sell you on us, you're correct!'"

Lindsey went on to recount how the rest of the meeting went.

The slightly overweight internist Sam Epstein had been late. A little out of breath, he sat in the only empty seat at the table. After his first comments, his gaze landed on Dr. Francis Boyega, Chair of the School of Public Health in silent communication. Epstein lifted an eyebrow and nodded. *Go ahead.*

Boyega leaned forward and grinned at Lindsey. His teeth were startlingly white against his ebony skin. "Dr. McCall, it's my pleasure to add another incentive to your accepting our offer." The dean of A&M's School of Public Health was Nigerian, spoke eight languages, and had charmed Lindsey from the moment she'd first met him the previous night. "My wife Elena's parents want to sell their cabin on the edge of the Jones Forest." Dr. Boyega shook his head. "It's hardly a cabin. In fact, it may recall the 'cabin' our former governor gave to your husband."

Lindsey thought *They've done their homework on me,* including *my stint in Huntsville Prison.*

Boyega insisted on driving Lindsey to see the "cabin" later that day. It was actually a log house, and it was stunning. Lindsey approached the wraparound porch, walked up to the glass front door, and waited while Boyega unlocked it. With a flourish and a bow, he stood aside for her to enter.

The house had an open floor plan, including a great room with a cathedral ceiling and a massive stone fireplace. The other three walls were mostly glass, with stunning views of the pine forest surrounding the home.

The room was tastefully but sparsely furnished with brown leather furniture, glass-and-brass tables, and huge Navajo rugs covering the wood floor. On the left side of the great room was a chef-sized kitchen with matching brown appliances, granite countertops, and well-stocked cabinets. The iron stove and ovens were huge and looked as if they could easily handle meal preparation for fifty people. On the far right was an island with several leather barstools serving as the kitchen table. Nothing was out of place, and Lindsey couldn't see a single dust mote floating in the filtered light from the setting sun streaming through the western window.

"What a welcome back to Texas! It's as if Boyega's in-laws just moved Greg Bell's 'cabin' in the Piney Woods to College Station and parked it on the edge of the Jones Forest."

When former Governor Greg Bell persuaded Rich to take the job of chief warden at the Huntsville Prisons, his top perk was a fully furnished log cabin. Boyega's house was almost a facsimile of Bell's "cabin" in New Waverly.

Rich and Lindsey were in bed in the master bedroom.

Their move-in had been seamless. It felt like they'd lived there for years rather than a little over a week.

Like their former New Waverly home, the entire south wall was glass but with remote-control blinds, which were rolled up. The windows were also open, permitting the sounds of the forest at night to whisper through the screens.

Lindsey reached for Rich's hand and squeezed it. "Your remarks after last night's dinner about how much we love being 'step-parents' to LJ and Morgan, of course, cleared the way for her to explain the real reason she wants to stay here with us and go to A&M. I'm sure she appreciated your doing that."

Squeezing back, he turned to hug her. "Not many adults could have expressed themselves like she did about her fears of returning to old and dangerous habits."

Once the light was out, Lindsey lay wide awake, listening to the rhythmic breathing of her sleeping husband. This whole move had been executed flawlessly, but at the edge of her brain, Lindsey could almost hear the shoe about to drop. She knew the faculty member's complaints to Dr. Peterson weren't going away. Joey's death would have significantly amplified the person's animosity toward Lindsey.

At 11:00 that night, the doorbell rang repeatedly, accompanied by someone pounding on the door.

With Max and Gus barking, Morgan and LJ walked sleepily out into the hallway, and Lindsey sat straight up in bed, dazed. She'd just gotten to sleep.

Pulling on his sweatpants and telling everyone to stay put, Rich raced down the stairs. He opened the door, thinking about the business card he'd seen at Cassie Carmichael's house. The one from the lawyer from the Transgender Law Center.

As he stared at six FBI agents standing on his porch with guns drawn and heard Max barreling down the stairs, about to launch himself at the agent closest to Rich, Rich drew down on years of experience in life-threatening situations: he spoke slowly, clearly, and with menace.

"Put the guns down, gentlemen. If you kill my dogs, wife, or daughters with a stupid move, I swear by all that's holy, all hell will come down on you and your agency." Rich grabbed the snarling Doberman with his right hand. "Max, sit."

For a moment, no one moved. Then Rich nodded at the agents and repeated his words. "Put the guns down now, and tell me why you're here." Even standing in his sweatpants and bare feet, Rich had an air of authority. His voice's low pitch and cadence, combined with a cold, calculated expression, conveyed more than any words could.

The agent closest to Rich cleared his throat and holstered his weapon, signaling the other five to do the same.

"I'm Agent Mark Blankenship, and I'm here to arrest Dr. Lindsey McCall for conspiracy to commit a federal hate crime against the American transgendered community and the unintentional murder of Joey Carmichael."

Of course, Lindsey. You're happier than I've seen you since we moved to California. So naturally, you get arrested by the Department of Justice. What are the odds of two wrongful death arrests? And this time, I'll wager our intrepid reporter, Kate Townsend, will be sitting right next to you in the courtroom. Zach, buddy, I sure pray you know more about the federal court system than I do.

"I'm Dr. McCall's attorney," Rich said, sounding as calm as if he was nightly awakened by a SWAT team of FBI agents. "I'll go get her now. She'll be ready to accompany you in less than three minutes."

He closed the door, taking a deep breath and slowly letting it out as he prayed. "Thank you, Lord. Thank you, guardian angel." He wasn't sure they'd obey his demands and was grateful they weren't storming into his home.

He looked up at the three women on the landing. To LJ and Morgan, he said," Pack Lindsey a bag, enough for several days; I'll take it with me." He knew they needed something to do to bleed out some of the terror of this night.

Lindsey's face was pale, her expression frozen. Rich took the stairs two at a time, then held her tightly. "Come on. Get dressed," he said. Tipping her head back, he asked, "Do you trust me?"

Her eyes were enormous, but Lindsey nodded.

With far more conviction than he felt, Rich declared, "We'll beat this, Lindsey, I promise you."

After the FBI agents left with Lindsey handcuffed in the backseat of Blankenship's car, Rich gestured for the girls to come downstairs. "Let's make some cocoa."

LJ and Morgan padded down the stairs after him. Both dogs panted nervously as they followed.

Busying himself with finding the cocoa, cups, and milk, Rich's mind raced with the overwhelming list of tasks. But first things first.

"Talk," he said a few minutes later as he placed steaming cups of cocoa in front of each young woman seated on the dark brown leather barstools in front of the island.

Morgan shook her head, enormous tears starting their passage down her cheeks. "It's all my fault, Rich. This wouldn't have happened if I'd never—"

LJ placed her hand over Morgan's as she stirred her cocoa. Then she looked at Rich, her eyes imploring.

Rich said, "You're right, Morgan. It would never have happened if she'd never met Joey. But Lindsey knew the risks she was taking when she decided to help. One of the reasons we're here in Texas was a warning from the Cal Poly president. Joey's name wasn't mentioned, nor was transgenderism, but the message was clear." Rich watched Morgan. She looked vacantly at her hand, stirring the cocoa as if it belonged to someone else.

"Morgan, I think Lindsey loved Joey. Yes, you introduced the two of them, but when you think back, would you want to take away the joy that being with Lindsey's dogs brought Joey? Would you want to eclipse the hope that Lindsey's help him gave to him?"

Feeling tears in his own eyes, Rich pushed on, more than a little surprised at the passion stirring in his heart. "Guys, this is war."

LJ's green eyes widened, then she nodded. Again, she reached for Morgan's hand, but Morgan wasn't there. She'd hopped off her barstool and was staring at Rich. "War," she said. "Just like last year in China, only now it's here."

Rich was filled with pride and overwhelming love for these courageous young women. He walked around the island to put one arm around Morgan and the other around LJ, hugging them close.

"Where have they taken her, Rich?" LJ's gaze was like green lasers.

Rich scowled as he thought about those agents. "They were hardly forthcoming, LJ, but it's gotta be back to California. The California Federal District Court must have gotten a grand jury to indict," Rich said.

"I know you need to get out there ASAP. And we need to find some folks to care for the house and the dogs. But once you get Lindsey out of jail and start working on her defense, Morgan and I need to be there." The tears standing in LJ's eyes almost belied the force of her words, but just almost.

"We've just landed in San Francisco, Rich. What a surprise to hear from—" Kate's smile faded as she listened to Rich's command.

"Stay on the plane. If you have to fake a missing piece of luggage or a sudden illness, do it. Just sit tight until I get there." Before Kate could ask what had happened, he hung up.

Steve was half crouched, eager to get off the crowded plane once it reached the gate.

"Steve, give Lucinda a hand with Nicholas. Would you please?"

Glancing down at his wife, then across the aisle at the sleeping child in Lucinda's arms, Steve sat back down, giving his wife an incredulous look. "You want me to wake him up?"

Kate leaned close to his ear. "That was Rich Jansen. He wants us to sit tight until he gets here, using whatever means necessary."

Steve frowned, puzzled. "But they've moved to College Station. Lindsey told me she accepted A&M's offer and was excited about their house in the … oh dear God, no, they've arrested Lindsey!" Steve looked at his wife's steady, peaceful gaze. "Rich wants us to delay leaving the plane because they will arrest you once you reach the concourse. You're not surprised, are you, Lois Lane?" Without thinking, Steve leaned in and gave her a long, lingering kiss, ignoring the other passengers' muted whistles.

Less than an hour later, Steve stood at the curb watching a black SUV carrying his handcuffed wife speed away. Holding giant stuffed teddy bears for the boys, Rich's eccentric investigator, Toni, had intercepted Lucinda and the boys before they got to baggage claim. Toni and Lucinda had left the airport via the private car exit, sparing the children the trauma of seeing their mother swarmed by FBI agents.

Steve grimaced, "If anyone had told me that American citizens could be treated like terrorists, I'd never have believed them. But your proficiency at tranquilizing the mad dogs of our numero uno justice department is nothing short of miraculous."

"See one, do one, teach one," Rich muttered.

The two men had been casual friends for years. Steve was aware of Rich's background as a cop and former Marine, but the guy who'd met him and Kate when they had landed seemed like a stranger. Ignoring Steve's question of how he got through security and onto the plane, Rich looked at Lucinda, holding Nicholas in one arm and JH by the other. "Good. You go out now. Toni is waiting in baggage claim. She'll take you and the kids to Kate's house."

When they didn't move, he lowered his voice. "Move. Now. Quickly." They did. JH paused just before they left the plane and stared back at his parents, then turned and left.

Rich turned back to Steve and Kate, his eyes flat and expressionless. "The FBI agents will be outside the terminal passageway. We'll give it another minute. Then, Kate, you walk with me. I'm your lawyer." For a second, his face softened, and Rich looked into Kate's wide, terrified brown eyes. "It doesn't feel like it, Kate, but you've handled tougher stuff than this." He said it with such certainty that Kate believed him and relaxed slightly. "There will be between four and eight agents with bullet-proof jackets and guns. I'm guessing they'll put you in the same jail as Lindsey."

Extending his trembling hands, Steve glanced at Rich. "These hands are trained to handle life and death, but I'm still shaking." Then he remembered the determined set of Kate's jaw as the agent in charge of the six-member FBI team had handcuffed her and the smile she threw at Steve before they took her away as if to say, *We've got this, Steve.*

Steve took a deep, steadying breath as he regarded Rich. Now wasn't the time to tell him how grateful he was for his presence and boldness. The man was running on fumes. So, he merely nodded. "What now?"

Rich checked his watch. "Toni'll return to grab Zach and us. His plane gets here in about fifteen minutes. Let's head to the Southwestern gate since it's a hike. Here's the bad news. Federal prosecutors win ninety-five to ninety-eight percent of their cases. Emilio Martinez is one of the Northern Federal District Court of California's top prosecutors. He's on the fast track to somewhere and has never lost a case. Evidently, his boss sees this as an opportunity to quash the conservative resistance to gender ideology and has shoved everything else off the docket."

It took Steve a few minutes to register Rich's remarks as they hurried through the crowded airport. His staccato speech was hard to follow. "Voir dire starts tomorrow," he said, "and our first court day will be Monday."

Rich was speaking in a machine-gun cadence. With his jaw set, his mouth nothing but a thin slash, and his thousand-yard stare, Steve barely recognized him. Steve was more than a little awed. He thought *I'd hate to be unfortunate enough to be your enemy.* Rich Jansen, the former combat-hardened Marine and homicide cop, had stepped into the foreground.

Steve's analysis was right on. Rich had slept no more than an hour or two in the seventy-two hours since Lindsey had been taken to stand trial in California by the very government he'd fought for and watched far too many good men die for.

"Our fight will be on two fronts," Rich said, "the facts and the legalities of their case. We've filed twenty memoranda on different variations of abuse of the Bill of Rights and the age-old moral duty of a physician to do no harm. One of our first was requesting Kate's and Lindsey's release from jail."

Rich slowed for a moment for Steve to catch up, flashing a shadow of a smile. "We feel confident about that one. We think they'll be out tonight or, at the latest, tomorrow morning. Thanks be to God, the judge hearing this case isn't one of the progressive puppets. He's actually a constitutionalist. Imagine that! Their list of witnesses runs the gamut of the usual cast of characters from the IGLBTIA." Seeing Steve's nonplussed expression at the acronym, Rich spelled it out. "It's the largest of all the global activist groups—International Lesbian, Gay, Bisexual, Trans, and Intersex Association. It's astounding how much one can learn when fueled by desperation."

When they arrived at the Southwest gate, Rich waved at one of the strangest-looking people Steve had ever seen. *That must be Zach Cunningham,* he thought.

CHAPTER THIRTY-SIX

Toni had missed Steve's driveway, which was understandable because her boss and Rich had not stopped talking since they'd met at the gate, and she'd not heard Steve tell her the house number.

Zach was not a big man, but his voice was tremendous. Even when he spoke softly, Zach sounded like a coach at a football game. Masking her epithet with a cough, the fiery Puerto Rican investigator did a U-turn and headed back to Steve's house.

It's not my house anymore, Steve thought without a trace of regret. The closing on the house would occur at the same time as their new place on Rattler, nine days from now, assuming his wife wasn't in a federal California prison by then. *Isn't it amazing how the impossible becomes the everyday?*

Parking behind a gray sedan, Toni hopped out of the rental car and opened the doors for her passengers. Steve looked at the sedan, wondering whose car it was. He and Kate had left their two vehicles in the garage, and Lucinda's white rental was parked in front of the garage door.

Feeling useless, Steve followed the conversing gaggle of Toni, Zach, and Rich onto the house's covered archway. The door opened, and JH ran out, followed by Nicholas, as fast as his chubby legs could carry him, both boys hollering.

"Daddy, Daddy, Daddy!"

Bending down, Steve stifled sobs as he scooped up his two sons, no longer feeling so useless.

When he stood back up, the boys in arms, Steve found himself looking into Father John's luminous gray eyes.

"Sorry for the surprise visit, Steve, but Eleanor called to tell me that Kate would be arrested when you returned to California. And right after she called, Lindsey did." His generous mouth curved into a smile. "Lindsey persuaded her jailers to permit a call to her priest."

"Father John's here to check on the newest members of his flock," Rich said from behind Steve. Steve looked back at Rich, who seemed unsurprised at Father John's presence. With dark shadows under his red-rimmed eyes, Rich looked exhausted, but that awful thousand-yard stare was gone, and he actually smiled. "Welcome to Catholicism, Steve." Regarding Steve and Kate's becoming Catholics, Rich said, "Lindsey and I are sorry we missed the ceremony."

"No, Rich, I'm here to check on one of the older members of my flock." His gentle, generous smile still present, Father John turned to Steve. "While you get Mr. Cunningham and his assistant situated, is there somewhere Rich and I can speak privately?"

"Of course," Steve replied. Grateful to be busy, he set about helping Zach and Toni turn the living room and kitchen into their office. Then, he got to work, setting laptops on every hard surface and mountains of files on chairs.

Rich knew he needed to join them but didn't move, pinned by Father John's gaze. After Steve showed them to Kate's office and closed the door behind him, Father John motioned to one of the overstuffed chairs, suggesting that Rich sit. Rich did so, then blinked at the priest. After three days of constant motion and tension, he felt disconnected, as if he'd lost his bearings.

Father John pulled his chair closer so their knees were almost touching. As always, the priest was clad in black trousers and a black shirt with his white clerical collar.

Does he ever take it off? Rich wondered. *I've known him for over ten years and have never seen him in civilian garb.*

"I don't know how she did it, Rich, but Lindsey persuaded one of the agents to lend her his cell phone and call me. She asked me to come because she's worried about you."

The thousand-yard stare returned, and Rich's face turned to stone. "Let me get this straight, Father John," he said, his voice grating. "Lindsey's in jail for murder for the second time in four years, and she's worried about me?" Then his voice cracked, and he buried his face in his hands. "Bless me, Father, for I have sinned." Rich slid off the chair and onto his knees, tears coursing down his face.

Father John looked down at Rich's bowed head and pondered the warrior he'd known for over ten years. Rich's first wife, Laura, one of Father John's spiritual directees, had introduced them one Sunday after Mass at the Co-Cathedral of the Sacred Heart in downtown Houston. Rich had been polite but distant. Laura told the priest Rich didn't understand why she needed a spiritual director. What was so complicated about being a Catholic? He'd jokingly claimed he was jealous when Laura left for her weekly meetings with Father John, asking what they discussed. But when Laura tried to explain her deep desire to get closer to Jesus, Rich's eyes glazed over, so she dropped the subject.

Then, not long after Father John and Rich met, Laura was killed in a head-on collision with a semi-trailer on the I-45. At her funeral, Father John had told Rich things were going to get bad. "When they do, come see me." Rich was back at his job as homicide chief for Harris County the following day and worked seven days a week until he was forced to stop.

Father John barely saw him for four years. But the combination of suppressed grief, his forced retirement, and the long recovery following a shoot-out in the fourth ward in Houston that nearly killed Rich brought him to his knees. Father John would never forget what Rich said: "I don't know how to feel better, Father." So, the two—plus Rich's Doberman, Max—met each Saturday for years. One of the many demons riding him was a recurring nightmare from combat in Lebanon.

Rich had confessed the almost ecstatic bliss he had felt when he'd killed the sniper who had ambushed his squadron and killed two eighteen-year-old kids from Arkansas. He had never told anyone about the incident, pretending he had buried the memory. Still, it had crawled out in his nightmares during those six months of hell following his injury. Only this time, he saw the intense pleasure on his own face as he pumped the sniper's body full of bullets. The palpable evil on his face awakened him night after night, his body drenched in sweat. He'd knelt before Father John, sobbing his confession like he was now.

When Lindsey called to ask Father John to come to California, explaining how worried she was about Rich, neither she nor the priest needed to use many words. Instead, they understood what this could do to Rich's hard-won battle for serenity. The consequences of his intense need to "fix" those who misused their power could be very bad indeed.

Following his confession, Rich regarded the priest. "How do I deserve a woman like that? She's the one in handcuffs, and yet she's worried about me?"

"None of us deserves anything, good, Rich, but what we do deserve," the priest paused to finger the crucifix he wore under his collar, "he already bore. And yet he rains down his mercy and goodness on us daily." He looked at the exhausted man before him. "If you don't get some sleep, you'll be no good to anyone."

Unable to contain his yawning any longer, Rich nodded. Then he got up, walked a few steps, and collapsed onto the sofa bed in Kate's office.

CHAPTER THIRTY-EIGHT

"All right, all right, coming!"

When Dr. Turner opened the door, he saw a heavy-set sheriff, a thick document extended toward her in his meaty hand.

"Dr. Adam Turner?" He pushed the papers toward him, so Dr. T. had to take them from him.

"Yes, what—"

"You've been served. The court date is in the package."

For a big man, his pirouette off the porch and onto the walkway to the street was almost graceful. He practically ran to his truck.

He must have tried a few times to find me home, Dr. T. thought idly, fingering the thick packet.

"Really? Eleven at night? " Rubbing the sleep out of her eyes due to an early morning surgery, Nancy stood beside Turner and eyed the unopened package in his hands.

"She did it! By God, Cassie found someone to blame!" Nancy said. "Persistence will always get you what you want," she added, her voice full of sarcasm.

"Except this isn't state, Nancy. This is federal." Turner stared at the stack of documents under the title page "United States v. Townsend, McCall," followed by a long list of statutory offenses by Townsend and McCall, then looked at his wife with widened eyes and parted lips. "How on earth did Cassie get the feds interested in this? And why would she even think of a hate crime? Cassie only wants money. It's always money with her."

Fully awake now, Nancy turned toward the kitchen. "Let's

have some coffee. I'll never be able to get to sleep now."

Multitasking as usual, Nancy got some cups and Nespresso pods, then fired up the machine while searching Townsend and the *Houston Tribune* on her phone. Astounded at the number of hits, she handed the phone to Adam while preparing their coffee. Then she grabbed a couple of biscotti from the glass jar they kept filled.

When she turned around, Adam nodded, then frowned and grimaced as he scanned the text on the phone.

"OK, you agree but dislike and maybe hate what you're reading?" Nancy was joking but shocked when she saw tears in Adam's eyes. *Have I ever seen Adam cry? Even when the cat got run over, or I lost that kid on the operating table?*

"A reporter named Kate Townsend and Dr. Lindsey MCall have been indicted for conspiracy to commit a federal hate crime because of Townsend's four-piece series on transgenderism," Adam said. "She called it 'Creating Chemical Eunuchs: Corrupting America's Children.'"

Dr. T. read through the legalese so quickly that he missed the additional crime of the unintentional murder of Joey Carmichael.

Nancy whistled softly.

"She begins by explaining why she's doing this. Townsend's got two boys: a ten-month-old and a four-year-old. She talks about an incident at the kindergarten where a neighbor's three-year-old said he wanted to be a girl. So, the kindergarten teacher decided to have a coming-out party with the three-year-old boy dressed up in a skirt and all the kids circling about, singing, 'Come out, Susie, come out.'

"When the kid started screaming, Townsend found the trousers the teacher had removed and put them back on. She thought everything was fine because the kid was happy again. But then the kindergarten teacher began preaching, saying she'd studied under Dr. Matt Heathcock, one of the theorists who brought the diagnosis of gender dysphoria into the twenty-first century. Dr. Heathcock also wrote and passed the transgender education legislation pioneered in California."

Nancy's eyebrows knit together. "Matt Heathcock, why is that name familiar? And Lindsey McCall, isn't she that Cardiologist turned animal researcher at Cal Poly?"

Surprised at Nancy's questions, Turner's thin eyebrows met in puzzlement. Regarding Nancy, he wondered why she even knew McCall's name. But as he pondered that name, he realized it also rang a bell with him. Joey's English teacher, Ellen O'Brien, claimed that McCall had been the impetus behind Joey's desire to detransition. In fact, Ellen had gone to the university president to complain. O'Brien had been incensed about McCall's interference and was quite vocal about it. Turner said none of this to his wife, Nancy. Instead, he just said, "I don't know why Heathcock's name is familiar, likely because he's an activist. We educators have a rich tradition of activism," he added sardonically.

Nancy just looked at Adam. She was never sure what those sarcastic comments of his meant, so she said nothing and drank her coffee.

Momentarily nonplussed, Adam pondered his mixed emotions, unsure what it all meant or how he felt about Joey's tragically short life. "Dr. Heathcock's on their long list of witnesses." He looked up at Nancy. "So, why would Cassie even want to bother messing with this? Unless …."

"Someone's paying her," they said in unison.

Kate and Steve's spacious great room and dining room felt—and looked—like the military headquarters for strategic combat. It was filled with laptops, whiteboards, and flip charts.

They'd had an early win. It was expected, but it still counted and raised their spirits. The judge ruled that neither Lindsey nor Kate was a flight risk and released them on a minimal, for California, bail of $25,000 each. After a short celebration of their release from jail the night before, Zach brought them back to earth. After a quick dinner, they sat outside on the patio.

"We were lucky on this one. Judge Rhinehart's a new appointee from the previous administration, and he's got no apparent agenda. But Martinez wants to impress his many layers of superiors.

"Emilio Martinez has been named a fellow in the Association of Trial Lawyers and twice won California Lawyer of the Year, no simple feat. In California, that means winning against hundreds of thousands of trial attorneys. He's got four witnesses against you, Lindsey: the president of Cal Poly; Ms. O'Brien, Cal Poly faculty; and two MDs probably to testify about the medical risk of stopping testosterone and starting estrogen in a kid. There are six witnesses against you, Kate. Academic whizzes with resumes that weigh more than I do. And he's also got that teacher and the mentor she admires so much, the educational activist."

Lindsey nodded, unsurprised. The complainant against her had surfaced. And Peterson was there because she had to be. The docs? Plenty of medical experts were more than willing to claim all kinds of inimical effects of detransitioning. But they were merely opinions because no data existed. None. But, of course, would the jury doubt those experts? Quite clearly, the grand jury hadn't.

Kate gulped at the prospect of seeing Addison Meeks again, and listening to the person—Heathcock was his name— behind the California legislation Addison had parroted felt surreal.

Rich hadn't been listening but started paying attention halfway through Zach's rant. *He's scared,* Rich realized. *Zach is terrified of this guy.* Rich's heart rate and breathing began to accelerate. *If Zach's this worried, we're screwed.* Then he felt Father John's piercing gaze. *Rich, your lack of experience as a trial attorney didn't stop you from taking over the strategy for Lindsey's appeal. Back then, you didn't know Zach Cunningham existed.* The words felt as if they'd been spoken into his ear.

Zach paced in front of Steve and Kate, sitting side by side on the swing. Then he turned toward Lindsey, sitting on Rich's lap in the big lounge chair. He started to ask her a question but stopped suddenly to stare at Father John, sitting quietly next to Lucinda.

They were outside in the perfection of a California evening: a gentle breeze with the temperature in the mid-sixties. "We need all the resources you can marshal, Father," Zach said quietly. "Martinez is Goliath."

"Then all we need is one smooth stone, Mr. Cunning-ham," Father John replied, his gaze fixed on Rich. With a voice that emanated from a deep well filled with gravel, a scar that stretched from the right side of his upper lip to his right eye-brow, and his Rastafarian hair, grown back either in sympathy with or protest against Black Lives Matter, Zach Cunningham was a study in contrasts.

Zach chuckled, then laughed appreciatively. "One smooth stone, Father. Good one. But how do we find the right one?"

Before Father John could reply, Lucinda stepped in. "I'm not sure about a stone, smooth or otherwise. But how did things reach this point so fast?" Her British accent startled everyone else into silence. "This country prides itself on freedom of the press and went to war with England because you wanted religious freedom. So, Kate wrote a newspaper piece filled with verifiable facts about gender dysphoria. She included her experience with her son's kindergarten teacher's brainwashing and manipulating a toddler's fantasies to fit some weird agenda. Lindsey agreed to help a female-to-male transgender teen wean off the puberty-suppressing drug and testosterone injections that were making her/him miserable. And restarts estrogen in hopes of restoring her lost femininity.

"Consequently, the United States government arrested them for hate crimes against transgendered Americans and manslaughter of the kid.

"The US Constitution protects citizens from their government by requiring a grand jury to agree there's enough evidence to indict. Somewhere between sixteen and twenty-three citizens constitute the grand jury. So, these good people had to listen to Goliath and all his 'experts' and were asked to vote. Indict or not? If they got twelve to agree the evidence was adequate, what did they tell them? Don't you wonder what happened in those secret sessions and how many jurors were genuinely persuaded that crimes were committed?"

Rich regarded Lucinda as he toyed with Lindsey's fingers. His short nap had helped, and he could think again. "Leave it to a Brit to analyze the evident weaknesses in our justice system.

You're right, Lucinda. The US took the grand jury from the UK's justice system. But you guys were smart enough to dump it. We're the only Western country still using the expensive farce. Someone said years ago, 'You could get a grand jury to indict a ham sandwich,' referring to the fact that 99.99% of grand juries indict." Rich smiled at Lucinda, "But maybe this one had somebody who didn't swallow the expert opinions."

Rich looked over at Zach, who was all ears, his expression now curious instead of anxious. Rich's gaze drifted to Toni. "So, with your quasi-black hat hacker skills, Toni, can you get into the grand jury database and take a peek? This one could be the .01 that almost didn't get twelve out of twenty-four votes.

"If any of you is disturbed by the use of dirty tricks, sing out now." Rich looked around at the group sitting before him and was excited by their tangible change in energy. Lindsey sat up beside him, took his hand, and grinned. Kate and Steve were smiling, and Lucinda looked happy. Happier than Rich had noted in the short time he'd known the woman.

"Behold, I am sending you out in the midst of wolves. Be ye therefore as wise as serpents and as harmless as doves." Father John's words fell like a blessing on the group. As well as a tacit "Go for it" to Toni.

The following morning, Lindsey stood at the whiteboard filled with erasures. On the left were the strengths of the prosecution's case, and on the right were the weaknesses. The list on the left was long and formidable. The one on the left was pitifully short.

Rich and Zach brainstormed and critiqued one another as they formed their strategy. First, they had to decide who would take each of the state's imposing list of witnesses and work out the holes in the case. Overall, they agreed that Zach would handle the prosecution's list of witnesses against Lindsey. And Rich those against Kate. Rich's suggestion to call Detective Cindy Ralston to testify for the defense didn't fly with Zach. Over and over, the senior attorney said, "It's too risky."

On the other side of the great room, Toni played Martinez while preparing Kate for his attacks on her assumed prejudice against transgender persons, racism, and antagonism toward the American public school system. Although it was chilly in the house, Kate was sweating as she replied to Toni's barrage of questions.

"As a mother of two young boys, Ms. Townsend, you're naturally protective of small children. Given that fact, isn't it likely that you overreacted to Ms. Meeks' actions? Especially since she denies the Sugarman boy ever cried when she dressed him in a skirt?"

"I did not overreact; in fact, I was—"

"Tell the court again, Ms. Townsend, why you wrote your series," Toni said, cutting off Kate's answer yet again and changing the topic, as she anticipated Martinez would do. "You don't believe a person has the right to change gender, do you? In fact, your article series is intended to scare Americans into believing that gender affirmation is dangerous and immoral—evil. Isn't that the real reason you wrote it?"

"I wrote those articles because parents and children are being coerced into life-altering decisions by institutions and physicians who pledge to do no harm."

"Your answer then is 'yes,' it's true. You don't believe people have the right to act on their intrinsic desires to be whole. You've been looking for a way to get back in the game, and your son's kindergarten provided just the right ingredients for a new series."

Kate doubled over in her chair and groaned. "Toni, I need a break. I know we're on the clock, but I can't stand another minute of this. Surely, he won't be this awful."

Toni's hands were on her sizable hips as she looked down at Kate, shaking her head. Her voice raised half an octave, and Toni thickened her Spanish accent. "Oh no, Ms. Townsend, Martinez wins all his cases by being polite, gracious, and gentle." Then she extended her tattoo-sleeved arm and pulled Kate out of her chair. "I'm a walk in the park compared to what Martinez is gonna do. If you want, I'll show you some videos of him in action."

Kate stared at her, the two of them practically nose to nose. "Toni, I know you're not the enemy. And yes, Martinez will take a scalpel, cut me into little pieces, and feed me to the jury. Of course, he will. But I need to shower, put on some makeup and a dress, and make myself feel pretty right now. Thank you, Toni. I appreciate what you've done here today. You think we need way more time at this, and maybe you're right, but at least now I know what to expect."

To Kate's surprise, Toni smiled. "You're welcome, Kate."

Then she put her arm around Kate's shoulders. "Go get beautiful for your man."

Lucinda's hands flew in the kitchen as she layered homemade lasagna noodles with alternating layers of marinara meat sauce and three kinds of cheese. "Father, do we have a chance?" she asked without looking up, speaking so softly that he barely heard her.

The priest stopped assembling the salads and turned to the young woman. "What do you think?"

Lucinda clasped her hands together, unconsciously praying, her blue eyes suddenly swimming. "Oh, Father John, I'm so scared for these people. And for me! Kate and Steve think they're lucky to have me, but I'm the fortunate one. If they hadn't given me this job—" She stopped, blinking hard, her eyes darting around the room.

The priest waited. There was more, he knew, a lot more. But the young woman compressed her lips and shook her head in a herculean effort to regain self-control. Over the last couple of days, Father John had grown to like and admire Lucinda's grit, intensity, and courage. But like so many twenty-somethings, she had no clue about her capabilities. He inferred she had an older, accomplished sibling whom her parents had doted on, leaving Lucinda the role of rebel. It was a tired story but one repeated in family after family.

With no sign of Lucinda lowering her shields further, Father John returned to making the salads. A few minutes later, Lucinda turned from the oven, brandishing a mouth-watering lasagna and the smile she used to hide her deep sadness.

Without even thinking, Father John prayed for her, wondering if this young woman was one of the reasons he was there.

Moments later, he walked out of the kitchen and clapped his hands. "Chef Lucinda has prepared lunch, and what a feast you have in store!"

Just then, Steve walked into the house. "Well, thanks, Lucinda. I couldn't have timed my final departure from Stanford Medical School any better!" He placed the stack of books on the foyer floor and rubbed his hands together.

CHAPTER FORTY-ONE

Father John scanned the tired faces sitting in various chairs and couches in Steve and Kate's spacious living room. His gaze remained on Lucinda, who was sprawled on a giant bean bag chair. Sensing his attention on her, she looked up from the living room rug and gave him a quizzical look.

"Lucinda, you asked me last night if you thought we had a chance in court tomorrow." Waiting until she nodded, he smiled. Then he looked at Lindsey and Rich, sitting together on an upholstered loveseat. Kate was sitting in Steve's lap in an oversized leather recliner. Then she regarded Zach, perched on the edge of a long sectional couch with Toni stretched out on the other end. All of them looked back at the priest, their eyes curious.

"Every single person in this room is a baptized Christian," Father John continued, noting the uneasy shifting of Zach, Toni, and Lucinda, who looked everywhere but at the priest. "Each of you has privately asked me to comment on what I meant by my 'one smooth stone' remark in answer to Zach's Goliath remark on Friday night. You also told me what your faith meant to you as children.

"Look around this room!" His command was so strident that they all sat up straighter and looked at one another, embarrassed smiles blossoming on a few faces. "Do you think that's a coincidence?" he asked, lowering his voice to a whisper. "That each of us has been marked with the indelible seal of God?"

God's presence was *always* discernible if one was paying attention, Father John thought as he felt the air in the room change. It almost crackled, like how it felt before a thunderstorm.

"Don't think for one moment that we will face *people* in that courtroom," he continued. Zach, Toni, and Lucinda's heads snapped toward him, alarm and even shock on their faces. Father John regarded Kate with suddenly tender eyes, then Lindsey. "Which of you would like to explain?"

The two women stared at each other across the room, then Lindsey cleared her throat. "Until I read Kate's series a few months ago …" She stopped and blinked a few times, still looking at Kate. "Was it really only a few months ago?"

"Four," Kate replied, holding up four fingers.

"Right!" Lindsey's smile lit up the room as she looked at Rich and grabbed his hand. "You and Father John both said I should see Kate." She glanced at Lucinda. "And eat the most delicious scones in the world. Because I'd decided to help Joey." Ignoring the emotion-filled crack in her voice, Lindsey looked around the room. "Sorry, everyone. I'm not usually so incoherent." She turned to Zach, "I promise I won't do this on the stand tomorrow."

Lindsey cleared her throat twice before continuing. "Until I read your series, Kate, I didn't recognize what we're dealing with in this explosive surge of young girls thinking they should be boys. I thought it was just another crazy phase. But mere men and women couldn't make this up. My medical colleagues know basic biology. We can't change a girl's biology by removing her breasts and dosing her with testosterone. Joey knew that. A fifteen-year-old knew the whole thing was wicked. That's the word he used the last time we talked, 'wicked.'" Lindsey was silent for a few seconds and studied Father John, who watched her. "The spirit distinctly says in the last days, people will turn away from the faith and heed deceitful spirits taught by demons through plausible liars. I'm paraphrasing St. Paul, but Father

John, isn't that close to what he prophesied?"

The priest nodded in reply. Lindsey looked across the patio at Steve and Kate. "So, you recognized this for what it is. Way too diabolical for mere humans to cook up. But I sure hope that one smooth stone shows up in the next three days."

Abruptly, Zach stood, grabbed Toni's hand, and pulled her to her feet. "Let's pray." He began without waiting for anyone else. "Our Father in heaven, it's been too long since you've heard from me. And there's no reason you should listen today. Except for your mercy, Lord. Mercy that sent your only Son to suffer and die while we were still sinners. Mercy that redeemed the thief hanging next to you, merely by him admitting his guilt. And Your Majesty. Because somehow, during those three excruciating hours, he learned that you are really and truly God. And we're your creatures, capable of nothing without your grace. And so we pray the prayer as he taught us, Our Father, who art in heaven …."

Father John wiped the tears from his eyes as he prayed with them. "Thank you, Lord, for hearing and answering our prayers," he said when they were finished. He knew that somehow one smooth stone would appear.

Just then, Rich's phone rang. He looked at the call display and then answered it, listening for a moment after saying hello. "You're at the airport now? Great, we're on the way." He hung up and then turned to the group. "Can someone lend us a car to pick up LJ and Morgan? They just got here from Texas." Rich looked at his wife and said, "Come on, gorgeous, let's go get our girls."

Rich followed Zach through the doors of the glass-and-steel monstrosity that was the Philip Burton Federal Building and Courthouse on Golden Gate Avenue in San Francisco. Judge Rhinehart's tight schedule demanded voir dire to begin at noon on Thursday and last until they had twelve objective jurors.

After passing through electronic security and showing their identification to the gaggle of guards, the two men hurried to the elevator. It was just 11:00 a.m., and the area outside the fourth-floor courtroom was filled with people of all ages spilling out into the foyer. The crowd noise was noxious, not unlike the whine of a dentist's drill. *Not quite that bad,* Rich told himself. *Get a grip. Somewhere in this crowd are a dozen men and women who will decide Lindsey's and Kate's fates.*

Both sides were on the lookout for their ideal juror. The US attorney and his prosecution team sought younger, single, areligious, college-educated people. Race was immaterial. The defense wanted people who were married with kids, blue-collar, and Christian, believing that race and ethnicity were irrelevant in this case.

On the way to the courthouse, Zach brought up the practice of jury shuffling. The prosecution would have hired jury consultants who would have been employing all kinds of methods to determine the biases and prejudices of the 260 California residents from which the fourteen jurors—twelve with two substitutes—would be selected. After all, their funds were practically limitless. Neither Rich nor Zach doubted they could influence the numbering system by categorizing questionnaires that fit their profile. Jury shuffling could combat such dirty tricks. By requesting that the numbers dictating juror seats one through twenty-four be shuffled, people sitting in the higher-numbered slots, who were less likely to be selected, would end up with lower numbers.

But the jury shuffle had to be requested before the completion of voir dire. There was controversy on when voir dire began in counties like the one they were in, where written questionnaires were used to qualify jurors.

Since Toni's research had uncovered Rhinehart's antagonism to jury shuffling in previous cases tried in his court, they dropped the strategy. However, she had discovered that the US Attorney came close to a no bill—no indictment—from the grand jury. In the required "secret" daily recording, there had been extensive, at times, combative disagreements about the testimonies of the expert medical doctors and Dr. Peterson from Cal Poly. One juror had been convinced that there was insufficient evidence for an indictment. The man, a retired internist, repeatedly insisted that the "expert" physicians merely gave their opinions about the danger of testosterone withdrawal and estrogen initiation in biological female prepubescent teens. That was true, the juror claimed, because there were no data to be had. The juror was powerful and exerted enormous influence over the group, but he had gotten sick and left the panel.

It wasn't yet 11:30, but Judge Rhinehart had already started. His bailiffs were well-trained and moved quickly. Groups of people were called by number in increments of sixteen: twelve jurors plus four alternates. Before seating the first group of sixteen, Judge Rhinehart addressed the one hundred or so people sitting in the gallery.

"Now, for those of you still in the gallery, when we ask questions, please listen. Please tell us if you can't hear my or the attorneys' questions. As we ask questions of the people seated in the jury box, think about your own answer because it's likely that some of you will be brought in to replace prospective jurors currently in the box.

"So, in the interest of saving time, if you are called to replace someone, I'll ask you, 'Are there any questions you would have answered in the affirmative?' If you can keep this question in mind and the questions asked of those in the box, we can save your time and ours by not repeating the same litany of questions repeatedly.

"The purpose of what we will do next is to determine if you are qualified by law to serve as a juror in this case. That is, to ensure that you are unrelated to the parties and their lawyers, have no evident bias or prejudice in this case, and can act as a fair and impartial juror. To make this determination, I will ask several questions. The attorneys will then ask you questions on matters not covered by this court.

"You are obliged by the oath that you just took to answer each question thoughtfully and truthfully. If any of your answers reveal a legal basis for you to be excused as a juror, one of the attorneys will challenge you or ask that you be excused. If the court agrees with the reason stated for the challenge, you'll be excused, and another name will be drawn. Once we have enough jurors, the attorneys can issue another type of challenge called peremptory. Each side is permitted to challenge you for a reason or for no reason, and this court has no alternative but to excuse you."

Rhinehart leaned down and peered at the sixteen people in the juror box. "If this happens, it does not mean you have done something wrong, are a bad person, or need to worry. During the questioning, please understand that we only have one goal: to provide a group of twelve impartial, unbiased, and unprejudiced people. The integrity of our justice system depends on this."

Rhinehart turned to the attorneys, "Please introduce yourselves and read the list of witnesses you plan to call for this trial."

Ten minutes later, Martinez and Zach had completed reading the names of their co-counsels, investigators, and the fifteen witnesses who would be called.

"We'll begin now," Judge Rhinehart said. "Some of the questions I may ask require only that you raise your hand if your answer is in the affirmative. At that time, we'll explore the matter further. Please do not hesitate to raise your hand if you think it appropriate. Now, are any of you over age sixty-five?"

Six people raised their hands.

Rhinehart frowned. "By law, no one over sixty-five is required to serve on a jury. You are free to go if you are that age or above."

All six people left, along with another ten in the gallery.

"Are any potential jurors acquainted with the defendant in this case?"

There were no raised hands.

"Are any jurors acquainted with the attorneys?"

No one raised their hand.

"Are any jurors acquainted with any of the witnesses?"

Once more, no hands were raised.

"Has anyone read or seen information in the newspaper or heard anything on the radio or on television about this case?"

No hands were raised.

"Do you have anything other than a passing interest in the case?"

"What do you mean?" a woman asked.

"Do you have an opinion about how this case turns out?"

"Yes, I think the defendants are guilty."

"What?"

"I think the reporter and doctor are guilty of a federal hate crime against transgender people. These two women are obviously filled with hatred against the LGBTQIA-plus community."

"You're free to go, Ms. Smith," Rhinehart said, then addressed the entire group. "If there are persons here who have already made up their minds about the guilt or innocence of these defendants, you are free to leave. I request that anyone who has decided the guilt or innocence of the defendants leave now. You're not capable of being a juror on this case."

There were a few seconds of silence, and then about fifteen people left the courtroom, nine men and six women.

Eventually, twenty-four jurors qualified through their negative replies to Judge Rhinehart's screening questions. Intent on loading the jury with as many people who would likely be open to their respective points of view, the prosecution and the defense were careful to use their three peremptory rejections for cause.

"Are you married, Mr. Martin?" Zach asked one juror.

"I am not."

"Do you have any children from a former relationship?"

"I do not."

Zach turned to Judge Rhinehart. "I object for cause."

"Hello, Mrs. Davis," Martinez said to another juror. "I see you're a social worker in the emergency room at the University of San Francisco Hospital. How long have you worked there?"

"Five years."

"Mrs. Davis, you said you have two daughters and one son under twelve. Do you think that fact would preclude your ability to examine the facts presented during this trial and arrive at a conclusion of guilt or innocence?"

"As a trained social worker, I have been required to adopt a professional and scientific approach to the patients under my care. I am confident I can transfer that same objectivity to the evidence presented during this case."

Martinez directed his attention to Rhinehart. "Dismissed for cause, Your Honor."

On and on it went until twelve people were finally accepted by both sides. Rich and Zach had won with four jurors. Married women, most likely mothers. But had lost with a couple of twenty-somethings who were walking ads for liberal college kids.

The remaining six were black holes, at least to Zach and Rich. For all they knew, these six were hand-picked by the jury consultants sure to be out there.

Stan Kendrick couldn't believe his bad luck. His number had been 223. With such a high number, he was confident he wouldn't be selected. But there he sat, one of the twelve. He'd asked his boss at the software company where he was a middle manager if he could get excused because his workload was ginormous. But all that did was provide an excuse for the boss to start on a rant about the responsibilities of citizenship. Stan looked around at the other eleven men and women and groaned inwardly as he thought, *conspiring in a federal hate crime and, in the process, unintentionally murdering a transgendered teen.*

Although he was the quintessence of a computer geek, nerdy and introverted, Stan avoided all news and social media and didn't have a television in the house. He could care less about this stuff; it had no relevance to his life. Worse yet, according to the long list of people named as witnesses, this case would last more than a day or two.

"This is a landmark case, ladies and gentlemen of the jury. Hate in and of itself cannot be criminalized. However, such conduct may be classified as a hate crime when hate motivates criminal conduct. Defined by the Federal Bureau of Investigation as, and I quote, 'criminal offense against a person or property motivated in whole or in part by an offender's bias against a race, religion, disability, sexual orientation, ethnicity, gender, or gender identity.'

"Historically, such criminal activities are traditional offenses like murder, arson, and vandalism with an added element of bias. Recently, however, hate crimes have proliferated. As a result, our government has amended and added new provisions to American hate crime legislation.

"Hence, it has provided additional options for prosecuting hate crimes, explicitly prohibiting a conspiracy to deprive others of federally protected rights.

"Ms. Kate Townsend and Dr. Lindsey McCall conspired in a premeditated hate crime upon the community of transgendered Americans. Their conspiracy had an unanticipated consequence: the death of sixteen-year-old Joey Carmichael."

Martinez paused and scanned the faces of the jury's eight men and four women. Then, after glancing at Zach and Rich, he looked over to the left of the courtroom and the gaggle of prosecutors. Sam Eldridge, his co-counsel from the Southern Poverty Law Center, was an ambitious, intelligent attorney. Rachel Stawarski, a lawyer from the Transgender Law Center, was another matter. She had been a husband and father of three children but now dressed and identified as a woman. Martinez hadn't wanted Stawarski as co-counsel because she was unpredictable.

"Emilio, you can handle Stawarski," Attorney General Mark Dorman had told him. "Just keep her contained. How many cases have you won now? I've lost count."

Martinez had worked to keep his teeth grinding inaudible as he listened to the gratuitous remarks. He should have known he was on his own in this case. If he won, once again, he'd be golden. But if he lost, his career would come to a screeching halt.

Four more co-prosecutors represented the American Federation of Teachers, the ACLU, the Human Rights Campaign, Amnesty International, and the IGYLO. Sally Whitman from the Teachers Federation, Paul Lopez from the ACLU, Harvey Bernstein from Amnesty International, and Tedra Champion from the IGYLO.

If I were on this jury, I'd wonder why there were eight on one side and just two on the defense, Martinez thought. *Was the prosecution side so weak it needed eight lawyers?*

He remembered four weeks ago when the co-counsel lineup numbered in the double digits. He'd used one of his few precious bargaining chips with the AG to reduce the insane number from twenty-six to eight.

Get a grip, Emilio.

Martinez strode about the courtroom in a slim-fit Calvin Klein that hugged his athletic body. The good-looking, dark-haired lawyer didn't believe in flaunting his success—no $2,000 designer suits for him. The son of farm workers from Tijuana, Emilio's parents had nothing but love to spend on him and his six brothers. They had taught their oldest son that money was a tool not to be squandered, and he'd taken the lesson to heart.

Emilio's only jewelry was his wedding ring. But his hard-earned poise and confidence belied his feelings about this case.

It was eating him up. If he'd slept one hour last night, it was a stretch. He'd told his wife, Maria, that it was only pretrial jitters, but she knew it wasn't that at all. Emilio was acting very differently from any other case he'd ever tried.

Before the grand jury had begun their proceedings, Maria had pleaded with him not to have anything to do with the case. He'd regretted his quasi-blasphemous response the moment it left his mouth. "What are you, Pilate's wife? Telling me to have nothing to do with Jesus on trial?" He winced in response to Maria's pained expression.

Emilio's excuses to skip Sunday Mass had worn thin with Maria years ago. She was a devout Catholic, just as he'd been when they married. Then he decided to go for partner at the law firm he worked for. Matthews, Carson, and Otto was among California's top five firms, and Emilio was the first Hispanic partner in the firm's history. As a result, his formerly eighty-hour work weeks became one hundred, including Sundays.

Emilio's sharp retort to his wife was said because he knew she was right. That retired Dr. Johnson on the grand jury had hammered his two expert witnesses decrying McCall's intervention with the dead teen. The seventy-something-year-old kept writing questions for Dr. Sullivan and handing them to the bailiff. She'd become furious at the seventh piece of paper with yet another question carried to his expert. Johnson was just as relentless with the second witness for the prosecution, a young surgeon. And then Johnson had an anginal attack. During another witness's testimony, Johnson had collapsed and was taken to the hospital.

Martinez could not stop asking himself, "What if Johnson hadn't left the juror panel?" Even though he knew the answer.

Inwardly, he shook himself and resumed.

"Ladies and Gentlemen of the jury, the relationship between the defendant, Dr. Lindsey McCall, and reporter Kate Townsend is long-standing and close." Lifting a dark eyebrow at the jurors, he told them, "Ironically, they first met because of Ms. Townsend's Pulitzer Prize-winning investigative series on Dr. McCall's wrongful conviction for another unintentional murder." He paused to let his words sink in and was rewarded by whispered "Oohs and ahs" from several jurors.

"The government will show that a party in a kindergarten and a vulnerable young boy converged into the perfect formula for these two women to conspire in the commission of a federal hate crime against the transgendered community of America. Due to their longstanding relationship, Ms. Townsend naturally consulted with her friend, Dr. Lindsey McCall, when she wrote the medical aspects of her newspaper series. We just received email verification of that consultation and will enter those emails into courtroom records.

"Dr. McCall's medical intervention in sixteen-year-old Joey Carmichael's hormonal treatments resulted in his unintentional murder."

Martinez scanned each of the twelve jurors riveted on him and said, "I trust you will responsibly act on the evidence you will hear over the next few days and find these women guilty."

The judge looked over at the defense table. Compared to the prosecution side, Zach and Rich looked underequipped.

Rich stood up. And said, "Judge, the defense waives our opening statement."

Kate started to rise, thinking, *Email documents of me asking Lindsey medical advice for my articles? What is he talking about?*

Rich's grip on her arm forced her back down. *Show nothing, Kate,* she remembered Rich telling her. *No matter what is said on the witness stand, act like you're in the twentieth inning, and it's midnight.* Since she'd gotten out of the car and walked up the steps of the imposing glass monstrosity of the federal building, Kate had been dealing with a feeling of panic bordering on hysteria. All the calm and serenity she'd told Steve she felt had galloped away. She'd never experienced such terror. If she could, Kate would have laughed at the ease with which she'd told Steve to go ahead and see some patients who wanted to see him one last time. "I'll be fine," she had said.

Zach and Rich had hurried off the elevator ahead of her and Lindsey, eager to get into the courtroom and get the lay of the land. Lindsey stopped to look at Kate before they stepped into the hallway. "I know how you feel." Kate stared at her, wide-eyed, her heart racing so fast she felt dizzy. "Like you have no control. There's nothing you can do. You're trapped." Those intense green eyes bored into her. "And you're right. This is awful." Her lips compressed into a thin line. "More terrible than anyone can imagine until it happens to them."

"But what you *can* control is your breathing. Slow it down. If you don't, you'll hyperventilate and faint." Lindsey had watched her for a few seconds. "Now, Kate!" she hissed. "Slow your breathing down *now*."

Kate thought, *Breathe. In and out, breathe.* Lindsey was right; it helped. Toni and Zach had predicted dirty tricks. But forging emails between Lindsey and her?

"Dr. Sullivan, you head up the gender affirmation clinic at San Francisco Medical Center. Is that correct?"

The tall, thin, dark-haired, hawk-nosed woman nodded. "Yes, that's right."

"And you've got a most impressive background, Dr. Sullivan. A fellowship in gender dysphoria at Cleveland Clinic." Martinez paused as if waiting for applause.

"With four books and over one hundred articles, Dr. Sullivan, is it correct to consider you an expert in gender dysphoria and treatment?"

The physician nodded and said modestly, "Yes, my expertise in the field is acknowledged through my research and publications."

"Have you had experience with the detransitioning of persons who regret their gender alteration and want to return to their biological gender?"

The doctor frowned. Paused and said, "A little. That situation is uncommon among my patients."

"How uncommon, Doctor Sullivan?"

Looking up and to the left, as if calculating, Sullivan said, "I have somewhere around four to five hundred patients. In the ten years of my practice, only five had requested detransitioning."

The US Attorney looked shocked. As if this information were brand new, he looked over at the jury to make sure they, too, were amazed and was rewarded with a couple of gasps from two female jurors.

To ensure the math was understood, Martinez said, "So,

that's one percent of your large population."

Dr. Sullivan seemed unsure of what she was supposed to say to this so she merely said, "Yes."

"And in those five patients, Dr. Sullivan, did you switch hormonal therapy in these persons? For instance, had the patient transitioned from female to male, did you stop the testosterone and start estrogen?"

"No, I did not."

"And why is that?"

"Because of the high risk of embolic phenomena."

There was a chorus of comments from the last two rows and the rear of the courtroom.

Judge Rhinehart looked startled but recovered quickly as he looked at the many reporters, rapping his gavel sharply. And then he said, "Ladies and Gentlemen. Take your comments out of my courtroom." Then, in the sudden quiet, he said to Martinez, "Please continue, Mr. Martinez."

"The prosecution has no more questions for this witness, Judge."

At that, Zach stood and approached the doctor.

"Good morning, Dr. Sullivan."

Judge Rhinehart looked up, startled at Zach's distinctive gravelly growl. His slight five-foot-five, 150-pound frame was clad in a light gray Dolce & Gabbana wool-and-silk suit with a white shirt and vest.

The witness nodded at Zach, said, "Good morning," and waited patiently, her hands folded in her lap. She had done this many, many times.

Making a pretense of notes he didn't need, Zach said, "Dr. Sullivan, you treat adult, not pediatric patients in your practice; isn't that correct?"

The witness hesitated, suddenly drained of her composure, and looked at Martinez, who was looking studiously at a file in front of him.

The judge looked over and said, "Doctor, please answer the question."

"Yes, my patients are adults. I am not a pediatrician."

Zach nodded politely, took his right hand, extended it toward the witness, and said, "So, Doctor, it would not be correct to consider you an expert in the gender dysphoria or detransitioning of children, would it?"

The doctor frowned, looked at the judge, and said softly, "No, it would not."

Nodding once again, Zach said, "And the hormonal treatment for a prepubescent and or pubescent teen would be completely different from that of a mature man or woman, would it not?"

Cheeks bright red and lips compressed, Dr. Sullivan said, "Yes, that is correct."

"Just one last question, Dr. Sullivan, when you mentioned all the papers and publications on gender dysphoria and affirmation, that data are all in the adult population, are they not? That means, Doctor, you have no idea about the proper treatment for detransitioning a teen …."

"*Objection*!!! Counsel is testifying!" The US Attorney was on his feet.

"I withdraw the question, Judge. The defense has no more questions for this witness."

"Good morning, Dr. Peterson; you are the president of California Polytechnic Institute; is that correct?"

"Yes, I am."

She was highly uncomfortable. Lindsey could see her whitened fingertips; she held them so tightly together they blanched.

As she watched her former boss, Lindsey felt only sympathy. Twice, Peterson had glanced at Lindsey and almost winced.

Martinez nodded. "Therefore, you employed Dr. McCall in her former position in the Animal Research Center at Cal Poly."

"That's correct." Martinez could see this woman's nervousness and tried calming her down with a few soft, undemanding questions.

Assuming an appropriately grave expression, the Attorney said, "And you'd most likely seen Joey Carmichael around the campus or been aware of him."

"Yes, I approved his transfer to us from Chico State last year."

"Doctor, were you aware of Dr. McCall's relationship with Joey?" Martinez frowned, "I apologize; my question was not clear. Did you know of Dr. McCall's medical treatment of Joey?"

"Objection."

The judge looked at Zach, "On what grounds, Counselor?"

"Facts not in evidence."

"Sustained."

US Attorney Martinez hid his anger or hoped he did as he thought, *Stupid! You're making the mistakes of a rookie; this Cunningham is shrewd. You can't afford to be on autopilot.* Martinez had been unconsciously repeating his grand jury questioning of this witness, completely forgetting that he'd been unable to introduce the risks of embolic phenomena with both testosterone and estrogen treatments.

"Doctor, were you aware that Dr. McCall and Joey knew one another?"

"Yes."

"Was that because you had been informed of that relationship?"

Peterson looked at a chubby, blonde woman sitting in the row behind the prosecution's table and said, "Yes, Ellen O'Brien, Joey's English professor, told me of her concern about Dr. McCall's treatment of Joey. Ellen believed Dr. McCall was helping …."

"Objection! Hearsay, your Honor." Zach was up again.

"Sustained," Rhinehart said, looking at Martinez quizzically.

Martinez smiled thinly. "Dr. Peterson, did you meet with Dr. McCall because you were concerned about this situation?"

"I did."

"And what was discussed at that meeting?"

Dr. Peterson shifted. She began to speak and then stopped. Finally, she said, "Since it's been several months, I cannot recall precisely what was said, but I asked Dr. McCall if she was aware of the university's commitment to diversity, whether ethnic or sexual and when she said she was, I asked if she had any concerns or questions about our policy. Dr. McCall said no that she understood and supported it." She looked almost apologetically at Martinez and continued, "I had no direct knowledge of any details, certainly not of any treatment, so there was nothing more to be said."

"Thank you, Dr. Peterson. I have no more questions."

"Does the defense wish to cross-examine the witness?"

Thinking, *That laid a big goose egg, Martinez, thank you,* Zach said, "The defense has no questions for this witness."

Judge Rhinehart called a twenty-minute recess.

"What do you know of emails between you two?"

Lindsey, Kate, Zach, Toni, and Rich sat in the conference room reserved for the defense outside the courtroom. Zach was doing his best to act calm and failing.

"Nothing."

He looked at Kate and said, "You're sure."

"Zach, Lindsey never even read any of the articles before she got to my house; she didn't even know I'd ...."

"It's faked," Lindsey interrupted. "Somebody with the know-how and or money had to have created them."

"She's right," Rich said, thinking, *Rachel Stawarski, the lawyer who left her card and had shown Lindsey's articles to Cassie. Transgender Law Center. They have know-how and money.*

Quickly, he found the image of her card on his phone and scribbled her name and organization on a page torn from a legal pad. Then handed it to Toni, who said, "I'm on it." Once she was gone, Rich explained what he thought he knew. Zach's "Whew!" evoked smiles as they sipped their cups of cold coffee.

CHAPTER FORTY-FIVE

"Good morning, Ms. O'Brien. You teach English at Cal Poly, is that right?"

"Yes."

Ellen O'Brien smiled nervously; this was very new to her.

"And the late Joey Carmichael was one of your students, correct?"

The witness's pale blue eyes welled up, and her voice quavered as she said, "Yes, that's correct." It was evident to everyone in the courtroom that Ellen O'Brien had been very fond of Joey.

"Ms. O'Brien, what prompted you to go to the university president and complain about Dr. Lindsey McCall?"

"I met Joey a couple of months into our semester. Although he had missed extensive materials, Joey was attentive in class and, although shy, eager to participate in class discussions. I knew he was trans and asked if he'd like to come with me to the Cal Poly GLSEN meeting that evening because Joey could use some friends." She smiled. "It worked because the club elected him their president not long afterward."

"Ms. Obrien, can you explain to our jurors what GLSEN stands for?"

"Of course! Gay, Lesbian, and Straight Educational Network."

"Objection, relevance Judge?"

"This is all very interesting, Mr. Martinez, but I'm also having trouble understanding the relevance here." Judge Rhinehart looked at Zach and then at Martinez and said, "I agree with the defense, Mr. Martinez. Is there a point coming here soon?"

Martinez had decided to strike his second medical expert.

The young surgeon had testified well for the grand jury, but like Dr. Sullivan, his practice was adults, not kids. So, he was winging it—fishing— hoping that something useful would come from the English teacher's testimony.

"Yes, Judge." The US Attorney smiled at Ms. O'Brien in a way he hoped she would find comforting and willed her to give him something tangible.

"You are talking about Joey's early behavior in your class, Ms. O'Brien, because why, exactly?"

"Because he changed. At the meetings, he began to withdraw. And act sad. Joey stopped participating in class, and when I asked some of the other GLSEN members about it, they said he changed when …."

Before Zach could shout, "Hearsay," Martinez thanked her and returned to his seat.

"Defense, do you want to cross-examine the witness?"

Zach was already on his feet when he said, "Yes, Judge."

"Ms. O'Brien, my deepest sympathies for losing a student you clearly had deep feelings for." His sincerity was genuine, and the witness knew it as she whispered, "Thank you."

Zach said in the same soft cadence and tone, "I've just one question. Do you have any *direct* knowledge of Joey's relationship with the defendant? Or the details of her treatment of him?"

The witness blinked. "No, I do not."

"The defense has no more questions for this witness."

Looking at the giant clock on the courtroom wall reading 12:30, Judge Rhinehart said, "The court will break for lunch and resume at 1:30 p.m."

LJ looked at Morgan and whispered, "Let's go find something to eat."

"They have sandwiches brought to Rich and Zach's conference room."

"Aren't you sick of sandwiches?"

Morgan looked at her friend. "How can I be? We've not had one yet. This is the first day of court, or have you moved to another dimension?"

"Do I need to beg? Come on, this is San Francisco. Let's go take a walk."

Within ten minutes, the two walked down Golden Gate Avenue; LJ was studying the map on their phone.

"Where are you going, LJ?"

"Shovel's Bar and Grill. It's about three blocks east, then two north."

LJ felt Morgan's hand grab her upper arm and squeeze hard.

"Hey!"

"Turn around, now." LJ hadn't noticed, but two youngish-looking hooded guys were tracking them.

They did a 180 and walked rapidly back to the courthouse. LJ was grateful that Morgan hadn't remarked on the stupidity of walking alone in a city she knew nothing about. But LJ had felt like she would jump out of her skin if she'd stayed in that courtroom a moment longer.

As they entered the federal building through the massive glass doors, LJ looked at Morgan, "What do you think?"

"About those guys?"

"No, about this trial."

Morgan studied her friend. LJ was trying to act casual, as if FBI agents, the sudden death of a classmate, and federal trials were the stuff of everyday life. But Morgan knew she wasn't sleeping. And hadn't since the middle-of-the-night arrest.

So she grabbed LJ's hands and squeezed them. "I think this coming week will be horrid. And scary and ugly. And more."

LJ stood utterly still, willing herself not to cry and knowing the truth of what Morgan said. Neither young woman noticed any of the bustling men and women impatiently moving around them. "But LJ, I do not believe that God has or will abandon them for a second." Those varicolored, long-lashed, coppery eyes blinked, and Morgan smiled one of her rare joyous grins. "Lindsey and Kate will be found not guilty."

Now LJ's tears released. But not because she was sad but because of relief: she believed Morgan. Morgan looked at her phone and said, "We've got to move, LJ; the afternoon session is starting."

"Ms. Meeks, you are the kindergarten teacher who once taught the defendant, Kate Townsend's son. Is that correct?"

"Yes, I am. In fact, I—"

"Just answer my questions, please, Ms. Meeks. Thank you." Emilio's gentle smile took the bite from his interruption, and Addison smiled back at him.

"I think you may have been about to tell the jury that you were a student of Dr. Matt Heathcock, the man who pioneered the first transgender legislation in the country. Am I correct?"

Concentrating on Addison sitting on the witness stand, Kate fought the terror again. Counting, she kept her breaths under twenty per minute. One breath every three seconds. Lindsey's counsel worked. When she slowed her breathing, her heart rate came down, too. Amazingly, her terror began to subside, and she could pray again. *Jesus, I trust in you. I do; I trust in you.*

Addison was a lovely young woman. Kate smiled inwardly at a memory. She'd been speaking with Father John about how he made each moment holy. "When I feel myself begin to criticize someone," he said, "I twist my thoughts around to find something to admire about the person. Sometimes it takes so long that I forget what I'm criticizing."

After only two brief introductory questions, the US attorney quickly got to the heart of Addison's testimony. "The child who wanted his name changed from Danny to Susan cried when Ms. Townsend took off the dress you purchased for her coming-out party?"

With a quick glance at Kate, Addison nodded. "Of course

he did! It was obvious that Danny no longer wanted to be a boy." Then, the young teacher frowned. "I didn't realize what Ms. Townsend was doing and why she was so aggressively preventing the child from becoming Susie. But then when I read—"

"Objection! Conjecture!" Rich had jumped to his feet before even thinking, casting an apologetic look at Zach as he did so. They'd agreed to let her testify unchallenged, but Judge Rhinehart nodded at the objection. "Sustained. Ms. Meeks, please keep your remarks to answering questions."

During Addison's testimony about Dr. Heathcock's theories, Kate's mind wandered as she reflected on that afternoon that changed her life. But she alerted when Addison began talking about the afternoon party for Danny Sugarman.

The young teacher had changed every single detail, precisely as Toni had forecasted she would do. Kate listened while Addison portrayed herself as the victim of a reporter on the lookout for context for her fanatic assault on gender dysphoria and transgenderism. Addison's eager young face shone as she told the jury that Danny had been dancing and singing, "My name is Susan, Susan Sugarman." She claimed that Danny clapped his hands at the cake with "Come Out Susan" written on it and was delighted with the change from "boy clothes" to "girl clothes."

Listening to the young woman's testimony, Kate realized that Addison had convinced herself it was the truth. *She's not lying. She's suppressed Danny's hysteria about being forced to wear his older sister's clothes.*

Kate had seen the Sugarmans in the packed courtroom earlier and could not imagine what was going through their minds. Of course, Kate had told them about what had happened that afternoon. She had brought each article to them for approval before it was published. But she'd never used Danny's name. So, this trivial incident from an imaginative child might result in his name being "slipped" and Danny Sugarman's whole "coming out party" dissected by pundits on both sides of the yawning chasm dividing the country.

"So, Ms. Meeks," Martinez said to pound the nail again, "to be clear for the jury, the child never cried or showed any distress until Ms. Townsend arrived early to pick up her child."

"Yes, that's correct."

Martinez looked at the judge and said, "The government has no more questions for this witness."

Judge Rhinehart leaned forward, "Does the defense wish to cross-examine this witness?" Rich and Zach had decided beforehand that cross-examination of Addison would be pointless. It was Kate's word against the teacher's.

Rich stood and shook his head. "No, Your Honor. The defense has no questions for this witness."

"Yes, I'm Dr. Matt Heathcock." The tall seventy-something man smiled at Martinez.

"You have a weighty curriculum vitae, Dr. Heathcock." Martinez smiled back as he walked to the prosecution table to consult his notes, then strode back to his witness. "Would I be correct in stating that you have published more than one hundred fifty articles, chapters, and books on gender dysphoria?"

Heathcock nodded. "You would."

Martinez gazed over at the jury. "With that volume of publications in gender dysphoria, Dr. Heathcock, we can acknowledge you as one of the top experts in that field."

Heathcock remained silent, waiting for a question. He looked comfortable in his conservative black suit, blue oxford-style shirt, and military-style haircut, and he looked at least fifteen years younger than his stated age. Testifying in court was routine; he'd clearly done it a lot.

"Have you read Kate Townsend's articles, Dr. Heathcock?"

"Yes, I have."

This guy is a perfect witness. Maybe too perfect? Zach thought. Unlike many expert witnesses Zach had encountered, Heathcock resisted the temptation to soliloquize about their expertise before a captive audience.

Watching each move Martinez and Heathcock made, Zach's almost photographic memory reviewed Heathcock's publications in his mind. He stopped on one. It was written in the late 1990s. It stood out because Heathcock had argued against proposed legislation advocating that children of age twelve be permitted to change their gender.

Writing a note on his pad, he looked back into the court-room for Toni and was momentarily stunned. *Where did all these people come from?* Two rows of men and women were standing in the back, holding up cell phones. There were even a few with legal pads and pens. Suddenly, Toni appeared, crouched in front of him. She grabbed the note and moved as fast as she could through the crowd.

Martinez moved on to Heathcock's role in pioneering transgender legislation in California.

"Dr. Heathcock, do you believe the dangers of too-early transitioning, as stated in Ms. Townsend's articles, have merit? Are there risks to youngsters that must be evaluated?"

"Yes, of course, there are risks," Heathcock said. He'd sat with his hands steepled before him the whole time he'd been on the witness stand. But now, he let his hands drop into his lap as he bowed his head. Then he looked back up at Martinez, his expression grave. "Gender dysphoria is a phenomenon where the chromosomal sex of the person is discordant with his or her identification as a male or female. This dissonance can be severe enough for some youngsters to commit suicide."

Kate was riveted by this mesmerizing man. He acted more like a minister or a counselor than an administrator. Compassion seemed to eke out of every pore. She could see that the jury felt the same way.

"Judge, the government has no more questions for this witness."

Once again, Judge Rhinehart looked at the defense and started to say something but was interrupted by the bailiff. He nodded in response and looked at the clock. "Dr. Heathcock, you may step down. The court will recess for twenty minutes and resume at 4 p.m. sharp."

Zach looked about in frustration. And then asked Rich, "Have you seen Toni?"

"No, didn't you send her to grab something, Zach?" Rich watched as Zach muttered something unintelligible and strode down the courtroom aisle and out the door. Toni had found the former grand jurist retired internist, Dr. Johnson, and made an appointment with him to take a call from Zach. He'd told Toni he would love to testify for the defense. But the doctor had suffered another heart attack only three hours ago and was dead. Still reeling from this devastating loss to his defense, Zach rushed to find Toni, desperate to get his hands on that article.

"What's wrong?" Both Lindsey and Kate watched Rich anxiously.

"I have no clue."

CHAPTER FORTY-EIGHT

Zach stood up. "Permission to approach the bench, Your Honor?"

"Judge, I'd like to enter into the record a May 1999 article from *Psychoanalytic Psychology* by Dr. Matt Heathcock. The piece is titled 'Arguments for Conversion Therapy for Gender Dysphoric Children Under the Age of Twelve.'"

"Objection!" Martinez leaped from his chair so abruptly that several files toppled to the floor before the prosecutor's table. Martinez strode around the scattered documents and stood in front of the bench a few feet to the right of Zach.

"Judge, the government has no knowledge of this article, but quite clearly, in their desperation to impugn the government's open-and-shut case, the defense is using the tired tactic of surreptitiously entering evidence at the eleventh hour."

Rhinehart said nothing, just looked at Zach.

"Your honor, this surreptitious eleventh-hour evidence can be found in the curriculum vitae of Dr. Matt Heathcock," Zach said, pausing for a millisecond to glance at Martinez. "Dr. Heathcock's CV was provided by the government—if anyone cares to read it."

Judge Rhinehart pounded his gavel in response to the growing hum of voices in the courtroom. He lifted his sizable frame from his seat when their reaction became even louder. "Order! This is a United States federal court of law, not a reality show. If you wish to observe the proceedings, you may do so, but only if you keep your mouths *shut*!

"Look around, and you will see bailiffs at each door. Open your eyes wider, and you will see armed police standing next to each bailiff." Judge Rhinehart was practically smiling, but the movement of his lips looked more like a grimace as he addressed the back rows where the reporters were standing or sitting. "Once you are asked to leave my courtroom, you will *not* be allowed back in."

Suddenly, the silence in the courtroom was tangible. Then, nodding with satisfaction, Rhinehart resumed his seat, cleared his throat, and glanced at Martinez and then Zach. "Please enter 'Arguments for Conversion Therapy for Gender Dysphoric Children Under the Age of Twelve' into the record. Counselor, you may proceed with your cross-examination of this witness."

"Dr. Heathcock, this paper you published nearly twenty years ago lists more than a dozen reasons for adopting a 'wait and see' response to children with gender dysphoria." Then, correctly interpreting Heathcock's expression, Zach corrected himself. "Doctor, I know I've oversimplified your paper, but for novices like me and the jury, 'wait and see what happens' is easier to understand —and seems far gentler—than the concept of conversion therapy."

As he smiled at the witness, out of the corner of his eye, Zach watched Martinez half rise in objection when prompted by a large man dressed as a woman sitting beside him. But Martinez changed his mind and sat back down. His associate leaned in and whispered. Martinez's hissed rebuke could be heard by those who were listening, and the jury was indeed listening.

Fully aware of the effect of his smile and his comment about conversion therapy, Zach watched as Heathcock tried not to stare at the grotesque distortion made by the quarter-inch scar running from Zach's left eyebrow diagonally down through the right side of his mouth when the damaged muscles responded. Heathcock's imperturbability began to slip as the seconds ticked by.

"How is it then, Doctor, that just two years after the publication of your article, you decided to enjoin the California legislature to instruct teachers and schools to do the exact opposite of what you knew to be best for these kids?"

At that, the courtroom exploded, and Martinez and all seven of his associates were on their feet. "Objection!"

Judge Rhinehart stood, looked at the jurors, and said, "The court will recess for fifteen minutes." He lowered his voice and looked at the prosecutors. "Everyone in my quarters, now!" He gestured to Rich and Zach. "You two, come, too."

The rows of reporters emptied out as they raced outside to file their stories.

Along with his fellow jurors, Stan Kendrick filed out of the courtroom via the juror hallway adjacent to the jurors' benches. He could hear snippets of conversation among a few groups that had formed: three middle-aged women had sat together at lunch. They chatted idly about the appearance of the lawyers, judge, and defendants. A few men around his age wondered how long they would be stuck in the case, and the youngest members, a twenty-something man and a woman, paired up. The woman listened to whatever her tall, blonde companion said as if it were gospel. A tall, elderly African-American man held the door for Stan and said, "I think it's going to be a very long week."

Stan looked up at him—he had to be at least six-feet-four or -five inches tall, and Stan was struck by his expression of kindness. He surprised himself by saying, "I tried to get out of this case, begged my boss to write one of those letters pleading that my work is essential. He became irate and lectured me about the responsibilities of citizenship. So, after listening to all these people today, maybe he's right."

The man nodded appreciatively, and they exited the courtroom silently, each lost in his own thoughts.

The ten attorneys stood before Judge Rhinehart's enormous, scarred wooden desk. It was a real feat because the office was barely large enough for Rhinehart's office furniture. They'd been standing there for fifteen minutes when the six-foot-six former UCLA linebacker walked in. Saying nothing to anyone, Judge Rhinehart squeezed past the line, walked behind the desk, and dropped into a sagging facsimile of an ergonomic chair.

Pushing his chair back, the judge placed his two humongous loafered feet on his desk.

"US Attorney Martinez."

"Yes, sir." Martinez almost saluted as he snapped to attention.

"Must we review why only one attorney can speak in a court of law?"

"No, sir."

"Does the remainder of your team understand that another incident where multiple prosecutors speak at once will earn your team a citation for contempt of court?"

"Yes, sir."

"I need to hear it from each man individually."

All six members replied except for Rachel Stawarski, who regarded the judge with animus. "I am not a man. I'm a woman."

Rhinehart leaped to his feet with astonishing speed and agility and stared at Stawarski. "What did you just say to my instruction about maintaining order in my courtroom?"

Glaring at him, Stawarski raised her chin, jaw extended. "I *said* I am not a man. I am a woman and refuse to answer until you address me as such."

"US Attorney Martinez," Rhinehart said, holding Stawarski's gaze, "please accompany this lawyer and the rest of your team out of my office." Stawarski opened her mouth to object again, but he cut him off. "Now, Martinez, unless you want that contempt citation, keep this person out of my courtroom for the extent of this trial."

As the door closed behind the prosecuting attorneys, Rhinehart looked over at Rich and Zach. "For now, this court is giving you latitude. Cunningham?"

"Yes, sir!"

"You seem familiar. Have you defended a case in one of my courtrooms before?"

"No, sir."

Rhinehart frowned. "I could have sworn I've seen your unforgettable face before." He nodded. "You're clever, Cunningham. Very shrewd. That's not really a compliment, so be careful."

"Yes, sir."

"How is it then, Doctor, that just two years after the publication of your article, you decided to enjoin the California legislature to instruct teachers and schools to do the exact opposite of what you knew to be best for these kids?" That was the question Zach wanted to ask Dr. Heathcock a second time. However, as he stood in front of the man and let his gaze scan the faces of the jury members, he realized most of them were waiting for the show to continue.

The absence of Dr. Rachel Stawarski was inadvertently conspicuous because the prosecutorial team now sat in one row behind their table. Stawarski's girth had made that impossible before.

Of course, they're waiting for another farcical occurrence. Rhinehart inadvertently set the stage for it when he shouted, "This isn't a reality show!" Father John's counsel must be causing my sympathy for Stawarski. It's not people we're facing here, he said, but these onlookers can't know that. Smiling inwardly, Zach thought about the implausibility of such self-restraint before he'd met the priest.

"Dr. Heathcock, I will rephrase my question of fifteen minutes ago." Zach looked up at the psychologist for the first time after the break and was surprised at his countenance. No longer unflappable, the man looked wan and wary.

"Can you explain to the jury why you changed your mind about the dangers of gender affirmation for pre-pubescent youngsters? A change so complete that you developed legislation instructing California teachers to regard a three-year-old as competent to change his gender?"

"Objection, Your Honor! Defense is testifying and harassing the witness!" Martinez was on his feet but lacked the passion Zach expected from him.

Judge Rhinehart lifted an eyebrow at Martinez. "Testifying, Counselor? How about asking consecutive questions that the witness can't answer?" He steepled his massive hands in thought. "Harassment? Overruled." He turned to Heathcock. "Please answer the question."

Dr. Heathcock blinked rapidly; his confidence bled away, and he looked confounded for the first time.

Thanks, Father John. I'm totally winging this, but it's evident that I'm not alone up here. When was the last time I prayed like I did last night?

"Well, there are times when one must discount theory when the evidence reveals the need to act," Heathcock said.

Zach stared at him in wonder. After waiting to see if the witness would say anything more, Zach cleared his throat. "I apologize again for my ignorance in these matters, Doctor." He saw Rhinehart's eyes glitter out of the corner of his eye and could almost hear him hiss, "Watch it, Counselor."

"Could you please explain what you mean by 'evidence revealing the need to act'? Perhaps you could give an example so we can understand how your theory gets trumped."

"Objection!" This time, the passion was back. Martinez was almost frothing at the mouth. "Your Honor, the defense counsel is doing everything possible to belittle Dr. Heathcock in front of the jury."

Rhinehart whispered something to the bailiff, who nodded and addressed the crowd. "Court is adjourned for the day. Proceedings will reconvene at 9:00 tomorrow morning."

After the jurors had filed out, the bailiff approached Zach

and Martinez. "Judge Rhinehart would like to speak with you both in his chambers now."

Moments later, the three men were standing in the chambers. Zach looked tiny next to Rhinehart and Martinez.

"Unless you two change tactics, we'll be here for the rest of our lives," Rhinehart said. If he was annoyed, his expression showed no evidence of it. In fact, he looked both sympathetic and grave as he regarded the two men. "I agree with your questions," he said to Zach. Then he glanced at Martinez. "And your objections are reasonable. But the afternoon is gone, and this witness has replied to only one question from the defense." The big man rubbed his jaw, then lowered his hand. "I wouldn't want to prosecute or defend this case." Then he stared down at Zach and then across at Martinez. "But you two drew very short straws. And somehow, you must figure out how we can move through these witnesses in a way that will not inflict any more harm. You both know there will be no winners here." The judge pinned them with an intense and profoundly sorrowful gaze.

Zach shook his head. "No, Your Honor, that's for damn sure." Then Zach extended his hand to Emilio. He stared at it for a beat, then shook it, nodding silently.

Emilio and Zach closed the door to the judge's chambers and walked toward the empty courtroom. Glancing at the prosecuting attorney, Zach thought Emilio looked quite different from the confident young prosecutor he had appeared to be just a few hours earlier.

Chastened schoolboys, Zach thought, *both of us.*

Zach reflected on Father John's intriguing observations the night before, or more accurately, very early that morning.

After tossing and turning for hours in a futile effort to sleep, Zach had wandered into Steve and Kate's great room, which had become their office. He found Father John standing in front of the whiteboard on which Lindsey had been writing.

Sensing Zach's presence, the priest turned, nodded, then went back to whatever contemplation the board evoked.

Father John's early comment about their opponents not being people but "powers and principalities" had been echoing in Zach's brain since the words were spoken. "Father John," he whispered, aware of all the other people who were, hopefully, asleep down the hall, "I agree this case is suffused with evil." The priest turned toward him in the dim light and pointed to Kate's office on the far side of the room, indicating they could talk there.

Once inside the office, Zach closed the door and sat in an upholstered chair across from the priest. They looked at each other in the soft light of the desk lamp that Father John had turned on. As Zach regarded the man in black, he saw a curious mixture of joy and sorrow, weariness and vitality in a face that wasn't much older than his own. Zach was sixty-eight and figured the priest was maybe a couple of years older.

Realizing Father John was waiting for Zach to continue speaking, he did precisely that. "Like Lindsey noted earlier, and Kate wrote in her articles, the concept of evil hasn't been in my lexicon. But none of us can look at the details of this case and not understand this is something different … other." Zach leaned forward. "But when you said we're not dealing with people, did you mean you think the people involved aren't responsible? That they're somehow possessed by dark spirits pulling their strings?" As he listened to his own words, Zach felt ridiculous, foolish, and yet eager to hear Father John's response.

"I suppose one could say they're not responsible, Zach." The sorrow deepened in Father John's intelligent gray eyes. "For the same reason that Christ begged the Father to forgive those who tortured and crucified him. If they'd known that the Galilean Jew was the King of the Universe, they would never have done what they did."

It wasn't cold in the room, but Zach shivered.

"You and I could spend the rest of our lives trying to understand evil and why it's permitted and never get any farther than we'll get here. Now." The priest fingered the crucifix that hung around his neck. "Each human being is created in the Creator's image and likeness. When he breathes life into us, he also breathes knowledge of his law: our conscience. Uniquely among all God's creatures, we have an intellect and a will to develop that conscience." The volume of his voice dropped. "His great gift to humanity: free will, Zach. Either we choose to follow the laws we know to be true—or declare ourselves gods."

Zach and Martinez had made their way through the courtroom and opened the doors to the corridor when Zach surprised himself.

"Emilio."

Startled, the younger man stopped and looked back. "Yes?"

"Do you know a place where we can grab a beer? I'll buy."

"Do you like Cajun Creole?"

Zach raised an eyebrow, "Sounds like my kind of place." Both men were eager to get some air and a little exercise. They were on Polk within fifteen minutes, heading into Brenda's French Soul Food.

They ordered, found a table in the corner of the funky restaurant, and sat, waiting for their food. Zach looked at the US Attorney and said, "We need to get rid of a problem, Counselor. I'm happy to keep it between us if you are."

Startled, Martinez said, "What are you talking about?"

"Those emails. Your co-prosecutor, Stawarski, faked them. We have the proof." Zach opened his phone, clicked on a file from Toni, and handed it to Martinez.

CHAPTER FIFTY-TWO

At precisely nine the following morning, the bailiff appeared and bellowed, "All stand for the Honorable Donald Rhinehart." The judge swept in, robes billowing behind him, and sat behind the bench. He looked at Zach and said, "Please continue your cross, Mr. Cunningham."

"I call Dr. Matt Heathcock to the stand." The educator rose, walked slowly to the witness stand, and sat, his face a study in weariness.

"Could you please explain what you mean by 'evidence revealing the need to act'?" Zach asked, as he had the day before just before court was adjourned. "Perhaps you could also give an example, so we can understand how your theory gets trumped."

Dr. Heathcock looked at Martinez, but the prosecutor's head was down, focused on a thick folder. The witness waited for a beat, then another. Perplexed and increasingly anxious, his gaze scanned the seven attorneys at the prosecution table. Each of them was studying something that commanded their undivided attention.

Judge Rhinehart looked at Heathcock. "The witness will answer the defense's question."

Zach waited while Heathcock shifted in his seat, then coughed. "I apologize, but can you please repeat your question?"

Zach did so.

Perspiring and looking far older than his stated age of seventy-two, Heathcock nodded. "Well, it's complicated."

"Yes, sir. I'm sure it is," Zach replied.

Rhinehart tapped his gavel at the wave of titters spreading over the courtroom. But there wasn't much energy behind it. Like each of the jurors, he was glued to the exchange between Zach and Dr. Heathcock.

"You see, there are data, persuasive data that factor in, specifically, the threat of suicide in these youngsters."

"Are these the same data that you demonstrated were exaggerated and, in some cases, fabricated?"

Eldridge, the lawyer from Southern Poverty Law Center, pushed his chair back, but at a gesture from Martinez, he remained in his seat.

Heathcock merely stared miserably at Zach. Once again, Judge Rhinehart looked at the witness. "Please answer the question."

"When I learned about the unfortunate situation of several young people's state of mind, I became concerned," Heathcock said. "So concerned that I agreed to author the California bill."

"Dr. Heathcock, you said you *agreed* to author the bill? Please tell us who actually wrote the legislation for you to sign."

This time, four chairs clattered as the attorneys for Human Rights Campaign, Amnesty International, IGYLO, and the American Federation of Teachers jumped to their feet.

"Mister Martinez!" Rhinehart bellowed.

Sullenly, the co-prosecutors sat back down.

Rhinehart's glare at Heathcock loosened his tongue. Staring at Sally Whitman, the American Federation of Teachers attorney, he gulped. "It was Ms. Whitman's predecessor, Ms. Lois Burkheim. She wrote the bill, and I agreed to sponsor it."

"Could it be, sir, that you did this to ensure your retirement and good standing with the California and federal educational systems?" Zach asked.

Martinez was on his feet. "Objection, Your Honor, facts not in evidence."

"I withdraw the question," Zach said before Rhinehart could sustain the objection. "No more questions for this witness."

Rhinehart nodded at Dr. Heathcock. "Sir, you may step down. Call your next witness, please, Mr. Martinez.

CHAPTER FIFTY-THREE

"My name is McKenzie Stanfield."

"And Ms. Stanfield, you are currently the Human Rights Campaign president. Is that correct?"

The attractive African-American woman smiled, "Yes, I accepted that position last February."

"The Human Rights Campaign is the largest lobbying organization for LBTGQ plus rights in the country. Is that correct?"

"Yes, we can claim that distinction."

"Objection, Your Honor. Relevance?"

Rhinehart blinked at Rich, then nodded. "Mr. Jansen makes a good point, Mr. Martinez. How are this organization's lobbying efforts relevant to this case?"

"Your Honor, Ms. Stanfield represents thousands of transgender individuals who have developed a petition denying most of Ms. Townsend's claims in her articles. I would like to read the petition for the jury and enter it into evidence."

"How many signatories are on the petition?"

Ms. Stanfield opened a folder and read from it. "Your Honor, there are 844,929 signatures on the petition."

Rhinehart glanced at the defense table, but Rich and Zach remained seated. Clearly, the defense had no objection. He turned back to Martinez. "OK, I'll allow it."

Martinez strode over to the judge and handed him a document to be entered into the court records. "Ms. Stanfield, please read the petition for the jury."

In a pleasant, controlled fashion, she began to read. "We, the undersigned members of the transgender community of the

United States, do hereby deny the following assertions published by the Houston Tribune's April 2021 series, 'Creating Chemical Eunuchs: Corrupting America's Children.'

"Gender is not defined at birth. Gender is an identity that develops over time as the individual person matures. Sexual and genital anatomy is a malleable construct, one that is controlled through the autonomy of each individual. Making the decision to change one's gender is a freedom protected in the Constitution.

"'We hold these truths to be self-evident, that all men are created equal, that they are endowed by their Creator with certain unalienable Rights, that among these are Life, Liberty and the pursuit of Happiness, that to secure these rights, Governments are instituted among Men, deriving their just powers from the consent of the governed.'

"Government has no implied right to dictate the terms of its citizens' personal decisions to alter sexual identity, anatomy, or hormonal makeup. These decisions are an intrinsic right free from parental or governmental constraints.

"American educators are charged with the duty and obligation to protect persons from such prohibited constraints. Although we accept that hormonal therapy has possible inimical effects upon persons, it is their right to imbibe or inject such treatment if the individual deems it desirable for their happiness.

"Ms. Townsend asserts that those of us who decide to alter our identities and those who help us achieve our desired gender are evil. We claim such a statement is unconstitutional and constitutes a federal hate crime. The use of such language is prohibited by federal law.

"We further decry Dr. Lindsey McCall's medical interference with deceased trans-Joey Carmichael and her collaboration with Townsend's bigotry."

Ms. Stanfield closed her folder and looked at Martinez.

After two more similarly mind-numbing testimonies from the executive directors of Amnesty International and the ACLU, Martinez returned to Lindsey's decision to help Joey detransition.

"My name is Cassie Carmichael. My son Joey was killed by—"

"Objection!" If anyone had been asleep in the courtroom, Zach's thunderous growl awakened them.

"Mr. Martinez," Rhinehart barked, giving him a stern look, "please control your witness." He narrowed his eyes. "We'll have no more misspoken verbs during this case now, will we, Mr. Martinez?"

"Absolutely not, Your Honor." Martinez turned to his witness, "Ms. Carmichael, you didn't mean to say Joey was *killed*, did you?"

Cassie shook her head like a puppet on a string. "No, sir, I apologize." Then, using a wadded tissue, she wiped a non-existent tear from each eye. "The doctors said that Joey died from a blood clot in his brain."

If she hadn't identified herself, Rich wouldn't have recognized the well-dressed, attractive forty-something-year-old blonde woman as the person who'd shouted at the detectives and him from her dilapidated trailer mere months before. Cassie's eyes were a clear blue, and her make-up subtly erased the ravages of drugs and alcohol. She was a lovely woman. Twenty years ago, she would have been a Gal Gadot—albeit strawberry blonde—clone.

"Can you tell the court how you learned your son had died?"

She dabbed her dry eyes once again. "I was awakened in the middle of the night by three detectives from San Luis Obispo." Cassie looked over at the jurors and said," Joey was a sophomore at Cal Poly." She smiled for a moment, looking just like any other proud mother. "Joey was always super smart. Even as a kid, she loved to read and had a great memory."

Rich watched Cassie closely and thought, ironically, *I guess nine in the morning is the middle of the night if you've been drinking and popping pills most of the night.*

Martinez smiled back. "And the SLO detectives told you your son was dead?"

"No, they said he'd been found unconscious by two friends, also sophomores at the college, near the cattle pens. They told me the doctors had used medication to break the clot keeping Joey in a coma. But that it hadn't worked yet. They still hoped it would."

This time, the tears looked real. "Joey loved animals. He always did. Didn't matter what kind; Joey loved them all." She frowned. "I guess the medicine didn't work because Joey died in the hospital about a week later."

"Did anyone tell you why a clot had formed in your son's brain?"

"Joey began taking testosterone back when her name was Zoey." A sad smile appeared. "That's the name I gave her when she was born." Cassie blinked a few times and then said, "But Zoey decided she didn't want to be a girl anymore. In fact, Joey was planning to get a top job, but then this happened right before the surgery." Cassie spoke as if she were discussing a change in hairstyle.

"Did you permit your child to get these shots?"

Cassie stared at Martinez, uncomprehending.

"You said you knew your daughter wanted to become a boy, so did you agree to her taking testosterone?"

Cassie's blue eyes widened. "Well, sure, it was something Zoey wanted, and you know, I'm a mom, so I wanted the best for my little girl." She coughed. "If she no longer wanted to be a girl, that was OK. An awful lot of people are deciding they want to switch these days."

"And, Ms. Carmichael, were you aware that testosterone could cause possibly fatal blood clots in the brain?"

The real Cassie broke through. She leaned forward, her face contorted, her neck veins bulged, and her teeth bared. "Now, what kind of mother would I be if I'd known this thing would kill my Joey?" she hissed. Half rising from her chair, she pointed at Kate and Lindsey, "Someone needs to pay for his death! Your articles and your messing with Joey's hormones took him away from me!" She turned back to Martinez. "That's why I agreed to come here! And that's why I took your lousy ten thousand—"

"Thank you, Ms. Carmichael. Stop!" from Martinez and Judge Rhinehart's "Madame, STOP TALKING!" finally registered, and Cassie shut up.

Martinez glanced at Rhinehart as if for approval. "I have no more questions for this witness, Your Honor."

Rhinehart studied Cassie. "Madame, this is a United States federal courtroom. Nothing justifies behavior like you just exhibited. Can you assure me that you can control yourself for the remainder of this trial?"

Chastened, Cassie hung her head. "Yes, sir."

"Ms. Carmichael, I'm so sorry for the death of your son." Zach paused and stepped closer to the witness, lowering his voice. "And Joey was your *only* child, I understand." He shook his head. "I have three kids. I can't imagine the pain of losing one, especially my only one."

Cassie's lower lip trembled. "Thank you. It's been awful."

Zach regarded her with sympathy. "The ten thousand dollars the government gave you to testify here barely covers the cost of—"

"Objection! Defense is testifying to facts not in evidence, Your Honor." Martinez's calm, assured demeanor was cracking. Frustration and anxiety erupted from every pore as he stomped around the prosecution desk to stand before Rhinehart.

"Actually, Mr. Martinez, the government's witness introduced this fact," Rhinehart said. He raised a thick, bushy eyebrow. "Do we need the court reporter to read it back and refresh your memory?"

"No, Your Honor, that won't be necessary."

"Mr. Cunningham, you can continue this line of questioning, but make sure you arrive quickly at the question."

"Thank you, Your Honor." *Here's the one smooth stone that was just lobbed into your lap,* Zach told himself. *Don't screw this up, Cunningham.*

"Ms. Carmichael, please tell the court how you happen to be here, testifying in this case."

Cassie's eyes narrowed, suddenly defensive and suspicious. "All I did was answer the phone. There's no crime in that, is there?"

"No, ma'am, there is not. And when you answered the phone, who was on the line?"

Cassie squinted at the seven prosecutors. "I don't think it was any of those people." Then she redirected her attention to Zach. "It sounded like a man, but he called himself by a woman's name." She paused for a moment to think. "Rachel. His first name was Rachel, and his last name began with an S. Uh, it was an odd name—like Star Wars." She closed her eyes, then opened them, her face jubilant. "Stawarski, Rachel Stawarski. That was it."

Judge Rhinehart's gavel raps in response to the swell of murmuring in the courtroom were perfunctory. Like everyone there, he was hanging on Cassie's every word.

One smooth stone, all right, Father John. Zach knew the priest was somewhere in that courtroom, praying. It took every ounce of self-control to stay on point, to restrain himself from turning around to look at the prosecutors' table, to search the courtroom for the priest, or to holler at the top of his lungs, "Lord! You are truly Lord!"

Instead, Zach nodded calmly at the witness. "OK, thank you, Ms. Carmichael. What did Mr. Stawarski have to say?"

"Actually, he preferred to be called she, Ms. Stawarski." Cassie smiled and shrugged. "She said she was from the Transgender Law Center and wanted to talk with me about Joey. So I said sure, but I had a few questions of my own first." Blinking rapidly, Cassie swallowed hard. Then again. For the first time, Zach thought he was looking and listening to the Cassie Carmichael who might have existed before all the drugs and alcohol.

"Ms. Stawarski answered my three questions. No, she did not know Joey. But had talked with people from the Cal Poly

GLESN club who did know him because Joey was president of the Cal Poly chapter." Her eyes sparkled like any proud mother. "President," she whispered. "Imagine that."

Neither Martinez, Your Honor Rhinehart, nor Zach interrupted her surprisingly coherent and heartbreaking testimony.

"Ms. Stawarski told me she was calling because she was transgender, just like Joey. At age forty, she told me she'd realized the reason for her depression, anxiety, and overall misery. She was not a man but a woman trapped in a man's body.

"So, I told her everything I knew about my daughter, who became my son. Ms. Stawarski asked me if I would be willing to testify today. She said my testimony would help protect the freedom of young people like Joey to affirm their gender identity and would dismiss the lies told by doctors like Lindsey McCall and reporters like Kate Townsend. She brought me copies of Townsend's articles that said Joey was evil."

Zach considered asking the woman if she'd read the articles because Joey was never mentioned. Nor had Kate ever written that those who decided to transition were evil. Zach had considered objecting to Human Rights Campaign McKenzie Stanfield's statement that Kate's articles contained phrasing like that. But he had decided he wasn't up to explaining distinctions between the entity of evil—Satan and his minions—and calling persons evil. Kate had very carefully explained the origins of the evil overtaking this world, but he didn't recall her words well enough to refute Stanfield's statement. So he'd let it go. Hearing this again, Zach wondered if he'd made a mistake in not challenging Stanfield. And should object to Cassie's statement.

But as he looked at her, Zach could guess how and why she'd become like this. *Sick, perverted men, most of whom never get caught.* Zach could feel his jaws clench, and only by sheer will kept himself from continuing down that path. And so he let her continue talking.

Cassie blinked at Zach. "I told Ms. Stawarski I couldn't afford to come here. Our car wouldn't make it that far, plus I didn't have money to stay in a hotel. So, Ms. Stawarski sent me a cashier's check for ten thousand dollars. She told me it was her own money."

Zach had been so engrossed with Cassie's transformation that it took him a few seconds to recover when she stopped talking and looked at him.

It wasn't the government who paid you but a person who genuinely believed in the rightness of this case, he thought. *Because Kate's newspaper series and Lindsey's helping Joey wean off the testosterone threatens everything she stands for.*

Zach looked at Judge Rhinehart. "I have no more questions for this witness, Your Honor."

After waiting to see if Martinez would redirect his witness, Judge Rhinehart looked at the massive clock on the adjacent wall, which read 4:45 p.m. "Court is adjourned for the day," he said. "We will reconvene tomorrow morning at nine o'clock."

Lucinda stood in the foyer, holding Nicholas, half asleep, in one arm and holding JH's hand with the other. Unlike his little brother, JH was wide awake. They would take time for dinner this evening; Lucinda had persuaded them late the night before.

"Mommy!" he said, holding his arms out to be picked up. Kate squatted down and reached for him, feeling the tears that had been threatening her throughout the preceding two-year-long days.

Nope, Townsend, she told herself as she held her son to her chest. *No crying. Maybe after this horrific thing is over, but not now.*

Zach, Toni, Lindsey, Rich, and Steve trailed in, with Morgan, LJ, and Father John ending the lineup of combatants, or at least that's what they all looked like to Lucinda. Their expressions were somber, their eyes filled with sadness as if they'd been in the bloodiest of battles.

"So, it isn't going well?" Lucinda asked Toni, who was nearest to her. "We're going to lose?"

"No, I think we'll win this case, Lucinda," Toni replied. "Zach's pulled so many rabbits out of the hat that Martinez can't figure out what blew in from Mustang, Oklahoma."

"Then why do you all look so funereal?" Her British accent lengthened the word by three more syllables.

Kate pulled her face back from JH's neck. "Because there won't be any winners when this case is decided. I believe the jury will see Lindsey and me as not guilty and that none of what we did was motivated by hate but, on the contrary, love." Her voice shook, and her eyes shone wetly. "But the witnesses on the other side are heart-breaking. My dear, gracious God, Luce, what tragically terrible plights can we humans get ourselves into!"

Lucinda stared at Kate. She was awed by the raw emotion and grit on her employer's face.

Missing none of this interaction, Toni looked at her boss heading to the great room/office. The emotional weight of the two seemingly endless days was pressing down on all of them, especially him. She doubted he'd slept three hours of the last seventy-two. Zach was dead on his feet. His usually vibrant expression was absent. Instead, he looked hollowed out. Zach desperately needed to free his mind, even if for only a few hours.

Toni glanced at Lucinda, whom she'd grown fond of. "I'll bet you have dinner close to ready. So, while we eat whatever you and Gordon Ramsey have cooked up for your starving minions, I'll educate you all about Serendipity and the four thousand dollars I made on an Amazon strangle yesterday. Sound good?"

Toni got the reaction she intended. Eight pairs of eyes were riveted on her, each filled with a single word: "Huh?"

"All right, Toni, help me plate the veal chops and mushroom risotto," Lucinda said.

For a few minutes, the only sounds were of contentment as everyone enjoyed their meal. Then Lucinda sat back from her plate. "Please explain what you said before we sat down to eat, Toni. Surely that four thousand dollars was not serendipitously achieved by strangling Amazon, although I suspect a good number of folks in the world would like to do just that, strangle Amazon."

It felt good to laugh even though no one was sure what they were laughing at.

Toni looked over at Kate. "Can you guess what I'm talking about?" Then she glanced at Lindsey, "How about you?"

"Hank Reardon!" Lindsey and Kate had said the name simultaneously, both of them grinning at Toni. Then Kate's eyes softened with remembered affection and respect.

"I forgot, Toni. Hank met you in Puerto Rico, hired you, and taught you so much about the stock market that you took over his portfolio. So, an Amazon strangle is a market option you two do, and Serendipity is a software program he introduced you to?"

Toni nodded. "That's right, Kate. It was our last conversation."

Quiet descended on the room as each of them remembered the man's genius and goodness.

"I've often wondered what would have become of me if he hadn't pursued me to the village where I lived with Abuela," Toni said, her voice uncharacteristically soft and tender. "Hank pushed right through all my fears, insecurities, and prejudices against you Anglos. It was as if he didn't even see them. Instead, just from a stupid comment I made to him, all Hank could see was what he called 'raw potential' waiting for activation." She paused, looked around the table, and said deliberately, "Even after I defiantly told him I was a lesbian, Hank just shrugged and continued explaining his plans when I arrived in Lucerne to work for him." Remembering Hank Reardon cost her, Toni swiped both eyes quickly, hoping no one would notice.

Missing nothing, Lindsey's smile was sad. Ignoring Toni's comment about her homosexuality, she said, "I never heard 'raw potential' from him, but it sure sounds like the guy who annoyed me into pushing forward with a drug that revolutionized cardiovascular disease. He cast aside all my doubts and fears, too." She looked at Toni, who smiled back, thinking, *They all knew you were gay … you make it pretty evident with the tats, the way you talk and act.* But still, she was relieved to have said it.

"Is he dead?" Morgan asked. "It sounds like you're talking about someone who's no longer here." She asked the question that LJ and Lucinda didn't and Zach couldn't.

No one noticed that Zach closed his eyes to mitigate the pain of losing his best friend. They'd met when Zach was in law school and Hank at medical school at Columbia. The friends' lifelong connection began with their dislike of their graduate programs. Had Zach not encountered William Kunstler, he would never have practiced law. Hank never practiced medicine after graduating from Columbia Medical School because he realized he had zero interest in working with sick people for the rest of his life. It was Hank who'd introduced Zach to each one of these people.

"Yes. It was a skiing accident close to Hank's house in Lucerne. He and his daughter, Lisa, went skiing, and Hank decided to do a black diamond run. He crashed into a copse of trees and died instantly."

Steve watched Kate brushing her teeth, running her fingers through her thick, curly hair, and throwing water on her face. Only when she got next to the bed did she notice his stare.

"What? Why are you looking at me like that?"

He sat up and reached for her. "Come and let's cuddle, love of my life. And tell me what you told Lucinda. I want to hear those words again."

"What words?"

"That you think the jury will find you and Lindsey not guilty."

Kate plumped down on the side of the bed. "Oh."

She was staring at the wall, and Steve guessed, was seeing nothing. When abruptly, Kate brought both hands to her face and began to sob. Stammering as she did so, "I promised myself I wouldn't do this, Steve; I'm so sorry!!"

Steve moved over to her side of the bed, stood, and pulled her up tight against him while she sobbed.

Shuddering amidst the sobs, she gasped, "It's all so awful, Steve."

He stood there holding tightly to this woman he knew grace had given him. Thinking as he did so, *You knew—saw it—felt it in your perfect humanity, dear Jesus. In Gethsemane, you ingested this ugliness, depravity, and wickedness and annulled it.*

CHAPTER FIFTY-SEVEN

"Where are you going, Morgan? They told us to sit back here."

"Yes, I know, LJ. You stay here, but I'm going up close, so he can be sure to see me."

LJ was puzzled. She had no idea what Morgan meant or who she was talking about, but Morgan had an intensity that LJ recognized. Not infrequently, Morgan operated in another dimension. Taking the seat Morgan had pointed to, LJ watched her friend stride up to the third row on the left behind Zach, Lindsey, Rich, and Kate. Rich turned and winked at Morgan as she sat in the row behind him.

Morgan talked to Rich. Told him she wanted to sit up front so "he could be sure and see me." Just as LJ realized whom Morgan had been referring to, the bailiff asked them all to stand for the Honorable Judge Donald K. Rhinehart.

After convening the court, Rhinehart turned to the prosecution. "Call your first witness, Mr. Martinez."

"My name is Dr. Adam Turner," he said as he took the stand.

"Dr. Turner, you are currently a professor at California Polytechnic Institute. In fact, you are the head of the Department of Gender and Queer Studies. Is that correct?"

"Yes."

"And did you know the deceased, Joey Carmichael?"

"Yes." Turner stared at Lindsey. "I've known Joey since he was in my second-grade class in Strawberry Elementary School. He was Zoey then. I'm the one who paid for the testosterone, helped him transition, and paid his Cal Poly tuition." Turner's face hardened. "I was planning to take Joey for his top job at

UCLA when he got a blood clot in his brain."

Rhinehart ignored the hum in the courtroom, too engrossed by Turner's testimony to notice.

"Dr. Turner, you haven't stopped looking at the defendant, Dr. Lindsey McCall, since taking the stand," Martinez said. "Do you know her?"

"No. We've never met. But I know who she is—was—at Cal Poly. She was head of the Animal Research Center, and she was helping Joey detransition."

"Helping Joey detransition. Can you explain what that means to the jury—to all of us?"

Turner's jaw pushed out, a vein on his forehead bulged, and his lips compressed. He opened his mouth to speak, but nothing came out. Instead, he saw Morgan, who mouthed, "Good Morning, Dr. T." It happened so fast that almost no one saw the interaction.

Martinez's back was to Morgan. When he turned around to see who had captured his witness's attention, he saw only a young woman with glasses sitting behind the defense table. He hadn't seen her before, and he wondered who she was, but the thought was cut off when his witness began to answer his question.

"Detransition means to stop all hormonal therapy: stop the puberty suppression drug and testosterone and start estrogen."

All the previous signs of anger were gone. Instead, Turner's manner was as serene as a summer lake.

What just happened? Martinez wondered.

His musings were cut off when Turner continued speaking. "Joey got to know Dr. McCall because he loved her Dobermans. She worked with Dobermans with a genetic cardiac disease. While at Cal Poly, Dr. McCall developed a dietary regimen and supplement that slows the progression of the disease and lengthens their lives.

"Stopping testosterone too suddenly can be dangerous. Joey asked Dr. McCall if she'd help him get off it because he hated how it made him feel. Moreover, Joey had decided he no longer wanted to be a boy."

Martinez was stunned. *This is not the person I spoke with two weeks ago. Back then, he was raging against McCall. And Townsend.*

Then he did what lawyers should never do: he asked a question to which he didn't know the answer.

"Dr. Turner, did you read Kate Townsend's series, 'Creating Chemical Eunuchs: Corrupting America's Children'?"

"Yes, I did. I read each article three times, in fact."

"You read them so often because you disagreed with the content?"

Turner's gaze drifted to Morgan, but the seat she'd been sitting in was vacant. Then Turner refocused on Martinez. "I gave Zoey the idea of transitioning to a boy." Blinking rapidly, Turner frowned. "I did that because I was convinced I was saving Zoey from a life of drugs, addiction, and prostitution and from a mother I was convinced was the incarnation of evil." Turner scowled and narrowed his eyes. "Like my own mother."

Turner regarded Kate. "Those articles are compelling. You've forced me to think honestly about what I was doing with Joey and why. I *knew* he hated his body and felt neither like a boy nor a girl. I knew he feared the top job and didn't want it. But he would have done it because Joey always did what I wanted him to. Always."

Turner redirected his attention toward Martinez. "But that

reporter's articles forced me to *see* Joey's misery. A misery that a top job would have worsened." Turner paused, then took a deep breath. "All I accomplished was substituting one evil for another." The witness stared at Lindsey. "And Dr. McCall tried to undo the damage I'd caused—she could see what I refused to."

Martinez stared at his witness, uncomprehending. The silence in the courtroom had a reverential quality.

After a few seconds, Judge Rhinehart seemed to virtually shake himself. He blinked several times at Turner, then looked back at the prosecutor. "Mr. Martinez, do you have any other questions for this witness?"

"No, Your Honor."

When neither defense attorney stood to cross-examine, Judge Rhinehart nodded to Turner. "Dr. Turner, you are excused. Mr. Martinez, your next witness?"

"The prosecution rests, Your Honor."

"Call your first witness, Mr. Cunningham."

Zach moved slowly. Not because he was tired. Far from it. He had just witnessed a miracle. One that had somehow included that girl, Morgan. Like Martinez, Zach had expected this witness to be one of the government's most vital witnesses. He'd watched the young woman slip into that seat. Then Zach saw the force field between the witness and Morgan; there wasn't any other way to describe it.

Zach Cunningham was in awe for the first time in his life and blinked tears from his eyes as he approached his first witness.

Lea and Samuel Sugarman had, after the first day in court, insisted that Danny testify. Lea and Samuel had waited outside the courtroom to speak with Kate, Steve, and their lawyers. Both of them were on the medical staff at Stanford and, therefore, knew Kate and Steve well. Initially, Kate protested. "Are you sure, Lea? Won't this bring up all the stupid things at the kindergarten party?"

"And won't this taint you both in the eyes of the administration?" Steve asked.

Samuel smiled. "I've been asked to interview at San Antonio. Their head of pulmonary medicine just retired. Lea and I went to med school there and would love to return. So maybe you could put in a good word for us." He was currently the chief of pulmonary medicine at Stanford Medical School.

Steve and Kate grinned at the thought of their friends moving to Texas. "Of course, Sam," Steve said. "It would be a privilege to endorse you."

"Actually, Kate, we think this will help Danny put this behind him," Lea explained. "He's been having nightmares ever since it happened. He wakes up screaming about being in Mia's skirt and unable to get it off."

Early Tuesday morning, the Sugarmans, Zach, and Rich met with the US Attorney to explain why they wanted their four-year-old boy to testify for the defense. To his credit, Martinez listened and agreed the child be added to the defense's list of witnesses. When they got to the judge's office before court began, Martinez and Zach met with the judge.

Zach explained the addition of Danny to his witness list

and the reasons. And handed Rhinehart the notarized document that the child's parents had signed.

The judge scanned the document, nodded, and placed it in his folder to hand to the court reporter when the trial resumed. The two lawyers began to leave the office when the judge said, "Mr. Martinez, why are you agreeing to this legal but irregular witness addition?"

"Judge, I have a four-year-old son at home."

Rhinehart narrowed his eyes and grimaced slightly.

Then, Judge Rhinehart said to Zach, "And you feel comfortable with this young a witness, Mr. Cunningham?"

Then suddenly, the judge snapped his fingers. "*That's* how I know your face, Cunningham! Texas law changed because of that appeal you won. Most of our law schools in this state show a simulated video of your interrogation of that little girl. She had certainly been molested, but not by the Army Ranger veteran charged with doing it. Brilliant work."

"Danny, I'm Danny Sugarman."

The little boy was dwarfed by the immensity of the witness chair. The bailiff had brought out a stool, so the four-year-old child could climb up to the chair. He sat perched on the edge, swinging his legs and waving happily at his mother and father, then at Kate. "Hi, Kate," he said with a grin.

Zach smiled at Danny, and the child's mouth became a perfect O as he watched Zach's facial scar distort the right side of his face. He raised his little hand as if to touch Zach. "What happened to your face?" he asked in a way that only innocent children can.

"When I was about your age, a furious man hurt me."

"Did you know the man?" Danny asked with widened

brown eyes through round black-rimmed glasses.

"He was my father."

"I hope someone punished him. That's not right to do to a little boy."

"Someone did punish him, Danny." Zach stepped a little closer to Danny and leaned in. "Now, is it my turn to ask you some questions?"

"Of course, that's why I'm here. Daddy told me you would be asking me questions, right, Daddy?" The child waved at a bespectacled man of about forty, who waved back and nodded.

"Right, Danny, that is precisely why you're here. Now, do you know the difference between the truth and a lie?'

Danny nodded vigorously. "Of course. The truth is what is real. What you see and know. A lie is what you make up. So, it's wrong to lie."

"OK, then, Danny, do you remember the party at the kindergarten where Ms. Meeks baked a cake with the name Susie—"

The child frowned. "How can I forget? I have nightmares about that party almost every night."

"Why did Ms. Meeks do that, Danny? Did she lie about you saying you wanted to be a girl named Susie?"

Danny heaved a huge sigh that could be heard throughout the courtroom. "No, she didn't lie. She told the truth." His face contorted as if he were about to cry, but he composed himself and looked at Zach. "I was angry at Dad. He couldn't make my hamster start breathing again. I thought he knew how to bring Herbie back to life." His lower lip quivering, Danny pushed on. "I thought he wouldn't do it because Herbie smelled up the house."

A tear fell, but Danny impatiently wiped it away. "So, I

told Ms. Meeks I didn't want to be a boy like Dad anymore. I wanted to be a girl like Mom because she cried when Herbie died.

"Ms. Meeks said, 'OK, you can decide to be a girl, Danny. What would you like your name to be?' So I told her, Susan. Susan Sugarman." His large eyes widened. "But when she put that girl's skirt on me, I realized it would mean I'd have to wear girl clothes like Mia! So, I wanted the skirt off!"

"What happened then, Danny?"

His tiny finger pointed at Kate. "Kate showed up to pick up JH. She saw me and asked me why I was crying. I told her I didn't want to wear Mia's clothes. I wanted mine. Kate took off the skirt and put on my trousers."

"And that made you happy?

"Yes! Of course! I'm a boy." He grinned. "I hate girls' clothes!"

"Thank you, Danny. I have no more questions for this witness, Your Honor."

Before Judge Rhinehart could ask, Martinez stood up. "The government has no questions for this witness, Your Honor."

CHAPTER FIFTY-NINE

After the lunch recess, Zach called Detective Cindy Ralston to the stand.

"You were the senior detective called to investigate the collapse of Joey Carmichael at California Polytechnic Institute on the morning of April 3rd of this year. Is that correct?"

"It is."

"Can you please describe Joey's condition for the jury, Detective?"

The attractive detective pulled out a notebook in her navy blue blazer from a pocket and read a detailed account of Joey's appearance and transport to French Hospital.

"Thank you, Detective."

"Can you provide an overview of your investigation and conclusions for the jury?"

This time, the detective opened a padded binder and gave the highlights of the interviews with Dr. Adams and Cassie Carmichael, the testimony from the hospital physician, and said, "We determined that death was accidental.'

"Thank you, Detective." Zach turned to Martinez to say, "Your witness."

Approaching the San Luis Obispo detective, Martinez was cautiously optimistic. He and his co-counselors had been surprised and pleased to see the name of the list of defense witnesses. There could be an opportunity to regain momentum in this case.

After watching her on the stand, he decided she was no-nonsense. So he went right for it. "Detective, thank you for your comprehensive report." He paused.

Ralston just stared at him. Expressionless.

"Didn't you consider that Joey's death could be manslaughter?"

Rhinehart rapped his gavel at the explosive reaction in the courtroom.

Coolly, the detective regarded the US Attorney through her huge black-rimmed glasses. "And what evidence would we use for that conclusion?"

Delighted, Zach sat still and ignored the tension pouring from Lindsey, who sat to his left.

If it looks too good to be true, then it probably isn't. Martinez was sure he would hear "Objection, facts not in evidence" when he replied to Ralston. But he kept barging ahead.

"Dr. Lindsey McCall prescribed estrogen for Joey, a known cause of emboli." And waited for an objection that never came.

Ralston reopened the binder. And pulled out a tattered leather book. "This was Joey's diary. I'll read two excerpts from it. The 'she' he refers to in the second passage is Morgan Gardner, one of the girls who found him:

> I feel better being off the testosterone. Way better. And I've lost ten pounds. I think the weight loss might be because of the estrogen. And, of course, the almost daily runs with Dr. McCall's dogs.
>
> But how do I tell him? He's been planning this for months. So, how do I tell him I don't want to be a guy anymore, that this has all been an awful mistake?

And the second passage:

> "A few weeks ago," she said, "I heard

Michelle asking when you would get your top done. You said this month, in a week or so, is that right?"

I nodded. Her emotionless reaction was helping me get control of myself.

"Joey, is this your idea or someone else's?"

She can't know about him. I've never said anything to her—or to anyone else—about him! "What do you mean?" I asked.

Morgan just sat there, studying me. She acted as if she could have waited for hours.

But as I sat there looking back at her, I smiled. "Can I tell you a secret, Morgan? Something I am happy about?"

Morgan looked surprised but nodded. I told her I was finally off the testosterone and had started taking estrogen, thanks to her friend, Dr. McCall.'"

Ralston closed the diary, placed it in her binder, and said, "I repeat, our office considers the death of Joey Carmichael a tragic accident."

Over the lunch break, Rich was energized because his risky idea of including Detective Ralston had paid off. He looked at his exhausted partner and quipped, "Why don't you take the rest of the day off? I've got this afternoon." Zach barely smiled, and Lindsey and Kate just stared at him. "Note to self, Jansen, no more jokes," he mumbled.

"Especially if they're not the least bit amusing," his wife said with a smirk.

"You are Kate Townsend, the Pulitzer-Prize-winning journalist of a 2016 Houston Tribune series, 'Murder in the Texas Medical Center'?"

Kate nodded to Rich. "Yes."

"You also wrote a four-article series for the Houston Tribune in April 2021 called 'Corrupting America's Children: Creating Chemical Eunuchs,' correct?"

"Yes."

She was astounded by the fact that she was not afraid. Even when looking at the crowded courtroom, with the double row of reporters ready to pounce, the singular emotion she felt was relief. They were finally *here*. There was nothing more they or she could do to prepare.

Kate had never been among a group of individuals who had worked so hard, not even back in San Francisco when newspapers still reigned, and deadlines terrorized them all. Zach's, Toni's, Rich's, and Lindsey's capacity for work seemed superhuman. None of them had slept more than a couple of hours a night.

And this man standing in front of her took her breath away. His wife was also facing a ten-year sentence— for unintentional murder. Because Rich believed Zach would be more effective and certainly more objective than he could be with Lindsey's defense, he took on Kate's defense with unswerving dedication. Last night, it wasn't Toni who had taken her through the mock cross-examination but Rich. They had gone through it until 3:00 a.m. Over and over, Rich said, "I want you to be immune to his intimidation. I want you to be fearless!" And by God, he'd done it. She felt fearless.

She thought he was an attractive man, and strangely, the sudden stress-induced whitening on the sides of his hair and the accentuated planes of his face and around his face made him even more handsome.

I know we may lose this case, Lord, but I trust in you. Lindsey had given her a copy of the *Chaplet of Divine Mercy* when she visited that weekend a few months ago. Kate had begun praying the chaplet that day and had not stopped.

"Can you tell the court why you did it, Kate? Why you wrote a newspaper series that you knew might land you here?"

He'd asked her that question three times the night before, and her answer had been more or less the same. But now, when she opened her mouth, something else came out. "Each of us is given a gift or many gifts by our Creator. Mine is journalism. Investigative journalism. So, when I experienced the indoctrination of my son's kindergarten teacher—"

"Objection!"

Judge Rhinehart regarded Martinez, who had practically leaped over the prosecution table to stand before him. "On what grounds, Mr. Martinez?"

"Indoctrination? Come on, Your Honor!"

Rhinehart stared at Martinez, daring him to continue speaking, but he merely glared back.

"Overruled." Rhinehart turned to Kate. "Please continue, Ms. Townsend."

Kate nodded. "I felt I had no choice but to learn how and why American educators had been granted the authority to initiate gender change in toddlers."

Rich frowned at the change in her reply to his first question, but it faded quickly, for he was already on to the next. "Ms. Townsend, Ms. Meeks testified that you acted like a reporter looking for a story. After all, it's been a few years since you won that Pulitzer. Couldn't part of your motivation be the desire to return to the limelight?"

Rich had warned her that he might grab a few of Martinez's zingers. This was one of them. She suppressed the desire to laugh at the notion of "returning to the limelight." "It's true I've done little other than freelance work since the boys were born. Truthfully, I was anxious about leaping from breastfeeding and diapers into investigative journalism. So, I did argue with myself for the first couple of weeks." With a half-smile, Kate glanced at the jury and then said wryly, "You may have heard, the limelight's not all it's cracked up to be."

They went through another eight questions and answers they'd practiced into the night's wee hours and were done. Then Rich turned to the judge. "No more questions for this witness, Your Honor."

Rhinehart nodded to Martinez. "Your witness."

Martinez watched the shock on Judge Rhinehart's face when Eldridge rose and walked over to the reporter to do the cross. *Any regrets, Emilio?* The US Attorney thought about last night's meeting following last night's text message from Rachel Stawarski.

"Uhhh, I haven't been home before midnight for the last—"

"I think you need to hear from your associates, Emilio. They're not happy."

Grudgingly, he took the next exit off the freeway and drove back into the city. As he entered the pub, he saw all seven of them, Steve at the head of the table and Rachel at the end. Taking the empty chair in the middle, Emilio sat. "Do you really want to talk about the case here?" He looked around at the couples and singles at the bar. Sam looked at Stawarski, who rose to ask for a private room.

Martinez knew their main complaint: They were losing this 'landmark case.' In the middle of Heathcock's testimony, Cunningham produced the expert's article refuting gender affirmation for children. That document changed the momentum of the entire case for the prosecution. It started downhill and quickly gained speed as each day passed. Worse yet, four-year-old Danny Sugarman's testimony had pierced Martinez to his core.

Rachel's fraudulent emails between the defendants were the tipping point. Martinez was disgusted and angry, mostly with himself. He'd accepted Cunningham's gracious offer— early that morning, he had removed the fabricated evidence from the record.

He thought about Cunningham, that meal they'd had together the other night. After eating, the older lawyer leaned forward on the small table and placed the chin of his remarkably ugly face into both hands. "Look, I get it. You're on the fast track. Good for you. You've got the looks, brains, and the guts. But Emilio, is this case worth losing your soul over?"

Rachel found the room. The table was barely big enough to accommodate them, so Martinez stood and listened while the others—primarily Rachel, ranted about his poor job with this case. Finally, after twenty minutes, he'd had enough.

"What do you want?" he asked, feeling exhausted.

"Let me do the cross on the reporter tomorrow," Eldridge said. "You've lost your edge. You won't be hard-nosed enough." Eldridge's stare felt heavy as Martinez listened to his following words. "Your Catholic bigoted upbringing won't let you go after her with the vehemence the jury needs to hear."

Martinez regarded the intense Southern Poverty Law Center attorney with a half-hearted chuckle, "Maybe you're right, Sam. Go ahead, take over."

Stunned, all jaws dropped.

Recovering first, Eldridge said, "Just for clarification, Emilio, do you mean just the reporter's cross," he paused, "or the rest of the case?"

"Take it, including closing arguments."

Then, into the shocked silence of the stuffy little room, Martinez looked at Stawarski and said, "Do I need to report you to the ABA for falsification of those emails, or will you do it yourself?"

Shortly after nine, the following Thursday, Kate watched the man who had sat quietly beside US Attorney Martinez all week approach her with a dazzling smile.

"You've had an impressive career, Ms. Townsend. A series on homelessness in San Francisco that's still used in many colleges and universities. And, of course, that powerhouse of a series, 'Murder in the Texas Medical Center.'" Eldridge smiled. "Your analysis of American culture and the rise of 'the most successful corporation in history: American medicine' makes excellent bedtime reading."

During their daily update before today's court session began, Zach told Rich and Kate about his talk with the US Attorney the night before. Zach believed that Martinez was troubled about this case and may hand it over. To Kate's "Who would take over?" Zach replied, "Eldridge."

"So, is that good or bad for us?" Kate asked.

"I know zip about Samuel Eldridge, aside from his being a lawyer with the Southern Poverty Law Center, which indicates he's radically anti-everything you stand for."

Kate returned to the present and concentrated on this smiling man's words.

"That was followed by a fascinating series on another wrongful conviction, an Army veteran who, on appeal to the Texas Supreme Court, was found not guilty of sexually abusing a six-year-old girl."

Eldridge paused to study Kate, who regarded him coolly, waiting. *This is a curious way to attack,* she thought. *Compliment like crazy, so I won't be ready for the blade to my ribs.* Kate felt her muscles tighten as if she were back in fencing lessons, preparing for a feint. *He's cleverly brought Lindsey into play.*

"I stayed up past midnight last night finishing it. A commendable piece of work that rightly earned you distinction among your peers," Eldridge continued. "So, it's logical that you'd be looking for a way to get back into the action." He paused for effect. "And naturally, you'd consult your good friend, Dr. Lindsey McCall, on the medical aspects of your articles. Probably also on your decision to convert to Catholicism like she did." While surfing the net last night, he'd wondered if McCall was a Catholic, too, and found her Cal Poly bio, which listed her as Roman Catholic. The "coincidences" kept adding up.

"Objection! Counsel is not only testifying but attesting to facts not in evidence."

"Sustained."

"I apologize, Your Honor," Eldridge said, working to suppress his smile because the women's friendship, collaboration, and shared religious dogma felt precisely like a conspiracy to him; maybe it would to the jurors even without the emails.

Eldridge glanced at his notes. "You told defense counsel that quote, 'I felt I had no choice but to learn how and why American educators had been granted the authority to initiate gender change in toddlers,' when Mr. Jansen asked why you decided to write these articles. But *learning* is a far cry from writing an explosive series in a newspaper. So, why did you decide to do that, Ms. Townsend, if not to regain notoriety?"

This was precisely why Rich had told her to stick to the script. Such questions were a minefield. They seemed harmless, but stepping on them could destroy the person answering them.

Kate studied Eldridge. His expression was neutral, and his eyes unreadable.

"You omitted the first part of my statement, Mr. Eldridge. I prefaced what you said with this remark: 'Each of us is given a gift or many gifts by our Creator. Mine is journalism. Investigative journalism.' Most of us learn early in our lives that these gifts can be a blessing or a curse. And, not infrequently, our use of them incurs huge cost."

Pausing momentarily, she regarded the lawyer. "We just heard Danny explain why he told his teacher that he didn't want to be a boy anymore. Danny's reasoning made sense even if we're not parents. The child clearly explained his anger and hurt at his father for refusing to save the life of his beloved hamster, Herbie. Hurt that resulted in Danny wanting to distance himself as far as possible from the father who'd let him down."

Kate paused momentarily to examine the twelve men and women charged with determining her guilt or innocence. And then returned to Eldridge.

"But once he said those fateful words, 'I want to be a girl,' his kindergarten teacher, Addison Meeks, did what she had been trained to do by this state's educational system. Teachers like Ms. Meeks are taught to listen and watch for behaviors indicating gender dysphoria in the children under their care."

Kate leaned toward the attorney as she almost hissed. "Once Danny declared, 'I'm a girl,' the words *couldn't be taken back*. The gender transition protocol gets implemented independent of parental consent or knowledge." She looked intently at the attorney. "I wrote the series, Mr. Eldridge, so fathers and mothers like them," she pointed to the jury's eight men and four women, "will know what can happen to their children in our kindergartens and elementary schools."

Toni and Rich had preached over and over for her to be brief and only answer the question, no more, so she resisted the temptation to continue.

Eldridge blinked. And thought of his three-year-old boy at home. And he felt a little sick about Rachel's teary confession about the faked emails between this woman and the doctor last night. Those emails had been planned to be a primary thrust of this cross. As he struggled to regain momentum, he noticed the absolute stillness in the room.

Even the reporters in the back of the courtroom were quiet, aware this was no ordinary trial. Instead, something else was happening in the room. Although no one could put it into words, something like a presence could be felt.

Eldridge asked a few more perfunctory questions but decided to follow his gut and end this. He said, "I have no more questions for this witness."

The judge declared a twenty-minute recess.

Stan Kendrick stood, stretched, and headed to the coffee and pastry bar reserved for the jurors. Usually, he skipped it, but he needed caffeine. The reporter touched him. When she'd talked about why she'd done this series and pointed at him and his fellow jurors, he'd felt like she looked directly at him. And had taken this gigantic risk to let parents like him *know*. To open their eyes. Even that new lawyer had been affected. She'd thrown him off with her replies.

Funny, Stan mused, the head guy Maritnez must also have some reservations about this case. Why else would he now be sitting on the bench?

"Dr. McCall, did Kate Townsend contact you at any time for advice about the medical facts of her investigative series, 'Creating Chemical Eunuchs'?" Zach was dressed down this morning. He wore a camel-hair sport coat with dark-brown pants and a light-blue striped shirt with a bright red tie.

"She did not."

"Doctor, you and Ms. Townsend have been friends for several years, correct?"

"We have."

"Doesn't it seem strange that Ms. Townsend wouldn't have spoken with you about such an important decision like returning to her career?"

"No. Ms. Townsend's been very busy with her small children. And I've been occupied with my job at the Cal Poly Animal Research Center and my family."

"Even though Ms. Townsend decided, like you did, to convert to Catholicism, did you think it odd that she didn't tell you until you read about it in her articles?"

Lindsey looked at Kate and smiled broadly. "I did. But I guess she wanted to surprise me."

"You no longer work at Cal Poly. Is that because you were fired?"

Lindsey looked wryly at Zach. "No, I decided to leave before that happened."

"Why do you say that, Dr. McCall?"

"I met Joey Carmichael about six, maybe seven months ago. Joey was a classmate of my daughter's. Morgan knew Joey loved animals and suggested he come to ask if he could work with the dogs."

Listening in the courtroom, LJ grabbed Morgan's hand in delight at Lindsey calling her her daughter. Both girls understood she'd said that to avoid the confusion of explaining how she'd come to live with them. But it was fun hearing it, and Morgan's blush belied her impassive expression.

"There were fourteen Dobermans in my lab, so naturally, I agreed to the offer of help to exercise them."

"Did you advise Joey about how to detransition, Dr. McCall? How to stop the puberty suppression and testosterone he was on?"

"I did."

"Why?"

Taking a deep breath, she whispered, "He begged me."

Rhinehart leaned over and said, "Doctor, please repeat what you just said so the jury can hear you."

Clearing her throat, Lindsey said, "Because he begged me to help him."

"Why did he beg you, Dr. McCall?"

"Joey had suffered from severe osteoporosis due to the high doses of testosterone he was on. In the last three years, he'd broken his ankle, wrist, the tibia in the leg, and humerus in his arm. He was at least fifty pounds overweight and morbidly depressed. He felt and said he looked like a monster. Joey wanted to become the girl he'd thrown away."

Lindsey looked up at Zach, the judge, and then the jury.

"I've never encountered an unhappier human being in my life. I could not say no."

"What did you do?"

"Slowly, for twelve weeks, I decreased the testosterone injections he'd been on since he was eight. Then, I started him on a low-dose estrogen oral medication.

"Did you alleviate his suffering? Did his depression ease?"

"No, and no." Lindsey grimaced. "The only time Joey was happy was with the dogs. And then he transformed; he became vibrant, excited, and alive."

"Did you tell him about the dangers of clots from the change in his hormones?

"I did. But didn't need to. Joey knew all about the risk of emboli. Clots are a well-known risk of long-term testosterone therapy."

"One last question, Dr. McCall. Had Joey lived, could he have returned to—" Zach made quotation marks in the air with his fingers, "the girl he'd thrown away?"

"No. Joey's body had been arrested at a prepubescent female state. Eight years of suppression and testosterone therapy caused his uterus and ovaries to atrophy and lose muscle tone and function."

"Then why did you prescribe the low-dose estrogen?"

Lindsey sighed. "In the hundreds of anecdotal cases I found online, I read of one case like Joey's in which the biological female regained her fertility. But she'd not started all this until she'd begun menstruating. I explained all this to Joey, and he still wanted to try it." She smiled thinly. "Joey said, 'At least my brain will know I'm getting some estrogen even if the rest of me doesn't.'"

"No more questions for this witness, Judge."

Judge Rhinehart announced, "The court will recess until 1:30."

"Dr. McCall, your relationship with journalist Kate Townsend began when you were convicted of murder and incarcerated in a Texas prison for two years, losing your medical license and your position as a cardiologist at the University of Houston Medical School. Isn't that correct?"

A clever way to get a ginormous amount of information bolused to the jury with one question, Lindsey thought. And said, "Yes."

"Dr. McCall, you are a medical physician, but you work with animals. Is that correct?"

"Yes."

Eldridge shuffled some papers. "Is that change in practice due to your previous incarceration?"

"Objection!" Zach was on his feet. "Counsel defames the witness with facts he knows to be incomplete."

"Sustained." Judge Rhinehart regarded the co-prosecutor sternly. "Mr. Eldridge, be careful here; defamation of a witness's character endangers your entire case." To the jury, Rhinehart said, "Disregard this last question."

And to the court reporter, "Strike that last question from the record."

"You may continue, Mr. Eldridge."

Eldridge said, "Pardon me. I'll ask the question a different way. Why did you stop practicing adult medicine to work just with dogs?"

Lindsey stared at the lawyer, thinking. "After more than fifteen years in practice, I decided to take a break from the high stress of my cardiac practice. And I love research. So, I decided to do it full-time. I wanted to see if the drug and supplements I'd created for humans in cardiac failure would work in dogs."

"And did they?" Eldridge asked.

"They did."

"And," Eldridge said, "that's how you met Joey Carmichael."

"I was the head of the animal research labs at Cal Poly, and Joey enjoyed walking the dogs from the lab."

"Tell us again, please, why did you advise him about his testosterone dosage?"

"As I said earlier, Joey talked with me numerous times about the stress, fractures, facial hair …."

"And did you try to talk Joey into becoming Catholic like your good friend Kate?"

Lindsey's mouth dropped open. *Where did this come from? But of course, make this about orthodoxy; why not?* Just as she completed the thought, Zach said, "Objection, Judge, relevance, and facts not in evidence."

Rhinehart peered unpleasantly at Eldridge. "Sustained."

"Dr. McCall, you've treated dogs, not people, for several years. You've said so yourself. Are you qualified to discuss testosterone?"

Lindsey paused before responding. Although she knew this lawyer could persuade the jury to put her back in prison, she was fed up with this game. Lindsey also knew better than most what a game this was. Filled with resolve, she fixed her emerald-green eyes on his. "Mr. Eldridge, I'm a medical doctor with a Ph.D. in cardiovascular physiology. I'm boarded in three medical specialties: internal medicine, cardiology, and emergency medicine. Those qualifications make me at least as qualified as Planned Parenthood unlicensed personnel to counsel people about testosterone and estrogen."

Judge Rhinehart ignored the wave of titters in the courtroom.

Eldridge's cheeks warmed, but he recovered quickly. His interrogation of Lindsey went on for another ninety minutes. Covering much of the same ground Zach had already reviewed,

Eldridge tried to get Lindsey to misspeak. Or contradict herself.

Zach objected more than twenty-five times. Fifteen were sustained, and ten were overruled. Finally, Eldridge dismissed her.

Judge Rhinehart looked at the giant clock on the wall. It was 4:30. "Court adjourned," he said. "We'll reconvene tomorrow for closing arguments."

CHAPTER SIXTY-TWO

"Father John, can I talk to you?" Lucinda asked, looking shyly at the priest.

"Of course. Just give me a few more minutes to finish my breviary." He was concentrating on a thick black book she'd seen him with before.

Lucinda couldn't handle idleness well. Even when not in the middle of a crisis of gigantic proportions, work kept her mind from digesting itself. But no one wanted dinner. Steve, Kate, Rich, and Lindsey had decided the best thing for them was a five-mile run in a park near Stanford. The girls had gone with them, and Zach and Toni had gone somewhere else. The boys were bathed and in bed, and the kitchen was sparkling.

She wandered outside and tried to enjoy the beauty of the flowers and the clarity of the California spring air but kept thinking about the case. *What if they get convicted? What if Kate has to spend ten years in jail for writing the truth?*

Of course, Lucinda was worried about herself and her job, but Kate was exceptional. Lucinda had never met a woman like her. It wasn't just that she was smart or pretty. Almost all the women Lucinda had ever known were both. It was her goodness, Lucinda decided as she reflected on her boss. *Goodness. What do I mean by that word?*

Father John's cough was fake. He did it, Lucinda knew, so she wouldn't jump out of her skin. He was sitting on the swing where Kate and Steve usually sat because it was near the baby monitor. He patted the space beside him. "Want to join me?"

"How do you do it?"

"Sit or drink iced tea?" He had just taken a drink from a

glass of iced tea and lemon. His gray eyes twinkled in the setting sun.

Lucinda smiled. "Act so calm. Behave as if this is a typical day as if tomorrow Kate won't be sentenced to ten years in federal prison for writing ..." To her horror, Lucinda began to cry. Not just ordinary tears but enormous, choking sobs as if her heart were breaking into a million pieces.

The dam has finally broken, Father John thought. *How long since this child of yours has cried out all the sorrows, betrayals, and losses of her young life, Lord? Ten years? Fifteen?*

Several minutes elapsed before the emotional tsunami eased, and Lucinda could finally speak. "Father," she croaked, "I'm so sorry! I ...."

He took her trembling hand. "Child, don't be sorry. Never apologize for using one of the best cleansing agents our gracious Lord has given. Tears."

Smiling, Lucinda's breathing slowed. She turned to look at Father John, trying not to care about her messed-up mascara and eyeliner. "Have you always had such complete faith in God?"

He erupted with laughter. "No! Although I was raised Catholic, it all began to fall apart somewhere in my late teens." His gray eyes filled with sorrow. "But I did nothing to stop it. So, I was an atheist for most of my academic years."

Lucinda's blue eyes widened in shock. "Really?"

Father John nodded, accustomed to such reactions to his testimony. "You are fond of Kate, aren't you, Lucinda? In fact, you love her, don't you? That's why you're so worried about what will happen tomorrow." *Because whoever you've made the mistake of loving in your past has disappeared.*

The tears returned, but this time, they were silent and

healing. Lucinda reached for the priest's hand and squeezed it. They sat there in silence as the sky darkened.

"I'm Rich Jansen, Mr. Cunningham's associate, and I'm doing the closing arguments for the defense because we decided the jury needed to know the whole story of Dr. Lindsey McCall's incarceration, not just—"

"Objection, Your Honor. Defense counsel is testifying!"

"Mr. Martinez, you opened this line of questioning—twice. I suspect you remember doing that?" Judge Rhinehart peered at the prosecutor, his eyebrows raised. "Overruled. Continue, Mr. Jansen."

"Thank you, Your Honor. You must understand the *whole* story, not just Mr. Martinez' and Mr. Eldridge's carefully redacted versions. I met Dr. McCall when she was a prisoner in the Huntsville Prison system, where I served as chief warden." Rich ignored the thrum in the courtroom and the mumbled remarks at the prosecution table.

"After graduating from Harvard Law School, I practiced criminal defense law for maybe six months. I disliked it so much that I did a four-year hitch with the Marines and then became captain of the homicide division for the Houston Police Department. But because of wounds sustained in a north Houston shoot-out, I had to retire. So, Texas Governor Greg Bell asked me to take the job at Huntsville." He smiled. "You Californians have probably heard of the federal government's ten-year oversight of the Texas prison systems. Well, it ended the year Governor Bell took office, and Bell didn't want the feds back."

He suppressed a smile as he saw jaws drop at the prosecution table.

He glanced at Kate, then turned back to the jury. "I'd read

Kate Townsend's newspaper series, 'Murder in the Texas Medical Center,' and I became curious about one of the few women ever incarcerated in Huntsville's male prison system. This was done for Dr. McCall's protection since Huntsville is one of the few Texas prisons with an isolated wing."

He looked at Lindsey, held her gaze for a moment, then returned his attention to the jury. "Like Ms. Townsend writes in her Pulitzer-winning series, it was a strange indictment with an even stranger conviction. Dr. McCall was convicted of the murder of her mother by giving her a non-FDA-approved research drug called Digipro, a drug that Dr. McCall created."

Even Rhinehart reacted to that. More than two-thirds of people with heart disease were on the drug, probably including some in that courtroom and/or their relatives.

Rich regarded the jurors' puzzled faces. "It doesn't make sense, does it?" A few jury members shook their heads. "Not to me either," he continued, "so I wrote the appeal for her case to be heard at the Texas Supreme Court." He turned back to Lindsey for a moment. "I thank Dr. McCall because her case persuaded me to return to criminal defense law."

And for marrying me, he added in his mind.

"In a suicide note left by Dr. McCall's older sister, Paula, Paula confessed to giving their mother the drug against Dr. McCall's wishes. As a result, all charges were dropped, and Dr. McCall's medical license was reinstated. She was offered the cardiology chair at the University of Houston Medical School but turned it down to become medical director at the Huntsville Prisons and work for me."

He turned to look at Eldridge. "That's why Dr. McCall is also a boarded emergency medicine doctor."

Until then, Rich had been pacing up and down in front of

the jury panel, wondering if his unusual closing argument would work—if a lengthy background like this would keep the jurors' attention. But each of the twelve jurors looked engaged. Even the young woman yawning throughout the previous day seemed attentive.

He paused and looked at his watch. "I've only taken twelve minutes to provide the complete story of Dr. McCall's first indictment for unintentional murder." Then he smiled at the jurors. "I need more than that for this current indictment, but I assure you, I'll be as brief and precise as possible. First: the reason we're here.

"A federal hate crime is defined as willfully causing bodily injury to another person because of actual or perceived race, color, religion, national origin, gender, sexual orientation, gender identity, or disability.

"The first federal hate crime legislation was enacted in 1968 after the civil rights protests, expanding the thirteenth amendment in this nation's abhorrence of slavery: the abolition of slavery. Since then, gender and sexual identity have been added to race in the personal characteristics needing protection under the government."

Rich strolled along the row of jurors, eyeing each one. "Your duty today is to decide if what you have heard from the prosecution proves beyond a reasonable doubt that Dr. McCall conspired with journalist Kate Townsend to commit a federal hate crime against transgendered individuals. According to the indictment, the two defendants' conspiracy caused injury to Joey Carmichael. This conspiracy resulted in Joey's death."

He noted a few jurors who looked troubled. "It's hard to wrap our minds around this, right?

"What evidence has been brought to support such serious

allegations against Ms. Townsend and Dr. McCall? Did their five-year friendship result in a conspiracy, and did Dr. McCall's decision to help Joey get off the masculinizing drugs he hated cause his death?

"Let's review the facts of this case. Kindergarten teacher Addison Meeks claims that then-three-year-old Danny Sugarman's decision to become a girl is irreversible. According to the government's witness, Ms. Townsend changed the facts of 'Susie' Sugarman's coming out party because it fit her prejudice against transgenderism and provided context for the newspaper series she was writing about the evil of transgenderism. Hence, the beginning of the conspiracy.

"But Danny Sugarman explained what happened. He told us that he was angry at his father and why. Danny's sequence of events was the same as Ms. Townsend's, saying he didn't want to wear girls' clothes. Danny told the court, 'Of course, boys can't become girls just by saying so.' By implication, four-year-old Danny is saying everyone knows that.

"Because he knew the dangers of gender affirmation in young children, the government's expert witness, Dr. Matthew Heathcock, wrote an article supporting a wait-and-see approach for children with gender dysphoria under age twelve. And yet, within two years, Dr. Heathcock's name was attached to the California legislation that mandates teachers like Meeks to affirm gender change and ignore the reality that small children don't understand the consequences of their words." Rich paused and looked gravely at the jurors. "That's why they can't drive, vote, get married, or go to war. Small children are *not competent* to make life-changing decisions.

"We've learned that Dr. Heathcock didn't write the legislation. Instead, he just let his name be used to stay on good terms with the American Federation of Teachers. After all, they control his retirement income.

"The subsequent four government witnesses never contradicted information found in Ms. Townsend's newspaper series, 'Creating Chemical Eunuchs: Corrupting America's Children,' because they couldn't. Ms. Townsend is an experienced investigative reporter and knows the importance of documenting her sources.

"However, each testified to their objections and disagreement with her introduction to the series, claiming Townsend's use of the Bible and writing that gender affirmation and its accompanying hormonal and bodily mutilation demonstrate hate and are highly offensive. And yet, the state's last witness, Dr. Adam Turner, stated that he had read 'Creating Chemical Eunuchs: Corrupting America's Children' three times. It was Doctor Turner who started Joey Carmichael down the road to transitioning from female to male." Rich lowered his voice. "And Doctor Turner said that Joey's transition was evil."

Rich paused long enough to regain the attention of the twelve. He could tell by their dazed looks and the fact they were no longer meeting his eye as he walked by that their minds were wandering. "Dr. Turner was asked if he'd read the articles so many times because he disagreed with their content. 'No,' Dr. Turner replied, 'I read them so many times because the information was *compelling*.'"

Rich returned to his rhythmic pacing. "Dr. Turner then testified that embolic phenomena are a well-known complication of testosterone therapy. However, he ignored that fact and continued to pay for Joey's injections. Dr. Turner told the court that he knew Joey did not want the double mastectomy or 'top job,' as it's euphemistically called. The government's witness stated that he knew Joey would have gone through with it even though he didn't want it because of Dr. Turner's influence over the teen.

"Last, Mr. Martinez asked SLO Detective Cindy Ralston why Joey's accidental death wasn't considered manslaughter."

Rich paused again and looked over at the prosecution table. Eldridge was taking notes, and Martinez met his gaze and nodded imperceptively.

"The question was a last attempt to implicate Dr. McCall in Joey's death. But Detective Lockwood read these words from Joey's diary. Rich took an index card out of the pocket of his suit jacket and read from it.

> I feel better being off the testosterone. Way better. And I've lost ten pounds; I think the weight loss might be because of the estrogen. And, of course, the almost daily runs with Dr. McCall's dogs.

> But how do I tell him? He's been planning this for months. So, how do I tell him I don't want to be a guy anymore, that this has all been an awful mistake?

> 'But as I sat there looking back at her, I smiled. "Can I tell you a secret, Morgan? Something I am happy about?"

> Morgan looked surprised but nodded. I told her I was finally off the testosterone and had started taking estrogen, thanks to her friend, Dr. McCall.'"

"These are Joey's own words we've just heard." Rich paused, stood still, and scanned the twelve faces looking at him.

"Have you seen even a shred of evidence of a *conspiracy* between Dr. McCall and Ms. Townsend? Or do you see two women who stuck their necks out in completely unrelated situations instead? Two women who could have easily decided to do nothing, fully aware of the risks they were taking in this politicized climate where so little can be discussed but so much condemned?"

Rich had decided to omit any remarks about Cassie's testimony. The woman had done a splendid job of perjuring herself without his help.

It's done. Dear Lord, I pray it's enough.

He looked at the judge. "The defense rests."

As Martinez watched Sam stride across the courtroom and stop before the jury, he reflected again on his decision to hand over the remainder of this case to Eldridge.

Last night, he told his wife, Maria, she'd been right about this case, that he should never have touched it. "Maria, when I lose this case, I'll get fired. Not right away, but soon."

She shrugged. "Is that such a bad thing?"

He pointed to the enormous window overlooking the vast lawn of the stunning home they'd been in for five years. Their three boys and two dogs were racing one another outside. "We'll lose this house."

She touched his cheek and smiled tenderly. "Emilio, it's just a house."

"Ladies and gentlemen of the jury, my name is Sam Eldridge. I'm an attorney with the Southern Poverty Law Center and have been helping US Attorney Martinez with this case. It's my privilege to do the closing arguments for United States v. Townsend and McCall."

Rubbing his hands together, Eldridge smiled, then pivoted toward the defense table. "That was quite a closing argument, Mr. Jansen. I enjoyed your comments, and I'm sure the jury also did." He turned back to face the jury. "But, ladies and gentlemen, we no longer live in the nineteenth or early twentieth century, where our society was constrained by religious superstition. No sir! We're in the twenty-first century, where science can work the miracles that previous centuries' faith failed to do!"

Eldridge was young, not yet thirty-five, but his girth added years to his face. And he had the oratorical skills of a preacher—an intriguing irony of upbringing. Although Eldridge had been affected by the reporter's cogent explanation for why she wrote her series, he'd brushed it away. Her comments momentarily evoked his Southern Baptist preacher father and childhood faith. But Martinez had given him a public platform by permitting him to take over the defendants' cross and do closing arguments. This could be the opportunity of a lifetime. In fact, he would give Martinez credit for his opening statements by quoting him.

"Last Monday, US Attorney Martinez explained why we are here." Eldridge smiled and turned toward the defense table. "Although Mr. Jansen did so, US Attorney Martinez's words differed slightly. They warrant a repeat." The smile disappeared, and Eldridge lowered his voice. "Mr. Martinez reminded us that hate in and of itself cannot be criminalized." The governmental legalese took on a grave, weighty meaning when heard by Eldridge's ponderous, solemn recitation.

"However, such conduct may be classified as a hate crime when hate motivates criminal conduct. Defined by the Federal Bureau of Investigation as a "criminal offense against a person or property motivated in whole or in part by an offender's bias against a race, religion, disability, sexual orientation, ethnicity, gender, or gender identity."

Eldridge paused and regarded the faces of the jury. All twelve were watching, no scanning phones or shifting around; he had their attention.

"Historically, such criminal activities are traditional offenses like murder, arson, and vandalism with an added element of bias. Recently, however, hate crimes have proliferated.

As a result, our government has amended and added new provisions to American hate crime legislation.

"Hence providing additional options for prosecuting hate crimes, specifically the prohibition of a conspiracy to deprive others of federally protected rights. And that is what we have spent the last five days deliberating." Eldridge raised his voice and nearly shouted, "Did Ms. Kate Townsend and Dr. Lindsey McCall conspire in a hate crime against the community of transgendered Americans? One that resulted in the unintended murder of sixteen-year-old Joey Carmichael? Have their actions deprived transgendered Americans of their *federally protected right* to define their sexual identity?"

Eldridge wrapped the passion of his words about himself. He dropped the volume of his voice almost to a whisper as he said, "American citizens are the most autonomous of any on Earth. And American science and medicine are the most advanced and influential among all other nations.

"Who are these two women?" he roared, causing all twelve jurors to startle. "What *right* do they have to call our science, our advancements, evil?"

Voice back a few decibels, Eldridge said, "Here's what we know, what we've been told.

"Ms. Townsend and Dr. McCall are close friends. And had been for five years before Ms. Townsend retired to take care of her two children." Sauntering up and down before the jurors' box, he stopped before the twenty-something blonde. He said, "Don't you think it would be difficult to leave the career that had afforded you the *Pulitzer Prize*?" Eldridge smiled as he got the nod he was waiting for.

Still standing before the young woman, he said, "And even harder to keep from talking with your close friend when the perfect recipe for another shocking investigative series appeared in your lap? Especially since your best friend had first-time knowledge of your subject through the detransitioning that Dr. McCall has admitted she initiated on Joey?

"Not only that, but the fascinating coincidence that Ms. Townsend and Dr. McCall share the outmoded religious dogma of the Catholic faith. A faith that explicitly rejects the right of transgendered Americans their right to define their sexual identity."

Voice dropping again, Eldridge began to move again. "But we can't find those emails."

Zach admired the guy's audacity. Stopping just short of lying, Eldridge was using classical logical errors like inference, correlation/causality along with the bandwagon and anecdotal evidence fallacies brilliantly. They must have conspired because Kate and Lindsey were simultaneously working on the articles and with Joey. Because gender change is a federally protected right, any subversion must emanate from hate.

Eldridge saved his best for last. Pointing to his black skin, he said, "We know the power of hate and of using Jesus and Christianity to embolden our colonial, privileged rights and properties. But it's just hate. And it must be stopped.

"Here and now."

He nodded to the judge. "The prosecution rests."

Zach and Rich looked at one another. An unsaid *Wow* lingering in the air between them.

Judge Rhinehart turned to the jury. "In your deliberations for this case, you cannot consult outside sources, whether an online search or other research materials. You must decide the guilt or innocence of these two defendants solely on the evidence presented in this courtroom." He paused to check the time. "It's nearly noon, so lunch will be served now." He whispered something to the bailiff, then turned back to the jury. "Mr. Kendrick, could you stand, please?"

The slight forty-something man sitting in the back row stood up.

"You have been selected as foreman of this jury. Do you accept that responsibility, sir?"

Stan blinked nervously as he looked at the judge. "Uh, yes, Your Honor, I do."

"Mr. Kendrick, please begin your deliberations no later than 1:00. If you need to review case documents, just ask the bailiff, who will be posted outside your deliberation room. In addition, each of you will receive a copy of Ms. Townsend's newspaper series, a copy of Dr. Heathcock's article, and an outline of the California legislation."

A few minutes after 1:00 p.m., the bailiff took the sandwiches and drinks away. Stan Kendrick sat at the head of the long table and looked at his eleven fellow jurors. They ranged in age from early twenties to late sixties. One middle-aged woman sitting in the middle on his right caught his gaze.

"Should we begin by introducing ourselves and a little about who we are and what we do?" she asked.

Surprising her and himself, Stan shook his head. "No. This isn't about us. It's about those two women there. Did they commit a federal hate crime by conspiring against transgendered Americans and, in so doing, inadvertently cause this kid's death?"

The woman scowled. Then she said huffily, "Well, excuse me!"

Three men began to speak simultaneously.

"Stop!"

Ignoring Stan, they continued talking even louder.

"Please." Stan looked at the three men, who looked like working men. "Look, I'm not trying to be rude."

They stopped talking. Glancing between them and the woman, Stan continued. "We're not here to become friends or chitchat. The judge asked me to keep us on track, so I will do my best. It's Friday afternoon, and like all of you, I'm pretty sick of this courtroom and hope to get this behind me and not return here on Monday, but we've got a job to do."

He pointed at the stack of articles and then the clock. "Let's take sixty minutes and read these through. Then, at 2:00, we can ponder what we've heard from the prosecution and defense. Then, at about quarter past two, I'll go around the table and ask for one word from you: innocent or guilty. That way, we can see how close we are to unanimity."

Stan worked in Silicon Valley. He was a middle manager and was accustomed to leading small groups. A natural loner, Stan quickly made it clear to the people who reported to him that they weren't his friends. Hence, if they were annoyed at him for the distance he maintained, so be it.

Before this case, he'd never given any thought to transgender issues. His employers flew the rainbow flag and celebrated Pride week, so he shrugged and went along with it. It didn't affect him, so he didn't care about others' sexual choices. But he didn't understand what transgender meant. Until now.

A computer whiz since high school, Stan took a logical, analytical approach to life. As a single father to a nine-year-old girl—his wife had died of cancer two years before—the tragic story of this teen so impressed him that he'd dreamed about the kid. And that four-year-old kid, Danny, explaining that he'd been angry with his father made sense. What made no sense at all was the teacher's reaction.

But evil? What did that even mean?

However, Stan had read the reporter's articles several times by the prearranged time. And he'd also read Heathcock's piece claiming it was best to do nothing with a little kid like Danny. That it was best to wait and see. And the California legislation mandating the explanation of gender identity and affirmation beginning in kindergarten was—Kafkaesque. Finally, the kindergarten teacher's insistence that Danny Sugarman had *inalterably* declared himself a girl was incomprehensible. What if that had been his little girl when she'd been such a tomboy? He shuddered at what could have happened.

So, that last witness—Turner—was correct. It was compelling stuff. Even Turner had used the word evil. Steve struggled to recall the summer Bible school his mom had insisted he attend when he was eight. He'd liked the classes and had gone the next three summers. Finally, a definition bubbled up: evil was the absence of Good, of God. Steve grasped and held onto that thought.

Once the allotted time was up, a couple of coughs got his attention, and he looked up. Except for the tall, older African-American sitting at the end of the table, all eyes were on him, waiting.

"OK, then, I'll start: Not guilty." The words fell out of Stan's mouth without even thinking.

The man sitting to his right looked at him somberly. "You said that with conviction." He looked about the table and asked, "Am I the only one wondering if they conspired? Like the timing of the reporter's articles and the doctor's intervention with the kid. Their friendship. Both are Catholic converts. Did you think about the string of those strange coincidences?"

Stan looked at him. The man was about his age. He's a big guy with a broad, open face. "Looks like a working man, maybe a contractor," he thought and nodded.

"Yes, I did. And I agree that the simultaneous writing of the articles and the doc's actions with Joey suggests they could have worked together. I thought the reporter's decision to frame this thing in some kind of diabolical evil was weird at first." Stan looked around the table. Everyone was listening. "But does any of you remember how evil's defined?"

Eleven faces stared at him. Some were quizzical, a few

skeptical, and the tall blonde kid looked bored. But his friend at the opposite end of the table smiled broadly. And then replied, "Yes, I do. Evil is the absence of goodness—of God."

Stan waited for him to continue, but he did not. The older man motioned with long, graceful fingers to Stan as if to say, *Go on, you've got this, son.*

"And the Catholicism convert thing is also ... another peculiar coincidence, just like Eldridge said." Stan steepled his hands again and looked around the table." But can any of you see their decision to become Catholic as relevant to this case? Remember high school temporal fallacies? Assuming a causal connection between two different events merely because they happened simultaneously?

"To me, the coincidences are just that."

Stan was grateful the man had asked him to explain because he hadn't understood why he was so sure of their innocence until now. Again, he scanned the jurors' faces and said, "But that's all distraction to the fundamental questions before us. Is publishing facts about an obvious risk to kids a hate crime? And is detransitioning a desperate teen 'unintentional' murder? We know that Joey knew about the risks of clots from testosterone, so could the doc starting the estrogen he begged for have caused the clot?" He shrugged and said, "Who knows? But is it the doctor's fault if it did? If anyone should be blamed, it's the mother and Dr. Turner. They're the ones who started the little girl on testosterone.

This doctor, McCall, was trying to help this kid. There's no hate crime or fault in either of these women." Stan looked at the man to his right and smiled slightly. "Thanks for asking me. I hadn't realized why I was so certain until you asked."

The man nodded and said, "Thank you. That helps me.

Not guilty."

"Not guilty."

"Not guilty."

"Not guilty."

The two twenty-somethings interrupted the continual string of "Not Guilty."

"Guilty."

"Guilty."

Stan looked at the clean-cut, good-looking blonde man, surprised at first and then not. The kid looked supremely, even supernaturally, self-confident, like a younger version of Stan's boss. The young woman beside him was clearly infatuated. Naturally, she'd follow his lead wherever it took her.

Once they'd heard everyone's verdict, the guy and the girl were the only two holdouts.

"Can you tell us why you think they're guilty of conspiring in a hate crime?" Stan asked, addressing the young man.

"Transgenderism is a federally protected right. Mr. Eldridge was correct when he stated that 'cis' resulted from capitalistic, colonial, racist thinking. This reporter's claim that transgenderism is evil is *the definition* of a hate crime. The reporter's a racist bigot." He lifted his long, muscular arm in a dismissive wave. "Her remarks about evil, about joining the Catholic Church because of the kid's silly kindergarten party, were superstitious dogma."

"First-year law at Stanford?"

Startled, the young man stared at the bearded African-American man at the end of the table who had just spoken. "How could you possibly know that?"

"Because I was on faculty there." His expression was somber, even grave. "Mr. Eldridge never said that man's long-held belief that human beings are created male and female or 'cis' results from capitalistic, colonial, racist thinking, son. But we hear what we expect to hear, particularly when we swim in the rhetoric."

"This case has nothing to do with the gender wars or racism," Stan said, taking advantage of his ally's intervention. "The question is this, did the reporter conspire with the doctor to create a hate crime against the transgendered American community?

"Did the simultaneous timing of the doctor's detransitioning the dead kid and publishing those articles indicate a conspiracy?" Stan regarded the arrogant young man for a moment before continuing. "What question did the reporter ask all the doctors who dealt with transgenderism she interviewed?"

The young lady was about to answer, but Stan held his hand to silence her. The young blonde man defiantly stared at Stan, his cheeks glowing slightly. "You didn't read the articles, did you?" Stan asked.

To his credit, the law student shook his head.

"Do you have a little sister or brother?" Stan asked.

The guy nodded.

"Which one?"

"Both."

"Will you please think about them while you read what this woman has written?"

Stan looked at the young woman seated next to him. "What about you?"

Her eyes widened, which was quite a feat, considering the black, heavy-looking fake eyelashes that looked ridiculous with her blonde-accented light-brown hair.

"What do you mean? Are you asking if I have sisters and brothers, too? I'm the youngest of four."

"No," Stan replied. "Please tell us why you think Townsend and McCall conspired in a federal hate crime against the transgendered American community and why you think McCall is guilty of unintentional murder for detransitioning Joey Carmichael."

"Well, it's obvious, isn't it?" she stammered, her long, bright red fingernails threading through her hair.

Several jurors studied the table.

"What do you mean?" Stan asked. "What's obvious?"

The girl just stared at him, her cheeks flaming red.

Stan looked at his ally at the end of the table. "Sir, could you please switch seats with our young friend here? I think she might be less distracted if you switch places." He wished he could smack the smile off the blonde Adonis beside her.

Stan looked around the room at the other jurors. "Why don't the rest of you take a break? The bailiff said drinks and snacks were in a conference room halfway down the hall on the right. Let's meet back here at 4:30."

Martinez looked at his watch. "I thought they'd be done by now. It's close to six and nothing."

He and Zach were at Brenda's Cajun Creole Soul Food—again. They were just finishing the Cajun substitute for the burger and beer that Zach had offered Martinez.

Zach looked around the tiny, funky room. "I'm going to miss this place."

"Why? It's kinda dirty and ugly."

Zach nodded. "Precisely. Whenever I get cabin fever in my Mustang home office, I'll think of this place, look out my picture window at the pasture, and say 'thank you.'"

Nodding, the younger lawyer popped his last crawfish into his mouth. "So, who influenced you the most in law school, Zach?"

Zach smiled at the memory as he swallowed the last of his meal. Then he picked up his napkin and wiped his mouth. "During law school? No one. In fact, by graduation, I didn't want to have anything to do with the practice of law. But Bill Kuntsler did our graduation speech, which changed my life."

Martinez frowned as he tried to place the name. "Kuntsler? Do you mean *William Kuntsler*?"

"Yes."

The strange combination of his diminutive stature and a voice that sounded as if it emanated from a 300-pound linebacker were gifts that Zach had used to significant effect in law school, graduating as a James Kent Scholar during each of his three years at Columbia. Roughly equivalent to the magna cum laude honor awarded at Harvard and some other law schools, the Kent Scholar award was rarely earned for a single year, let alone three. Zach was among the few Columbia law students who had ever reached the academic distinction, which was likely a significant factor in achieving a year-long internship with William Kuntsler.

When Zach graduated in 1968, Kuntsler spoke at his graduation ceremony. A Class of 1948 Columbia Law School graduate, Kuntsler was well on his way to earning the *New York Times* sobriquet as "the most hated and also the most feared lawyer in America." Director of the American Civil Liberties Union and defender of radical groups like the Weathermen, the Black Panthers, and the Chicago Seven, Kuntsler's legal philosophy diverged almost wholly from Columbia's faculty.

Zach studied the younger man. "I'll never forget the constipated looks on the faculty members' faces when ol' Bill turned to them, then us, and said, 'I only defend those I love. I'm not a lawyer for hire. I defend only those whose goals I share.'"

Martinez nodded to Zach, appreciating the anecdote. It was a heck of a thing for any lawyer to say. But at a law school graduation? No wonder this man was so special: he'd apprenticed under one of the best legal minds of the last century. Then Martinez said, "I looked online for that simulated video of your cross of the child during the appeal of the sexual molester. Rhinehart's right. You were brilliant with that little girl. I've never seen anything like it."

Zach merely nodded.

Still looking at the lawyer, "Quite obviously, the little girl couldn't return to her negligent mother; what happened to her?"

Zach's eyes softened, warmed, and lit up. "My wife Harvey

and I adopted her. Annie's just turned nine and has twirled this old man right around her little finger."

Stan steepled his hands as he looked at the helpful middle-aged woman and shook his head. "No."

She had suggested they call it quits for the weekend because the Stanford Law School kid and the girl were still stuck on "guilty."

She looked at the clock on the wall. "It's almost six, and we've been through this repeatedly. Maybe we can say we're a hung jury."

"Yeah," someone else chimed in. "You've done the count five times, and it hasn't changed."

"So, you're all fine with making those two women go through this again? Maybe keep them in jail until a new trial can be scheduled?" No one looked at him. Instead, they all stared at the floor or the table as if something terribly interesting was lying there.

Stan stood up, then asked everyone else to join him. Surprisingly, they all did. He looked at the young girl standing at the opposite end of the table. "The last reason you gave us for believing they're guilty was the California law that tells teachers to do what that kindergarten teacher did, right?"

Fingering her hair again, she nodded, though Stan noted she wasn't looking for direction from Stanford Law. "Did you read Dr. Heathcock's article?"

"No. I did not. I apologize; I'll do that now."

Fifteen minutes later, she changed her vote to "not guilty."

Eleven pairs of eyes regarded the Stanford Law student.

"You can't force me to change my vote!" he said. "Just because *she* caves, you want me to be a good little boy along with all you know-nothings?"

"Don't you dare!" the young woman hissed above the explosive reactions of the other jurors. The young woman's ferocity caused the group to shut up and wait to see what would happen next.

She held up Kate's and Heathcock's articles and shook them. "You didn't bother to read any of these, did you?" She walked around the table to him. "You've got a little sister and brother, and yet you don't care enough to see the results of your precious ideology?" She pointed at several underlined paragraphs in Kate's and Heathcock's articles. "Just read these, oh Mr. Wisest Person in the Room, and then tell us you think they conspired in a hate crime against the transgendered American community!"

At 7:30 that evening, the court was back in session. Judge Rhinehart turned to Stan. "Mr. Foreman, has the jury reached a verdict?"

"We have, Your Honor."

The bailiff took a folded piece of paper from Stan and walked it over to the judge. Rhinehart opened it, his face impassive as he read what was written on it. "Defendants, please rise."

Lindsey and Kate stood.

Right behind them sat Morgan, LJ, Father John, Steve, Lucinda, and Toni holding hands.

"In the matter of US v. Townsend and McCall, conspiracy to commit a federal hate crime against the transgendered American community, the jury finds the defendants not guilty. In the matter of US v. Townsend and McCall, conspiracy to commit unintentional murder, the jury finds the defendants not guilty."

Rhinehart looked over at Stan, who was still standing. "Mr. Kendrick, is this verdict unanimous?"

"Yes," Stan replied, nodding.

Rhinehart studied the twelve jurors. "In a case of this magnitude, we must hear this from each juror personally. He pointed to the juror sitting beside Stan. "Starting with you, please stand and state your opinion."

The blonde first-year Stanford law student stood and mumbled something. Rhinehart scowled. "Son, neither I nor anyone in this room could hear what you just said."

"Not guilty!"

After each of the ten remaining jurors had spoken, Judge Rhinehart nodded. "This court thanks you for your service. You are dismissed." Then he turned to the defendants and smiled. "Ms. Townsend and Dr. McCall, you are free to go." He tapped his gavel. "This court is adjourned."

"Not guilty of trans hate crime!" was the front-page headline of the *LA Times,* which sat on Adam's placemat. Nancy had grabbed a copy of the paper from a newsstand on her way home after an exhausting week. She'd had to search for a hard copy but knew Adam preferred the newspaper to online.

A plastic surgeon and head of the gender-affirmation team at UCLA, Nancy had performed five double mastectomies and three castrations in six days. Her recent decision to refuse trans surgery on patients younger than twenty-one was causing consternation with the chief of surgery and the administration. But what had happened to Joey Carmichael and her close read of Kate's articles had shaken her.

Turner was asleep when she got home a little before midnight and was still out cold at 7:00 a.m. Nancy stared out their enormous picture window at a massive boulder with waves crashing over it and wondered what the hell she was doing with her life.

As a plastic surgeon, Nancy had accustomed herself to a wide range of strange patient requests. A nose that looked fine to her was too long. Breasts that seemed perfectly sized weren't large enough. She was in cosmetics, after all. Whatever made the patient happy. So, six years ago, when UCLA decided to jump into the lucrative transgender business and asked her to head up the gender-affirmation team, she'd not given her decision much thought. It was more of the same, making people look how they wanted. She became a department head with tenure. Not bad at age thirty-eight. But as she sipped her coffee and stared at the crashing waves below, Nancy realized that none of those decisions had really been choices. Each one had been more a matter of, "Why not?"

She'd done exceptionally well in her surgical residency program. She was considering a specialty in trauma, but the chief surgical resident she was dating at the time suggested plastics instead. It offered better hours and better money, so she switched.

Then there was Adam. Nancy realized she'd married him to thumb her nose at men, especially Marine helicopter pilot types. Five years later, she was here, making more money than God, yet utterly miserable. Adam had gone to the hospital to see Joey the morning he'd died and returned less than an hour later. Nancy wondered what had happened in that hospital room. Several times, she'd almost asked but then stopped herself. *Do you really want to know?*

Nancy knew that Adam had testified in the trial, but she had no idea what had transpired in court, for they'd barely seen each other in the last two weeks. But even if they'd seen one another, Nancy thought sadly, Adam probably wouldn't have talked to her. Adam was more closed off than anyone Nancy had ever been with, and any hopes that she could make Adam happy had been extinguished long ago.

Yes, this house and everything in it is stunning. But I'm never here ... because I don't want to be.

What happened to the idealistic young doctor who wanted to join Doctors Without Borders? To help people improve their lives rather than wreck them?

Nancy heard Adam in the kitchen fumbling around, signaling her to come in and take over to make coffee and breakfast.

She took a breath and gazed out at that astounding view

of Pismo Bay for what could be the last time.

It's time, she thought. *In fact, it's way past time.*

Then she walked into the kitchen. "Adam, we need to talk."

CHAPTER SIXTY-NINE

It looked like a caravan as the ten people and two small children tumbled out of a truck and two Ubers at San Francisco Airport.

"Toni, get a move on. Our flight leaves in forty-five minutes," Zach growled at his assistant as she hugged Lucinda. His gruffness was an attempt to distance himself from the emotional goodbyes at the curbside. However, it wasn't working well because Zach grabbed Father John's hands as he climbed out of the Uber. "What happened in that courthouse was miraculous."

The priest nodded, then narrowed his eyes. "Life is jam-packed with miracles, Zach. But we're often not awake enough to see them." He held onto the hand that Zach was pulling away. "You've done great work for them, Zach and him." Father John looked heavenward.

Toni ignored the wetness in her boss's eyes as she caught up to him, carrying her travel bag. Extending her sleeve-tattooed arm to shake the priest's hand, she withdrew it and let the travel bag drop to the pavement, stretching out both arms instead. "Father John, I'm not a hugger, but you and Lucinda are exceptions. Do you mind?"

Rich jogged up just then. "Zach, what do you think about bringing Harvey and Annie to College Station for Labor Day weekend?" He turned toward Morgan and LJ, who were hugging JH, Nicholas, and Lucinda. "Those two have become quite the chefs." He grinned. "And I'm not bad either."

"You got it, partner," Zach replied. "I'm pretty sure we can make that work." He glanced at Lindsey in a three-way embrace with Kate and Steve. "Thanks to Lindsey, Annie's doing great.

She's playing soccer and started swimming competitively." Zach smiled broadly. "That Digipro plus the Longevive supplements keep her ticker just the right size."

Nine-year-old Annie was the adopted daughter of Zach and Harvey Cunningham. Despite their ages, the Cunninghams had been awarded custody of the child. Sexual abuse had been almost a constant in her life until Zach won the appeal of an Army Ranger named Gabe McAllister. During the trial, the negligence of Annie's mother was made sickeningly clear. Perhaps because of the stress of that early childhood, Annie had developed cardiomyopathy.

"What's up, babe?"

Rich saw Lindsey frown at a text as they hurried along the Dallas Airport concourse to the second leg of their flight home to College Station. Morgan and LJ were way ahead of them.

"Francis wants to meet us at the house. He said he needed to talk about something with me before Monday. He promises it won't take long."

As he watched his wife, Rich sent up a quick prayer. *Please, Lord, if you can make this something good rather than another crisis, we'd certainly appreciate it!*

Two hours later, they drove down the dirt road and parked the rental car in front of the house they had bought from Dr. Boyega's in-laws just a month earlier. LJ and Morgan tumbled out. "Max! Gus!" LJ shouted. "Where are you? We're home, and we sure missed you!"

Boyega opened the glass front door, and the two canines nearly knocked the girls over as they raced onto the porch and down the stairs. Boyega flew down the stairs almost as fast as the dogs. The tall, thin Nigerian stood beside the car with a humongous grin. "Welcome home, Dr. McCall and Mr. Jansen." As he had done the first time Lindsey had seen the wonderful house, he thrust out his right hand to shake hers. "There are a few very nice surprises in there."

CHAPTER SEVENTY

"Honey, wake up. We've landed."

Dazed, Kate looked around, realizing she'd slept the entire four-hour flight from San Francisco to San Antonio. "I've never been able to sleep on a plane, but the last thing I remember is closing my eyes while we waited to take off."

No one answered; they didn't hear her.

Steve was in the aisle, taking Nicholas, who was crying, from Lucinda. As Steve smiled and babbled to his son, Nicholas was so fascinated by his daddy's antics that he laughed and reached for Kate.

Kate grabbed thirty-five pounds of squirming boy and clutched him to her chest. *Did last week really happen?* she wondered. *Did Lindsey and I hear those words last night, 'not guilty'?*

She looked around at the crowd struggling to get their luggage out of the overhead bins, probably worried about making their connections. *Do they know how precarious their freedom is?*

Suddenly, Steve's warm brown eyes were close to hers. He kissed her on the forehead. Then he took Nicholas out of her arms and held him close while taking Kate's hand. "Come, my intrepid reporter. Let's go start a new life."

Kate saw Lucinda and JH walking down the causeway. JH disliked being carried, but he was only four, so with his short legs, their pace was slow. When they reached the waiting area, Kate saw a tall blonde woman with a shorter dark-haired man and an elderly woman with white hair.

Steve entertained Nicholas as they walked so he didn't see

the people waiting until Kate cried out.

"What on earth are Michele and John Smith and Eleanor Philbin …" Kate paused when a tall, lanky, dark brown-haired man approached Eleanor and handed her a coffee. "Steve, that's Jeff Simmons!"

"Why wouldn't they be here?" Steve asked. "Lois Lane, you deserve another Pulitzer for what you wrote and went through because of it, although I know they'd never consider it." He shook his head and chuckled, "But how do Eleanor and Jeff know the Smiths?" Shaking his head in wonder, he said," I'm sure we're about to hear."

He watched as Kate ran to Eleanor and Jeff and stretched out her hands to the Smiths. Lucinda and JH walked up, and then Steve finally got there.

Steve was content to stand there holding his little boy, watching. He was delighted to see his wife back. Her face flushed, her eyes vibrant, and she displayed her megawatt smile, which made his heart melt. He couldn't recall when he'd last seen it. He could have hugged each of them for making the effort, especially Eleanor. Wasn't she close to ninety now?

John Smith ambled over to him and grinned. "Need a ride home? Michele and I have the keys to 604 Rattler Pass, where Eleanor and Michele have been busy all week.

"Our four sons have made hundreds of copies of Kate's articles and posted them in their respective college and high school classrooms." Smith raised an eyebrow. "If there's been blowback, we haven't heard it."

John looked out the window at the street in front of the Southwestern gate. Then he turned back to Steve, his usually cheery expression grave. "I can't imagine what this week has been like for you and Kate, but on Tuesday, we got a call from

Eleanor, who had a proposition. We jumped at the chance to do something special for you guys."

He looked over at the diminutive, octogenarian, white-haired owner of the *Houston Tribune*, gazing up at Kate. Her beautiful, aristocratic face was filled with a thousand wrinkles of love. "You'd think that one of the ten wealthiest women in Texas would be obnoxious, condescending, or at least commanding. But that lady is like a lighthouse of grace. She's treating Michele and me as if we're the important ones here." He gave Steve a rueful look. "I'm sorry, man. I'm not usually so long-winded. You must be wiped out. So, here's the plan, if it's OK with you. Why don't you, Lucinda, and the boys drive to your new home with me in our truck?" He pointed out the window at a stretch limo. "Eleanor's gone all out for your wife and has asked Michele to join her, Kate, and Jeff in the limo."

Steve chuckled. Then he said, "A limo for Kate Townsend, also known as Lois Lane, intrepid reporter. Eleanor Philbin, you are the very best; thank you, thank you." Turning back from watching Eleanor to John, he said, "There's nothing I'd like better, John. Especially since I have no clue where the house is."

Steve woke up when John's car door shut. Lucinda had already taken the boys inside. He blinked several times, staring at their new house, a house that he couldn't remember at all. He saw the limo parked in the driveway and wondered how they had all arrived so fast.

John glanced over at him. "It's going to get even stranger, Steve, this sense of disorientation. 'They' say that moving is one of the most stressful things a person can do. So, a move and a week-long trial that ended just last night?" John took a deep breath. "Add twelve California jurors who held your life in their hands all week." He shook his head. "What am I saying? *You're* the doctor here!"

Steve's face suddenly conveyed nothing but deep weariness. As John studied his client, his heart went out to him. *With all due respect, Ms. Philbin ….*

"I'm not supposed to tell you this, but I'm guessing you might be like me and dislike surprises."

At Steve's puzzled nod, John continued. "Figured as much. Eleanor and Michele have spent the week staging the house."

Steve's look of confusion deepened. "Staging?"

"It's how we realtors use furniture, plants, and decorative objects to accentuate the best attributes of a home. Eleanor knows that Kate hates furniture selection and decorating with a passion."

Steve laughed. All traces of fatigue falling away. "So, Eleanor and Michele have decorated our new house?"

John nodded. "Yes. The whole thing is a gift for you guys

from the board at the Houston Tribune in gratitude for you and Kate. And since there was no price ceiling, yours is the most stunning staging we've ever seen!" John's eyes sparkled with mischief. "Too bad we didn't have it staged when we sold it to you the first time."

Before Steve could retort, John held up his hand. "Here's the real surprise. The one I wasn't supposed to tell. There's a party."

"A party?" Steve echoed.

"Yep. You've all been conveniently dead to the world while I drove around the hill country to see some properties Michele and I just listed. That gave Eleanor and Michele time to arrive before us and show Kate your newly appointed home."

Reading the confusion on Steve's face when he realized Lucinda and the boys were no longer in the car, John smiled. "Lucinda took the boys in the house a half hour ago to settle them and to supervise the caterers."

Steve followed John down the cement walkway and gaped at the unusual entrance to the stone house. Four pillars supported a wooden archway that led to a set of massive double doors made of glass and ebony wood.

Opening one of the doors, John bowed and extended his arm to Steve. "You first, Dr. Cooper."

They stood in the foyer. Steve's eyes were instantly drawn to the red and gold Chinese character oil painting hanging over a simple wood table against the end wall of the entry. The picture accentuated the red rug on the tiled floor. Matching faux nine-foot LED-lit birch trees complemented the wooden table. Against the pale walls, the effect was understated and elegant.

John looked at Steve, who was agape in disbelief. "Kate must love this," Steve said. "It's completely her taste!"

"Steve, you've seen nothing yet. As I told you before, Michele and I have been in the business for a while but haven't seen anything close to this. Each piece subtly accents the unique features of the house."

Heading to the left, they walked into the great room. It had windows galore with white and black leather furniture that looked clean, crisp, and classy.

And yes, there was a party.

Eleanor had thought of everything. A baroque trio—a harpist, cellist, and violinist—played Mozart in the corner of the great room. Everyone was dressed in Saturday casual but with extras. There were flowers everywhere. A young woman dressed in a modified tuxedo approached and asked Steve and John if they would like a glass of champagne.

"Sure, why not?" Steve said.

Julie Grayson spied them first. She, Lindsey, and Rich were talking in a corner across the room from the musicians. Grabbing Lindsey's hand, Julie weaved through a group of men until she reached Steve, her eyes shining. Joining them, Rich glanced at his watch. "Yo, Steve. Good to see you." He offered an excellent facsimile of a grimace. "I just didn't think it would take so long! It's been all of ten hours!"

Before Steve could answer, Lindsey cut in. "Steve, we knew nothing about any of this." Putting herself in Steve's shoes, Lindsey feared he'd feel all this activity had been planned behind his back. It had been but not by her. If she were Steve, she'd be annoyed, feeling intruded upon. But as she looked at her friend's serene expression, one she'd not seen since all the craziness had started, Lindsey thought for the millionth time since she'd known Steve Cooper, *I'm not Steve.*

"Eleanor contacted Francis Boyega," she waved at the tall black man standing with three others, "the School of Public Health dean. We bought our house from his in-laws. When we got home, he was waiting at our new house to tell us about Eleanor's surprise party." Lindsey looked around. "This is one stunning house, Dr. Cooper. We got here a couple of hours ago and got the grand tour."

Lindsey turned to John, seeming to have noticed him for the first time. "You must be John, right? Michele's husband? I hope you don't mind," she continued to Steve, not waiting for a reply from John, "but we're staying overnight. We've already picked out the blue bedroom down the hall."

Steve drained his champagne flute, then grabbed Lindsey and hugged her, holding Rich's hand as well. "No worries, former partner and her husband to whom I am unspeakably grateful. Wanna show me this house I feel like I've never seen before?"

Lindsey and Rich had just completed Steve's tour of his new home. They were returning to the great room when the music toned down, and Eleanor appeared, her arm outstretched to Steve.

Eleanor crossed the enormous room with Kate. Steve hadn't seen Kate since they'd landed at the airport hours ago, and he gaped as he watched her walking toward him. Dressed in a light gold and violet sundress, her dark-brown hair was arranged in a French braid with tendrils curling about her face. The effect was paradoxically innocent and as sexy as hell.

"Now come, you two," Eleanor said. They followed her to the other side of the room before the musicians. Apparently, the moment had been orchestrated because Kate's editor, Jeff Simmons, five men whom Steve assumed were *Houston Tribune* board members, Lucinda and his two strangely quiet boys, Michele and John Smith, and Lindsey and Rich had formed a line. The rest of the gathering fell in behind them. Steve realized they had created a receiving line and that each person intended to speak to Kate, to offer her their congratulations or their sympathies, whatever was proper in this most bizarre of situations.

Also included in the line were Francis and three other men whom Steve guessed were the deans of Medicine and Veterinary Medicine, the Health Science Center president from A&M. He saw no one from UT San Antonio. An oversight from Eleanor? Doubtful.

Steve managed to suppress the nervous laugh he felt threatening to erupt and looked appropriately genteel. But when he caught Rich's eye, he almost lost it again.

"Kate, dear, thank you all for allowing us to be here this evening. To let a group of virtual strangers take over your new home the moment you finally arrive back in Texas."

The warmth, love, wisdom, and sincerity flowing from Eleanor erased all the negative thoughts Steve had been having about the evening.

Eleanor stepped to the side, directly in front of Kate, placing her hands on Kate's arms as she leaned forward. "When you came to us with the idea of writing 'Creating Chemical Eunuchs: Corrupting America's Children,' we were skeptical," Eleanor said, eyeing a heavy-set man standing with Simmons. "John was opposed—the risk of litigation and worse was too great. But after the longest board meeting in the history of the Tribune, ten hours, we decided to follow our senior reporter's instincts, never dreaming the outcome wouldn't just be litigation but an indictment from the United States government." Eleanor's voice cracked at her failed attempt at humor. She swallowed hard. "Each of your investigative series has been excellent. But Kate, dear, this surpasses anything you or any other reporter has done." Tears glistened in Eleanor's eyes. "I am so proud of you, Kate. Proud of your grit and your faith.

"These last few weeks have been brutal for us but unimaginable for you all." Her blue eyes widened in shock at her gaffe of omission. "Dr. Lindsey McCall and Rich Jansen, you two get up here now!"

"Eleanor, I didn't write the story. Kate did!" Lindsey protested.

"Please?"

Grudgingly, Rich and Lindsey went and stood on Eleanor's opposite side.

"Thank you." The tiny but statuesque woman collected

herself, reached into the pocket of her flowing skirt, and brought out a folded set of eight-by-eleven pages, which she straightened out, scanned, and then crumpled up.

"The words I wrote last night can't convey the depth of admiration that I—" She paused and gazed at the thirty-five grave faces before her. "That all of us here feel for the four of you and for Zach Cunningham and Toni Martinez.

"We feel certain that the decision of those twelve jurors is the beginning of the cleansing of our nation. This case will profoundly affect our country and leaders, perhaps not today, this year, or within my lifetime, but the light of truth can't be suppressed."

She turned to look at the heavy-set man standing next to Simmons. "I'm John Jaworski," he said in a deep Texas drawl, "senior partner of Fulbright and Jaworski. Our monthly board meeting was extended until three in the morning because I insisted that the series Kate proposed was far too explosive for a privately owned newspaper to publish." He paused and surveyed the room. "The plaintiff I feared most was the US Justice Department."

He walked over to Rich and handed him two envelopes that he had taken from the inside pocket of his blazer. "Rich Jansen, on behalf of the Fulbright and Jaworski Law Firm, I am privileged to award you and your partner, Zach Cunningham, a check for one hundred thousand dollars." He glanced at Eleanor. "A week ago, I was banging the table in Eleanor's office and shouting that even God Himself couldn't beat the president's justice department." He turned to the crowd, both arms extended. "Can y'all imagine how ecstatic I am to be so totally wrong?"

The lawyer took Rich's hand in two meaty hands. "If you ever want to leave Cunningham, I'd make you a partner immediately. Just say the word."

The big man turned to Lindsey. "So, you're Dr. Lindsey McCall. I and most of my lawyers who are over fifty are on your drug. In fact, I wouldn't be here if it weren't for Digipro." He winked at Eleanor. "And I've got much more work to do before I'm ready to meet the Lord."

After accepting a large, beautifully wrapped package from a man beside him, he handed it to Kate. She held it awkwardly, unsure what to do. "Open it!" he said.

Inside was a stunning crystal sculpture of Joseph Pulitzer standing next to an excellent facsimile of Kate. Two pure gold facsimiles of the Pulitzer Prize for Investigative Journalism from Columbia University were included.

Eleanor lifted her champagne glass. "To you four warriors. And to our gracious, merciful God Almighty." Her blue eyes sparkled. "Let's party!"

"Air conditioning! Thank you, Lord, for the air conditioning!" LJ shouted as Max, Gus, LJ, and Morgan thundered onto the porch and into the cool College Station house.

Morgan's face was bright red. "Is it usually this humid here?"

"No, it's typically way more humid," LJ said. "No more dry California summers for you, Morgan Gardner!" LJ laughed at her friend's scowling face, covered in perspiration. "Sweating like crazy is good for the pores, Morgan. You'll get used to it."

LJ grabbed a couple of towels from the staircase and threw one to Morgan. Both girls wiped their faces and soaked chests following their six-mile run in the forest just beyond their house.

LJ grinned at Morgan. "We've got a few hours before Lindsey and Rich return home from San Antonio. How about us cooking them a gourmet steak meal?"

"Sure, but are there any steaks here?"

"Good point, oh wise one."

They headed into the pantry behind the kitchen to check the contents of the upright freezer. LJ stared in wonder at the vast array of frozen meats. "Nice of the former owners to leave all their food."

"Would people really do that?" Morgan asked. "There must be hundreds of dollars' worth of meat and fish here."

"Dr. Boyega told Lindsey that he and his wife made sure the kitchen was fully stocked," LJ replied. "They weren't kidding."

Closing the freezer, they exited the pantry with four good-size New York steaks and placed them on the kitchen counter to thaw. Then Morgan looked at LJ. "Let's make some breakfast for us and the dogs."

Several hours later, the steaks were marinating, a salad had been made, and baked potatoes were in the oven. They'd also spied a wine cooler stocked with Lindsey and Rich's favorite reds and whites. Morgan had selected one and uncorked it so it could breathe.

She looked over at LJ, sitting with an enormous physics textbook on her lap. The girls were in Morgan's bedroom upstairs, studying for the following day's classes. "Are you sorry you decided to go to A&M?" Morgan asked. She knew how stressed out LJ got with the sciences, especially organic chemistry and physics.

LJ looked up, startled out of her intense concentration. "No, actually. It makes more sense this time around." LJ pressed her lips together and sighed. "I think it's only been a little over a week since Mom and Dad Grayson were here thinking they would bring me back home to Friendswood and start at U of H. But when I reminded them that many of my high school friends were there and how afraid I was of getting back into that way of life, they both told me how proud they were of me." LJ blinked away the wetness in her eyes. "It makes no sense, being proud of an alcoholic teen, does it?"

Morgan stared at her, unblinking. "Actually, LJ, it makes more sense than most of the stuff that's happened recently."

Morgan returned to her physiology text, then looked up when she felt LJ's stare.

"Remember the day Dr. T. testified?" LJ asked.

"Yes."

"Why did you sit in the third row, where we weren't supposed to?"

"Dr. T. had to see me clearly."

"Why?"

"So I could mouth, 'Good Morning, Dr. T.'"

Flabbergasted, LJ's mouth fell open. "What are you talking about?"

Morgan regarded LJ with her coppery-brown gaze. "Dr. T. came to the hospital the morning Joey died. He didn't see me because I was no longer sitting at his bedside because Joey was no longer there; he was dead. I sat in a corner chair that Dr. T. couldn't see.

"He walked over to his bed, reached into his pocket, and pulled out a syringe that he started to fill with air."

LJ said, "Why would he fill the syringe with air?" Then her eyes widened, and she said, "Turner was going to inject air into his veins. To kill Joey." Her voice faded as she repeated, "To kill Joey."

"Yes, that's what Dr. T. planned to do."

Ignoring LJ's frozen, horrified expression, Morgan continued, "When I said, 'Good morning, Dr. T.,' he dropped the syringe, and it rolled toward me. I picked it up and told him he'd better put it away because Joey's monitor alarm was about to go off. Joey was already dead.

"Dr. T. was so scared, he started to shake. So, I stuck the syringe into my purse right before a nurse came in to turn off the alarm. The nurse asked if we were family, and I told her I was Joey's friend from college, but Dr. T. was family. She asked if we'd like to sit with Joey for a while. Dr. T. was crying hard by then, so the nurse left.

"'How did you know?' Dr. T. asked me once he calmed down.

"I told him that Joey had a diary and that I found it in his room the day we found him unconscious and took him to the hospital, that it was all there, about Joey initially being Zoey and looking exactly like his mother and about how determined he was to look nothing like Cassie. I also told him that Joey was afraid of him.

"I told Dr. T. that Joey hated how he was but how happy he was with Lindsey and her dogs on those afternoons. Joey loved Lindsey, I said. He had a framed picture of her with three of her dogs in his room. It was the only photograph there.

"I also said that the only reason Dr. McCall ever got involved with Joey was that *I* told Joey about her, the animal science center, and the Dobermans. I told him Joey begged Lindsey to get him off the testosterone, so she decided to help him.

"The two of us stared at each other as we stood beside Joey's body. Finally, Dr. T. asked if I was going to tell anyone about the syringe, to which I replied, 'Are you going to tell the truth about you and Joey?'"

Finally released from her shocked paralysis, LJ leaped up from the couch. She stomped to where Morgan sat and cried, "You can't let Dr. T. get away with it, Morgan!"

"Get away with what?"

Absorbed in her outrage, LJ missed the flash of intense anguish that transformed Morgan's usually placid countenance into that of a war-weary soldier.

Just then, both dogs raced downstairs. Rich and Lindsey were home.

Morgan studied LJ's still indignant posture and expression. Quietly, she asked, "Do you genuinely think that subjecting Dr. T. to criminal investigation for a crime he thought about committing—" Morgan gazed at LJ intently, "an act that may have been committed out of mercy, would accomplish anything good?"

LJ looked at her friend thoughtfully for a long moment, pondering Morgan's uncanny ability to see past the opacity of emotion to the truth.

AUTHOR'S NOTE

Like all of my novels, *Plausible Liars* is a work of fiction. The background, however, is based on actual events. Addison Meeks is my fictional version of a California kindergarten teacher who celebrated the gender affirmation of a three-year-old from boy to girl with balloons, cake, and a party.

Matt Heathcock is loosely based on gay rights activist James Sears. Sears' numerous publications on teaching sexuality in the classrooms and lesbian and bisexual culture can be found online. *Sexuality and the Curriculum: The Politics and Practices of Sexuality Education* is one of his well-known works.

Judith Butler is considered the leading philosopher for the idea that gender is malleable, a social construction aimed at constraining and bounding female identity. Her book, *Gender Trouble: Feminism and the Subversion of Identity*, published in 1990, became one of the leading handbooks for queer theory. Butler's academic and philosophic credentials made Monique Wittig's books, *Lesbian Body* and *One Is Not Born a Woman*, more accessible. Butler's book is the place to start if you're looking for background specific to these areas.

Kate's interviews with gender-affirming physicians are based on written materials from gender-affirmation websites at medical centers nationwide.

Cal Poly has no animal research center, and no Dr. Adam Turner is on the school faculty.

If you are Christian or Catholic or open to either, Henri Lubac's *The Drama of Atheistic Humanism* is enormously helpful in understanding how we got here, just as Kate writes. And if you have a philosophical bent, Eric Voegelin's *Science, Politics, and Gnosticism* is a good read.

St. Pope John Paul II's *The Sign of Contradiction* and *Theology of the Body* are brilliant, though dense, reads. As Father John told Kate, all the answers to humanity's questions are contained in Genesis. John Paul's two books expound on that statement in ways that startle and even shock.

Not infrequently, characters simply appear in my head. Morgan Gardner did so about a year before I started to write my novel, *Malthus.* She was "different," a teen who was smart but weird. At the suggestion of Susan Toscani, a helpful reader of all of my books, I decided to make Morgan autistic. Autism and autistic spectrum disorder are fascinating conditions that are just beginning to be fully understood. Since diagnoses of autism are increasing each year, there are scores of books on the subject. Based on the many I read, Morgan's qualities are a composite. Dr. Temple Grandin's books stand out as clear and practical, with an understanding of the condition that only an autistic individual could possess. Morgan's psychic and empathic qualities are unrelated to her autism, as they are uniquely hers.

When I began this book, I thought I needed to understand why we decide to do this to ourselves. So, I read several books written by men who had decided they were women. Unless you're interested in the details of the hormonal and surgical procedures, I don't recommend these stories, as the authors never get into the real reasons why they feel so disconnected from their bodies, probably because they don't know. I think Morgan nailed it for young girls who are considering female-to-male transition.

Eleanor and Marguerite Philbin were sisters who immensely enjoyed their notoriety as Houston publishers and businesswomen in the Lindsey McCall medical mystery series.

Michele and John Smith, thank you for permission to use your names and for helping us find our San Antonio refuge.

Wayne Pederson, thank you for scanning the courtroom chapters to point out errors in my language.

Kudos to my early readers: Susan Toscani, Margaret Caddy, Lori Ann Finn, and my husband, John. After seven novels, I have found partners in this intricate work of getting a story into your hands.

One that is plausible—pun intended.

One that will stimulate.

One that will challenge while providing a darn good read.

Kevin Miller, thank you for your flexibility in fitting me into your editing schedule. And for your challenging editorial critique.

It's a wrap. I hope you have enjoyed the book.

Reader Discussion Guide

1. Introduction

Plausible Liars is a gripping medical mystery that follows Dr. Lindsey McCall as she confronts a dangerous combination of scientific ambition, military secrecy, and powerful people willing to manipulate the truth. The novel blends ethical dilemmas, character-driven suspense, and high-stakes action, perfect for book club exploration and deep conversation.

2. Book Overview

Dr. Lindsey McCall is drawn into a crisis when a miscalculated medical decision places her reputation and safety at risk. While she tries to uncover what truly happened, she becomes entangled in a hidden project involving government agencies, suppressed research, and a dangerous cover-up.

As lies stack upon lies, Lindsey must rely on her instincts, her allies, and her commitment to truth, even when doing so pulls her deeper into a web of betrayal. The story challenges the boundaries between ethics and ambition, trust and deception, science and power.

3. Major Themes

• Medical Ethics & Responsibility
The novel asks what happens when scientific advancement conflicts with integrity and transparency.
• Power, Secrecy & Manipulation
Government, military, and corporate interests collide, raising questions about accountability.
• Trust vs. Betrayal
Characters must choose who to believe and how much trust to give.

• **Courage Under Pressure**
Lindsey's journey highlights personal strength when faced with overwhelming odds.
• **Human Cost of Scientific Innovation**
The story shows how discoveries that promise breakthroughs can also cause devastation when misused.

4. Character Spotlights

Dr. Lindsey McCall
Brilliant, principled, and determined, a scientist forced into a role she never asked for.

Rich
Her steady anchor who provides moral support and insight.

Lucinda and Cassie
Emotionally vulnerable characters whose stories raise questions about family, trauma, and hidden motives.

Government/Military Figures
Powerful forces operating in secrecy, shaping events from the shadows.

5. Chapter-by-Chapter Talking Points

Chapter 1: Joey's Beginning
Mini Summary:
Joey starts writing in a diary he found, hoping it will help him explain his story. He accidentally reveals his intelligence in class, surprising himself and his teacher.

He introduces his background: unknown father, small-town roots, and a dramatic mother. Early hints show he struggles with identity and wants to distance himself from his mother's influence.

Discussion Questions:
- What does this chapter reveal about Joey's personality or insecurities?
- How does the classroom moment set the tone for his story?

Emotional Observations:
- Early tension around identity and self-worth.

Key Elements:
- Introduction of Joey
- Background foundation
- Early foreshadowing of internal conflict

Chapter 2: LJ, Morgan, and the New Presence

Mini Summary:

The chapter introduces LJ and her best friend, Morgan, studying together with their two very different dogs, Max and Gus. Their friendship began in college registration lines, bonding instantly over honesty and shared vulnerabilities. As they study, Morgan becomes distracted by thoughts of Joey Carmichael, a new transfer student whose presence feels dark and unsettling to her. The chapter reveals the closeness of the girls' friendship and introduces a sense of growing tension surrounding Joey.

Discussion Questions:
• What does this chapter reveal about LJ and Morgan's personalities and friendship dynamic?
• Why might Morgan be so sensitive to the "darkness" she sees around Joey?
• How do the dogs help show the emotional atmosphere in the room?

Emotional Observations:
• Strong friendship bond between LJ and Morgan.
• Morgan shows anxiety, intuition, and heightened sensitivity.
• Subtle tension is introduced through her unease about Joey.

Key Elements:
• Introduction of LJ and Morgan's friendship
• Contrast between characters and their emotional styles
• First foreshadowing of Joey's darker presence

Chapter 3: New Connections

Mini Summary:
Joey returns to his diary after three weeks, sharing both good and bad developments. Ms. O'Brien surprises him by inviting him to a GLSEN meeting, giving him a chance to meet more students like himself. Joey also invites Morgan, a quiet and observant classmate who immediately recognizes he is transgender. Through Morgan, Joey learns about Dr. Lindsey McCall and her Dobermans, opening the door to a new opportunity. The chapter highlights Joey's growing sense of belonging and exploration of identity.

Discussion Questions:
- What does Joey's reaction to the GLSEN invitation reveal about his need for community?
- How does Morgan's blunt honesty affect Joey?
- What does this chapter suggest about Joey's search for identity and acceptance?

Emotional Observations:
- Rising hope and curiosity as Joey begins finding people who understand him.
- Vulnerability around his identity and being "seen" for the first time.

Key Elements:
- Introduction of Morgan
- First connection to Dr. Lindsey McCall
- Identity recognition and self-exploration
- Hint of new support systems

Chapter 4: Lindsey, Joey, and New Tensions

Mini Summary:

Joey arrives at Lindsey's lab, hoping to walk the Dobermans, enthusiastically taking on more than he can handle. Lindsey observes his weight and begins questioning his hormone therapy and overall health. Their routine is interrupted by the arrival of Jodi Tamarack and a new postdoc, Dr. Christine Phillips. Joey struggles with the dogs as he leaves, drawing curious attention from Jodi. The chapter closes with Lindsey explaining her background and research role.

Discussion Questions:
- What does this chapter reveal about Lindsey's concerns regarding Joey?
- How do the interactions between Joey, Jodi, and Christine set up future dynamics?
- What does Joey's excitement about the dogs show about his emotional needs?

Emotional Observations:
- Subtle tension around Joey's physical and emotional vulnerability.
- Lindsey's protective instincts and analytical worries emerge strongly.

Key Elements:
- Introduction of Christine Phillips
- Hints about Joey's medical/hormonal issues
- Lindsey's background and shift from human to animal research
- Early foreshadowing of Joey's deeper struggles

Chapter 5: Lindsey & Joey's Connection

Mini Summary:

Lindsey reflects on how Joey first entered her life and how quickly she bonded with him through their shared love of the dogs in her lab. Joey arrives late but glowing with happiness, showing rare signs of joy and trust. Lindsey gives him his medication, and his emotional reaction reveals how important she is. Through memories and advice from her friend Julie, Lindsey considers Joey's struggles with identity and what it means to support him. The chapter ends as Lindsey returns home to her family and pets.

Discussion Questions:
- What does this chapter reveal about Lindsey's compassion and instincts as a caregiver?
- How does Joey's behavior show his emotional dependence on Lindsey?
- What does the conversation with Julie reveal about Lindsey's concerns?

Emotional Observations:
- Lindsey feels protective, conflicted, and deeply connected to Joey.
- Joey shows vulnerability, relief, and attachment, especially when receiving help.
- Moments with her family contrast the heaviness of Lindsey's earlier worries.

Key Elements:
- Lindsey and Joey's growing bond
- Insights into Joey's identity struggles
- Supportive guidance from Julie
- Contrast between Lindsey's professional worries and home life warmth

Chapter 6: Joey's New Role & Morgan's Questioning

Mini Summary:
Joey becomes president of the GLSEN chapter, a role that surprises and excites him. After the meeting, Morgan invites him to dinner and reassures him it's not a date, just friendship. Their conversation turns deep when Morgan asks Joey if he's happy, a question that brings him to tears. Morgan then gently probes whether Joey's upcoming top surgery is really his choice, revealing concern for him. Joey

ends by sharing the secret that he has stopped testosterone and started estrogen.

Discussion Questions:
• What does Joey's reaction to becoming president reveal about his self-esteem?
• Why does Morgan's question "Are you happy?" affect Joey so strongly?
• What do you think motivates Morgan's concern about whether Joey's decisions are truly his own?

Emotional Observations:
• Joey experiences pride, confusion, vulnerability, and relief all in one chapter.
• Morgan shows emotional intelligence and a protective attitude toward Joey.
• Joey's tears indicate inner conflict and uncertainty about his identity and choices.

Key Elements:
• Joey's first leadership role
• Morgan as a grounding, truth-seeking figure
• Early questioning of Joey's transition decisions
• A deepening friendship based on honesty

Chapter 7: Dinner, Tension & a Dark Revelation

Mini Summary:

Lindsey, Rich, LJ, and Morgan share a warm family-style evening overlooking the ocean, enjoying food, movies, and lighthearted conversation. The relaxed atmosphere shifts when Morgan brings up Joey Carmichael, revealing his transition history and her concerns about his upcoming "top surgery." Lindsey learns that Joey may be under pressure from an unnamed older man who has been funding his transition. Morgan's emotional reaction and insights raise alarms, hinting at danger surrounding Joey. The chapter ends with a sense of foreboding as both Lindsey and Rich realize something is deeply wrong.

Discussion Questions:
- How does the peaceful family setting contrast with the disturbing revelations about Joey?
- What does Morgan's insight reveal about her character and her relationship with Joey?
- Why does the mention of an unnamed man funding Joey's transition raise red flags for Lindsey and Rich?

Emotional Observations:
- The chapter moves from warmth and comfort to tension and unease.
- Morgan shows rare vulnerability, highlighting her deep concern for Joey.
- Lindsey and Rich experience growing fear and protective instincts as the truth unfolds.

Key Elements:
- Contrast between comfort (home, family, dinner) and hidden danger
- Introduction of Joey's surgical crisis
- Foreshadowing of a threatening, possibly abusive figure
- Morgan's empathic and psychic insight

Chapter 8: Lindsey's Dilemma

Mini Summary:
Lindsey discusses Joey's situation with her husband, Rich, revealing her decision to help wean him from testosterone

and give a low-dose estrogen prescription. They worry about potential risks and powerful external influences affecting Joey. Rich advises Lindsey to act carefully but confidently, and they consider seeking guidance from Father John. The chapter highlights Lindsey's ethical struggle and the looming tension around Joey's care.

Discussion Questions:
• What does this chapter reveal about Lindsey's values and sense of responsibility?
• How do Rich and Lindsey complement each other in making difficult decisions?

Emotional Observations:
• Tension about the potential consequences of Lindsey's actions.
• A mix of care, worry, and moral responsibility.

Key Elements:
• Ethical dilemma regarding Joey's treatment
• Introduction of powerful external influences
• Father John as a trusted advisor

Chapter 9: Father John's Guidance

Mini Summary:

Lindsey seeks guidance from Father John regarding Joey's situation and the mysterious benefactor supporting him. Father John draws on past experiences with at-risk youth to advise her about the stakes and potential dangers. They discuss Joey's medical treatment, the university environment, and influential faculty. The conversation reinforces the complexity and risk involved, while highlighting Lindsey's commitment to helping Joey.

Discussion Questions:
- How does Father John's perspective influence Lindsey's decisions?
- What risks and responsibilities does Lindsey face in intervening for Joey?

Emotional Observations:
- Lindsey feels uncertainty and pressure but is motivated to act.
- Father John provides calm reassurance and moral perspective.

Key Elements:
- Joey's benefactor and unknown influences
- Ethical and emotional stakes for Lindsey
- Insight into institutional and social pressures

Chapter 10: Seeking Solutions

Mini Summary:

Lindsey continues reflecting on her responsibilities while reading Kate Townsend's investigative reporting on transgender issues. She considers collaborating with Kate to gain insight and guidance on Joey's situation. Meanwhile, Rich prepares for challenges in his upcoming trial, leaving Lindsey to focus on solutions. The chapter emphasizes problem-solving, support networks, and the personal stakes involved.

Discussion Questions:
- How does Lindsey balance personal ethics with professional constraints?
- How do external events (Kate's work, Rich's cases) influence Lindsey's actions?

Emotional Observations:
• Lindsey experiences relief, hope, and cautious optimism.
• Awareness of the stakes motivates her to act thoughtfully.

Key Elements:
• Collaboration with Kate Townsend as a resource
• Continued ethical considerations
• Exploration of external influences on decision-making

Chapter 11: The Trial Revelation

Mini Summary:
Blake Cameron's father confronts the legal team after learning they plan to withdraw from Blake's case. Evidence uncovered by Toni Martinez and Blake's former girlfriend reveals that Blake participated in a fraternity sexual assault dare under peer pressure. Overwhelmed by guilt, Blake confesses the truth, setting the stage for legal action against the responsible parties. The chapter highlights the complexities of privilege, accountability, and the consequences of choices.

Discussion Questions:
• How does this chapter explore themes of privilege and power?
• What motivates Blake's confession, and what does it reveal about character?

Emotional Observations:
• Tension and fear dominate the courtroom and personal dynamics.
• Shame and guilt are central to Blake's emotional state.

Key Elements:
- Confrontation and confession
- Evidence and investigative work
- Introduction of legal consequences

Chapter 12: Joey's Fear

Mini Summary:
Joey faces anxiety about an upcoming gender-affirming surgery and struggles with conflicting feelings about his body. He reflects on past experiences with hormone treatment and worries about irreversible changes. The chapter captures the intense fear, uncertainty, and anticipation associated with major life decisions, particularly regarding identity and body autonomy.

Discussion Questions:
- What does Joey's fear reveal about the challenges of transitioning?
- How does the chapter explore personal identity versus societal expectations?

Emotional Observations:
- Anxiety and fear dominate Joey's thoughts.
- Conflicted emotions about body and identity emerge strongly.

Key Elements:
- Inner conflict and self-reflection
- Pre-surgery apprehension
- Exploration of gender identity

Chapter 13: The Ideological Battle

Mini Summary:

Lindsey reads Kate's investigative series on the effects of radical gender ideology and puberty blockers on children. The articles connect religion, philosophy, and science, illustrating the perceived moral and ethical consequences of social engineering. Lindsey reflects on her own past when she prioritized science over faith, recognizing the potential societal dangers Kate highlights. The chapter blends personal reflection with broader ideological critique.

Discussion Questions:

- How does this chapter examine the tension between faith, science, and ethics?
- What role does personal experience play in understanding societal issues?

Emotional Observations:

- Lindsey experiences awe, shock, and moral contemplation.
- A sense of urgency and concern about societal direction is present.

Key Elements:

- Investigation into gender ideology and ethics
- Integration of religious and philosophical perspectives
- Personal reflection as a lens for broader social critique

Chapter 14: The Crisis Response

Mini Summary:

Joey is found unconscious on campus, prompting immediate intervention by friends and authorities.

Cody McManus, the DA, coordinates with Rich and Morgan to ensure Joey receives medical attention.
The chapter emphasizes rapid response, teamwork, and the protective instincts of those close to Joey. It sets a suspenseful tone and underscores ongoing threats to his safety.

Discussion Questions:
• How do the characters' responses reflect loyalty and responsibility?
• What does this event reveal about the dangers Joey faces?

Emotional Observations:
• Anxiety and urgency dominate the scene.
• Care and protective instincts highlight relational bonds.

Key Elements:
• Emergency intervention
• Teamwork and authority figures
• Suspense and immediate danger

Chapter 15: The Sierra Madre Dorm

Main Summary:
Rich visits Joey's dorm at Cal Poly and is struck by the unexpected luxury of the accommodations for a student from a modest background. The room is thoughtfully decorated, giving off a more feminine and personal touch, reminiscent of LJ and Morgan's own rooms. Morgan discovers Joey's diary, which mentions "Dr. T." coming to take Joey for the "top job," adding a layer of mystery. Rich and LJ notice the prominence of a photo of Lindsey with her Dobermans, which evokes subtle emotional reactions. Detectives and Cody are present, securing the scene and

discussing the diary's significance, setting the stage for deeper investigation.

Discussion Questions:
- Why do you think Joey's dorm is so extravagant compared to his background?
- How does the diary act as a plot device to reveal Dr. T.?
- What role do Morgan's psychic abilities play in shaping the investigation?

Emotional Observations:
- Rich experiences surprise and curiosity about Joey's lifestyle.
- LJ shows reflective sadness upon seeing the photo of Lindscy and the dogs.
- The group feels tension and anticipation in confronting the mysterious Dr. T.

Key Elements:
- Luxury dorm vs. modest background.
- Discovery of Joey's diary.
- Introduction of Dr. T.
- Interplay of intuition (Morgan) and investigation.

Chapter 16: Medical Complications

Main Summary:

Joey is in a coma due to a blood clot, not drugs, complicating the situation for his caregivers. Dr. Amanda Dyson outlines the treatment with Tenecteplase and explains the legal constraints due to Joey's status as a minor. Rich and the team learn that Dr. T. holds medical power of attorney, adding urgency to their actions. Cody works to secure emergency judicial consent, while Morgan's presence underscores the ongoing tension and concern for Joey's health.

Discussion Questions:
- How do legal and medical constraints affect emergency care for minors?
- What are the ethical implications of hormone therapy for teens?
- How does the collaboration between medical staff and investigators advance the plot?

Emotional Observations:
- Rich's frustration at being unable to act immediately.
- Morgan's quiet vigilance and concern.
- Anxiety and tension surrounding Joey's medical condition.

Key Elements:
- Blood clot and hormone therapy complications.
- Tenecteplase treatment.
- Legal and ethical considerations.
- Coordination between law enforcement and healthcare professionals.

Chapter 17: Identifying Dr. T.

Main Summary:

Morgan identifies Dr. T. as Dr. Adam Turner, a Cal Poly academic with a complex background and strong influence over Joey. Rich and the team examine Turner's credentials, noting his achievements in science, technology, feminist theory, and engineering. Plans are made to question him, highlighting the growing tension and uncertainty about his role and motives in Joey's life.

Discussion Questions:
- How does Dr. Turner's identity and pronoun use affect the narrative?
- What does Morgan's psychic insight reveal that conventional investigation cannot?
- Why might Dr. Turner be so protective or secretive about Joey?

Emotional Observations:
- Surprise and curiosity from Rich about Dr. Turner.
- Anticipation and tension as they prepare for the interrogation.
- Subtle admiration for Morgan's extraordinary abilities.

Key Elements:
- Dr. Turner's credentials and identity.
- Ambiguity of motives and gender presentation.
- Psychic insight versus investigative discovery.

Chapter 18: Personal and Professional Intersections

Main Summary:

Lindsey, Steve, and Kate discuss how personal and professional lives intersect during crises. Joey's medical situation and the risks associated with hormone therapy are considered, while family dynamics and potential relocation to Texas are also explored. The chapter balances humor, anxiety, and decision-making as characters navigate overlapping responsibilities and ambitions.

Discussion Questions:
- How do personal and professional lives collide in moments of crisis?
- What does this chapter reveal about loyalty, friendship, and decision-making?
- How do the characters' career ambitions influence family dynamics?

Emotional Observations:
- Humor as a coping mechanism during tense discussions.
- Mixed feelings about leaving familiar surroundings.
- Concern for Joey's well-being alongside excitement for future opportunities.

Key Elements:
- Career and family obligations intersect.
- Medical crisis and hormone therapy considerations.
- Decisions about relocation and future planning.

Chapter 19: Confrontation with Dr. Turner

Main Summary:

Dr. Turner is interrogated by law enforcement regarding Joey's care, yet remains evasive and cryptic. Rich notices Turner's ambiguous statements, suggesting that while he may be protective, his motives are unclear. The tension between the investigators and Turner builds suspense and highlights ethical and emotional complexity.

Discussion Questions:
- What does Dr. Turner's evasiveness suggest about his character and intentions?
- How do Rich and the investigators navigate authority and ethics in this scenario?

- What narrative purpose does this confrontation serve in building suspense?

Emotional Observations:
- Tension and unease during the interrogation.
- Frustration and curiosity from Rich about Turner's motives.
- Subtle admiration for law enforcement's skill in questioning.

Key Elements:
- Interrogation of Dr. Turner.
- Ambiguity of motives and ethical boundaries.
- Suspense and narrative tension.

Chapter 20: Political Assignments and Ethical Reflections

Main Summary:
Steve reflects on his assignment in China, navigating political challenges and cultural complexities. Kate discusses her investigative work, especially cases affecting children and transgender issues. Lindsey observes coincidences that highlight the influence of human intervention and ethical responsibility.

Discussion Questions:
- How do personal and professional responsibilities intersect in this chapter?
- What ethical dilemmas does Kate face as a journalist?
- How does Steve's assignment reflect broader systemic challenges?

Emotional Observations:
- Tension and relief alternate as characters reflect on challenges.
- Humor and camaraderie lighten otherwise serious discussions.
- Pride in personal and professional growth is evident.

Key Elements:
- Steve's China assignment and challenges.
- Kate's investigative reporting and ethical considerations.
- Human connection influencing outcomes.

Chapter 21: Safeguarding Zoey

Main Summary:
Dr. Turner focuses on protecting Zoey from a potentially harmful family environment. His commitment to tutoring and caring for her demonstrates both compassion and personal investment.

Discussion Questions:
- How does Dr. Turner's past influence his actions toward Zoey?
- What does this chapter suggest about surrogate parenting and responsibility?
- How does the author convey the vulnerability of children in complex family dynamics?

Emotional Observations:
- Compassion and protectiveness dominate the chapter.
- A sense of foreboding mixed with hope for Zoey's future.
- Empathy and frustration emerge through Turner's reflections.

Key Elements:
• Dr. Turner's motivations and past trauma.
• Zoey's vulnerability and potential.
• Family dysfunction and its impact.

Chapter 22: Hospital Crisis

Main Summary:
Joey is hospitalized after a medical procedure complication. Rich and the girls grapple with uncertainty about his condition, highlighting the tension and fragility of life.

Discussion Questions:
• How do different characters process fear and uncertainty?
• What role does family and community support play in crises?
• How are hospital and emergency scenarios emotionally portrayed?

Emotional Observations:
• Tension, fear, and helplessness dominate.
• Emotional strain is amplified by uncertainty over Joey's outcome.
• Compassion and care manifest in small gestures.

Key Elements:
• Joey's critical medical situation.
• Family responses to crisis.
• Communication challenges with medical staff.

Chapter 23: Spiritual Reflections

Main Summary:
Kate, Steve, and Lindsey spend a reflective day together,

exploring spirituality and Kate's journey toward Catholicism. Themes of faith, redemption, and moral responsibility emerge.

Discussion Questions:
- How does Kate reconcile past actions with her spiritual awakening?
- What role does friendship play in supporting personal growth?
- How does faith intersect with morality in this chapter?

Emotional Observations:
- Reflection, gratitude, and humility dominate.
- Emotional vulnerability arises in Kate's admission of past ignorance.
- Awe and admiration for faith practices provide contemplative moments.

Key Elements:
- Exploration of Catholic faith and morality.
- Friendship and mentorship.
- Kate's spiritual awakening.

Chapter 24: Family Preparations

Main Summary:
Rich cares for LJ and Morgan while preparing to meet Joey's mother. This chapter emphasizes the importance of planning, caregiving, and confronting difficult family dynamics.

Discussion Questions:
- How does Rich's role emphasize responsibility and compassion?

- What strategies are effective in gathering sensitive information?
- How are family dynamics portrayed in this chapter?

Emotional Observations:
- Tenderness and patience highlight Rich's character.
- Subtle tension in navigating responsibilities and potential danger.
- Comfort and normalcy through family routines.

Key Elements:
- Rich's caregiving and planning.
- Preparation for meeting Joey's mother.
- Family and community responsibility.

Chapter 25: Encounter with Cassie

Main Summary:
Rich and detectives meet Joey's mother, Cassie, confronting her denial and confusion. The chapter highlights parental responsibility and crisis management.

Discussion Questions:
- How do characters manage denial and confusion?
- What ethical considerations arise when communicating medical information?
- How does the setting enhance narrative tension?

Emotional Observations:
- Frustration and disbelief from caregivers and detectives.
- Sympathy for Cassie's struggle as a parent.
- Hope and perseverance in crisis communication.

Key Elements:
- Cassie Carmichael encounter.
- Explaining Joey's medical condition.
- Ethical and emotional challenges.

Chapter 26: Trauma and Caregiving

Main Summary:
Dr. Turner reflects on Joey's care and his own past trauma, highlighting the complexity of protecting children while managing personal and professional limits. Nancy provides emotional support.

Discussion Questions:
- How do past traumas influence Turner's decisions?
- How does professional responsibility intersect with emotional involvement?
- What does Nancy's role reveal about support systems in caregiving?

Emotional Observations:
- Anxiety and despair dominate.
- Grief and residual trauma emerge in Turner's reflections.
- Compassion and patience from Nancy provide grounding.

Key Elements:
- Turner's trauma and caregiving challenges.
- Medical ethics and protection of children.
- Emotional support through Nancy.

Chapter 27: Small Joys and Reflection

Main Summary:

Kate reconnects with small pleasures and shared moments with Steve. The chapter explores intimacy, reflection, and finding joy in everyday life.

Discussion Questions:

• How do small pleasures contribute to emotional recovery?
• What does the chapter reveal about balancing personal and professional life?
• How are intimacy and connection portrayed?

Emotional Observations:

• Joy, nostalgia, and intimacy dominate.
• Lightheartedness contrasts with heavier themes.
• Humor reinforces character connection.

Key Elements:

• Kate's reflections and joy.
• Couple dynamics.
• Importance of everyday pleasures.

Chapter 28: Stress and Support

Main Summary:

Dr. Turner faces stress from Cassie's interference and the complexities of Joey's care. Nancy provides emotional grounding while Turner reflects on his traumatic childhood.

Discussion Questions:

• How does stress affect decision-making?
• How do past traumas shape present challenges?
• What role does support from loved ones play?

Emotional Observations:
- Anxiety, stress, and frustration are prevalent.
- Emotional grounding through Nancy highlights stability.
- Reflection on past trauma creates empathy.

Key Elements:
- Turner's stress and trauma management.
- Nancy's stabilizing influence.
- Ethical complexity of caregiving.

Chapter 29: Career Opportunities vs Responsibility

Main Summary:
Lindsey receives a major career opportunity while balancing concern for Joey's well-being. The chapter explores ambition, moral responsibility, and emotional tension.

Discussion Questions:
- How do professional opportunities intersect with moral obligations?
- How does the author portray ambition alongside responsibility?
- What challenges arise when balancing personal and professional priorities?

Emotional Observations:
- Excitement and anticipation from Lindsey.
- Anxiety and guilt about Joey's situation.
- Hope and optimism are intertwined with responsibility.

Key Elements:
- Lindsey's career advancement.

• Balancing ambition with obligations.
• Joey's ongoing condition is a moral backdrop.

Chapter 30: Managing Life Transitions

Main Summary:
Kate balances family responsibilities, house hunting, and work commitments. The chapter emphasizes planning, multitasking, and adaptation to life changes.

Discussion Questions:
• How are work and family balance challenges portrayed?
• What strategies do characters use to manage multiple priorities?
• How does setting reflect life transitions?

Emotional Observations:
• Fatigue and stress from juggling responsibilities.
• Determination and problem-solving mindset.
• Sense of progress and adaptation.

Key Elements:
• Kate's family and work responsibilities.
• House hunting and relocation.
• Managing personal and professional life.

Chapter 31: Texas Moves and Spiritual Renewal

Main Summary:
Kate and her family finalize plans for their new Texas home while reflecting on the recent spiritual ceremonies that have brought them into the Catholic Church. They navigate house selection, close on a property, and experience

the emotional depth of baptism and confession. Father John and Father Greg play central roles in guiding the family through these sacred rituals.

Discussion Questions:
• How does the move to Texas symbolize both personal and spiritual transition?
• What role do Father John and Father Greg play in Kate and her family's growth?
• How do material concerns, like choosing a home, intersect with spiritual development?

Emotional Observations:
• Excitement and relief at securing the perfect home.
• Awe and reverence during spiritual ceremonies.
• Gratitude for guidance and mentorship from clergy.

Key Elements:
• Selection and excitement about 640 Rattler Pass.
• Baptism of the boys and confessions of Kate and Steve.
• Entry into the Catholic Church and spiritual affirmation.

Chapter 32: Running, Reflection, and Family Decisions

Main Summary:
Rich reflects on his physical recovery and the joys of returning to Texas. During a family run, he and the children discuss LJ's decision to remain in Texas to finish her education with Lindsey, navigating emotions around change and responsibility.

Discussion Questions:
- How does physical activity serve as a metaphor for resilience and healing?
- What are the implications of LJ's choice to remain with Lindsey and Morgan?
- How does the chapter explore parental guidance and adolescent autonomy?

Emotional Observations:
- Pride and joy in family cohesion and personal health.
- Mixed emotions as LJ asserts independence.
- Warmth and comfort from supportive family dynamics.

Key Elements:
- Rich's physical recovery and symbolic run.
- LJ's educational decision-making.
- Emotional support and guidance from Rich and Lindsey.

Chapter 33: Professional Progress and Hidden Concerns

Main Summary:
Lindsey's career opportunities at A&M unfold, with visits from influential faculty like Sam Epstein and Dr. Boyega. The family settles into the new house, enjoying comfort and security, but underlying concerns about professional and legal challenges remain.

Discussion Questions:
- How does Lindsey's career advancement intersect with her family responsibilities?
- What does the chapter reveal about social and professional networks in academia?

• How does the author build tension through subtle hints
of pending challenges?

Emotional Observations:
• Excitement and satisfaction at new professional
opportunities.
• Comfort and contentment in the family home.
• Lingering anxiety about legal complications.

Key Elements:
• Lindsey's meetings with A&M faculty and house
inspection.
• Family settling into their new home.
• Foreshadowing of upcoming legal challenges.

Chapter 34: Federal Arrest and Family Support

Main Summary:
FBI agents arrive to arrest Lindsey for conspiracy related to
Joey's death and alleged crimes against the transgender
community. Rich acts decisively to protect his family and
manage the situation. Morgan and LJ cope with fear and
guilt, while Rich reassures them and begins preparing for
legal defense.

Discussion Questions:
• How does Rich's authority and experience shape the
family's response to crisis?
• What ethical and emotional dilemmas arise during
Lindsey's arrest?
• How are fear, guilt, and reassurance portrayed in high-
stress situations?

Emotional Observations:
- Panic and fear as the FBI executes the arrest.
- Compassion and calm from Rich mitigating family trauma.
- Tension mixed with pride in resilience and courage.

Key Elements:
- FBI arrest of Lindsey McCall.
- Rich's protective and decisive actions.
- Emotional processing and reassurance for Morgan and LJ.

Chapter 35: Coordinated Legal Response and Escalating Stakes

Main Summary:

Rich alerts Kate to delay leaving the plane to avoid immediate arrest. He coordinates the safety of Steve, Lucinda, and the children while preparing for Lindsey and Kate's federal court case. The chapter emphasizes strategic planning, legal preparation, and the looming challenges of a high-stakes trial.

Discussion Questions:
- How do strategy and timing play crucial roles in managing legal crises?
- What does this chapter reveal about teamwork and trust in high-pressure situations?
- How does the author portray the scale and complexity of federal legal proceedings?

Emotional Observations:
- Anxiety and tension during airport maneuvering.
- Confidence and determination in Rich's leadership.

• Relief and gratitude as family members are kept safe.

Key Elements:
• Kate's delay to avoid arrest and coordination with Rich.
• Protection of Steve, Lucinda, and the children.
• Preparation for the federal court case and trial logistics.

Chapter 36: A Surprise Visit and Fatherly Guidance

Main Summary:
Toni, Steve, Zach, and Rich arrive at Steve's house. Introductions take place while Steve reconnects with his sons, JH and Nicholas. Father John unexpectedly visits, summoned by Lindsey, to check on Rich, who has been under extreme stress. Steve sets up a temporary office, and Father John begins providing spiritual support, guiding Rich toward reflection and healing.

Discussion Questions:
• How does the reunion with Steve's sons affect his sense of purpose?
• What role does Father John play in stabilizing Rich's emotional state?
• How does this chapter explore the intersection of professional and personal responsibilities?

Emotional Observations:
• Relief and joy in Steve's reunion with his children.
• Deep emotional vulnerability from Rich, leading to catharsis.
• The calm and grounding influence of Father John.

Key Elements:
• Arrival at Steve's house and family interactions.
• Father John's spiritual intervention.
• Establishing temporary operations for the team.

Chapter 37: Rich's Confession and Reflection

Main Summary:
Father John recalls his long relationship with Rich, from Rich's initial skepticism to the trauma of losing his first wife and a near-fatal incident in Lebanon. Rich confronts suppressed grief and guilt, confessing past actions and emotions. Father John reminds him of mercy, grounding, and the importance of rest.

Discussion Questions:
• How do Rich's past traumas continue to influence his current emotional responses?
• In what ways does Father John provide both spiritual and practical guidance?
• How do reflection and confession contribute to resilience?

Emotional Observations:
• Grief, guilt, and sorrow dominate Rich's inner state.
• Compassion and understanding from Father John create a safe space.
• Catharsis and emotional relief are achieved through confession.

Key Elements:
• Rich's emotional and spiritual confrontation.
• Father John's role as mentor and confidant.
• Healing through acknowledgment of trauma.

Chapter 38: Dr. Turner Served

Main Summary:
Dr. Adam Turner receives federal legal documents regarding Townsend and McCall, revealing charges of conspiracy to commit a federal hate crime. Nancy and Adam review the case and the involvement of influential figures, connecting it to Joey's situation. The chapter explores confusion, frustration, and the sudden escalation of legal consequences.

Discussion Questions:
- How does receiving the federal documents change Dr. Turner's perception of the case?
- What is the significance of connecting the legal case to Joey's experience?
- How are Nancy and Adam's dynamics used to explore emotional processing under stress?

Emotional Observations:
- Shock, disbelief, and anxiety dominate Adam's reactions.
- Nancy balances humor and support to manage tension.
- A sense of urgency and confusion permeates the scene.

Key Elements:
- Federal indictment of Townsend and McCall.
- Connection to Joey's case and implications for the involved parties.
- Emotional and legal tension.

Chapter 39: Preparing for Legal Battle

Main Summary:
Kate and Steve's home becomes a strategic command

center for planning Lindsey and Kate's defense. Bail is secured, and Zach, Rich, and Father John coordinate strategies for confronting an overwhelming prosecution. The team prepares for a high-stakes legal fight, exploring tactics, potential witnesses, and moral support.

Discussion Questions:
- How do the characters organize themselves to face a formidable legal challenge?
- What is the role of collaboration and mentorship in preparing for high-stakes situations?
- How does the chapter depict the tension between legal reality and personal values?

Emotional Observations:
- Anxiety and fear contrasted with determination and teamwork.
- Encouragement and humor provide moments of relief.
- Gratitude and trust develop between team members.

Key Elements:
- Setting up a strategic legal command center.
- Bail and initial legal positioning.
- Coordination of resources, witnesses, and defense strategies.

Chapter 40: Mock Trials and Strategy Sessions

Main Summary:
The team begins rigorous preparation with whiteboards, flipcharts, and role-playing to anticipate prosecution tactics. Toni challenges Kate with potential questions from the opposition. Lucinda assists with logistical and emotional

support, while Father John offers guidance. The chapter demonstrates meticulous preparation and highlights character dynamics.

Discussion Questions:
- How do mock trials and strategy sessions prepare characters for the real courtroom challenges?
- What role do mentorship and team support play in building confidence?
- How do characters balance emotional stress with practical preparation?

Emotional Observations:
- Stress and tension as Kate and team anticipate attacks.
- Empowerment and resilience through preparation.
- Gratitude and admiration for support from mentors and colleagues.

Key Elements:
- Mock trial preparations with Toni and Kate.
- Strategy sessions led by Zach and Rich.
- Emotional and practical support from Father John and Lucinda.

Chapter 41: Gathering and Prayer

Main Summary:

Father John addresses the group, reflecting on their faith and the idea of being "marked by God." Lindsey and others discuss Joey's case, the challenges of hormone therapy, and the moral implications. Zach leads a group prayer for guidance and protection. The chapter ends with Rich arranging to pick up LJ and Morgan from the airport.

Discussion Questions:
- How does Father John's spiritual guidance influence the group's morale?
- What role does faith play in interpreting difficult situations, like Joey's case?
- How does the group's unity shape their response to impending challenges?

Emotional Observations:
- Tension and apprehension about the trial.
- Comfort and hope inspired by prayer and reflection.
- Anticipation for reunion with LJ and Morgan.

Key Elements:
- Spiritual reflection and moral framing.
- Emotional support within the group.
- Planning and preparation for the next steps.

Chapter 42: Jury Selection

Main Summary:
Rich and Zach navigate jury selection at the San Francisco federal courthouse. They encounter the complexities of voir dire, biases, and jury shuffling. The chapter emphasizes strategic considerations for selecting jurors sympathetic to either the defense or prosecution.

Discussion Questions:
- How do biases and personal beliefs of jurors impact a trial's outcome?
- Why is jury selection considered a critical part of legal strategy?
- How do Zach and Rich manage challenges in the jury selection process?

Emotional Observations:
• Anxiety about unpredictable juror reactions.
• Frustration with complex procedural rules.
• Relief when key jurors are seated successfully.

Key Elements:
• Voir dire process.
• Jury biases and profiling.
• Defense and prosecution strategies.

Chapter 43: Opening Statements

Main Summary:

Martinez presents the prosecution's opening statement, framing Kate and Lindsey's actions as a premeditated hate crime. The defense waives its opening statement. The chapter highlights courtroom tension and the high stakes of the trial.

Discussion Questions:
• How does the prosecution frame the defendants' actions as a hate crime?
• What effect does waiving the opening statement have on the defense's strategy?
• How does the chapter establish tension for the reader?

Emotional Observations:
• Fear and anxiety for Kate and Lindsey.
• Anticipation of courtroom drama.
• Awareness of the moral and societal stakes involved.

Key Elements:
- Framing of the case by the prosecution.
- Defense's strategic choice.
- Courtroom tension and anticipation.

Chapter 44: Expert Witness – Dr. Sullivan

Main Summary:
Dr. Sullivan testifies about gender dysphoria and detransitioning cases. Her expertise and statistics highlight the rarity and risks of detransitioning, influencing the jury's perception. Courtroom dynamics intensify with juror reactions and judge interventions.

Discussion Questions:
- What role do expert witnesses play in shaping a jury's understanding of complex issues?
- How does Dr. Sullivan's testimony challenge or support the prosecution's case?
- How do courtroom reactions influence the perception of the trial?

Emotional Observations:
- Shock and surprise among jurors.
- Tension and anxiety in the courtroom.
- Cautious optimism from the defense team.

Key Elements:
- Expert testimony on gender dysphoria.
- Statistical evidence.
- Courtroom dynamics and procedural control.

Chapter 45: Witness – Ellen O'Brien

Main Summary:
Ellen O'Brien, Joey's former teacher, testifies about her interactions with Joey and the Cal Poly GLSEN meetings. Her testimony establishes the background context for Joey's experiences and Kate's involvement.

Discussion Questions:
- How does Ellen's testimony provide context for Joey's experience?
- What does her testimony reveal about the social and educational environment?
- How might this testimony influence the jury?

Emotional Observations:
- Emotional resonance due to personal connections with Joey.
- Nervousness from the witness under cross-examination.
- Sense of moral urgency in the courtroom.

Key Elements:
- Background of Joey's education and social interactions.
- GLSEN and its influence.
- Witness credibility and emotional impact.

Chapter 46: Witness – Ms. Meeks

Main Summary:
Ms. Meeks, a kindergarten teacher, testifies about Kate's interactions with a student, highlighting the emotional and behavioral responses of the child. Her testimony reinforces the prosecution's narrative of influence over minors.

Discussion Questions:
- How does Ms. Meeks' testimony impact perceptions of Kate's actions?
- What does the testimony reveal about child psychology and emotional responses?
- How does the defense manage the emotional weight of such testimony?

Emotional Observations:
- Tension from sensitive subject matter.
- Emotional empathy for the child involved.
- Anxiety from the defendants and their counsel.

Key Elements:
- Witness testimony on child behavior.
- Emotional weight of courtroom narratives.
- Defense and prosecution handling sensitive issues.

Chapter 47: Witness – Dr. Matt Heathcock

Main Summary:

Dr. Heathcock, an expert on gender dysphoria and legislation, testifies on historical perspectives and research. His credibility and expertise lend weight to discussions on age-appropriate gender affirmation.

Discussion Questions:
- How does Dr. Heathcock's expertise influence jury understanding of gender-related legislation?
- Why is historical context important in this case?
- How might the jury interpret conflicts between past and present research?

Emotional Observations:
- Admiration for expert credibility.
- Tension over controversial topics.
- Relief when clear expert testimony supports the defense strategy.

Key Elements:
- Expert witness credibility.
- Historical and legislative context.
- Gender dysphoria research impact.

Chapter 48: Evidence Submission

Main Summary:
Zach attempts to submit Dr. Heathcock's 1999 article as evidence. The prosecution objects, and the judge rules on courtroom decorum and procedural rules, demonstrating the tension around evidentiary strategy.

Discussion Questions:
- How does procedural strategy affect the presentation of evidence?
- What are the ethical considerations in submitting evidence at the last moment?
- How does the judge maintain courtroom order?

Emotional Observations:
- Tension and suspense in courtroom maneuvering.
- Anxiety over potential evidentiary rulings.
- Engagement of jurors and courtroom observers.

Key Elements:
- Evidence submission and objections.

• Judicial control of courtroom proceedings.
• Procedural strategy.

Chapter 49: Judge Rhinehart

Main Summary:
Judge Rhinehart asserts authority, ensuring proper courtroom conduct. He addresses both prosecution and defense, emphasizing decorum, and sets the tone for trial proceedings.

Discussion Questions:
• How does Judge Rhinehart's authority shape courtroom behavior?
• Why is maintaining decorum important in high-stakes trials?
• How do the judge's actions influence trial strategy?

Emotional Observations:
• Respect and tension under judicial authority.
• Anxiety for attorneys navigating strict rules.
• Awareness of procedural consequences.

Key Elements:
• Judicial authority and courtroom management.
• Legal protocol enforcement.
• Trial preparation and strategy.

Chapter 50: Defense Questioning

Main Summary:
Zach questions Dr. Heathcock about his past positions versus current stances on gender affirmation for minors.

The defense challenges credibility and legislative decisions, highlighting potential inconsistencies in expert testimony.

Discussion Questions:
- How does cross-examination reveal inconsistencies in expert testimony?
- Why is credibility central to a witness's influence on a jury?
- What strategies does the defense use to question legislative decisions?

Emotional Observations:
- Tension and anticipation during cross-examination.
- Anxiety from the potential impact on jury perception.
- Satisfaction when lines of questioning expose contradictions.

Key Elements:
- Cross-examination strategy.
- Witness credibility assessment.
- Legislative and research context.

Chapter 51: Reflections in the Judge's Chambers

Main Summary:

Emilio and Zach leave the judge's chambers, both reflecting on their roles and personal growth. Zach recalls Father John's early morning insights about "powers and principalities," which echo in his mind, suggesting that some battles extend beyond human opposition.

Discussion Questions:
- How does Father John's concept of "powers and principalities" influence Zach's perspective?

• What does the contrast between the confident prosecutor and the chastened Zach reveal about personal growth?
• How does reflection before action affect decision-making in high-stress situations?

Emotional Observations:
• Introspection and humility dominate Zach and Emilio's reflections.
• Tension is replaced by contemplative calm before the next day's proceedings.
• A subtle sense of awe and responsibility emerges

Key Elements:
• Judge's chambers as a reflective space.
• Father John's philosophical insight.
• Transformation of character demeanor under pressure.

Chapter 52: Dr. Heathcock on the Stand

Main Summary:
Zach calls Dr. Matt Heathcock to testify, probing his theory about "evidence revealing the need to act." Heathcock's weariness and hesitation reveal the challenge of defending complex theories under courtroom pressure.

Discussion Questions:
• How does Heathcock's demeanor affect his credibility with the jury?
• What does this testimony reveal about the intersection of education, theory, and practical application?
• How does Zach navigate the tension between technical complexity and lay understanding?

Emotional Observations:
- Anxiety and pressure are palpable in the courtroom.
- Tension mounts as attorneys and witnesses confront uncertainty.
- A sense of determination is evident in Zach's questioning style.

Key Elements:
- Testimony of Dr. Heathcock.
- Judicial procedures and courtroom tension.
- Exploration of complex theories in public testimony.

Chapter 53: McKenzie Stanfield and the HRC

Main Summary:

McKenzie Stanfield, president of the Human Rights Campaign, is questioned on her organization's relevance to the case. A petition from thousands of transgender individuals opposing Townsend's articles is introduced as evidence.

Discussion Questions:
- How does Stanfield's testimony illustrate the role of advocacy groups in legal proceedings?
- What is the significance of petitions in influencing jury perception?
- How does the courtroom handle objections regarding relevance?

Emotional Observations:
- Respect for Stanfield's authority and experience.
- Tension around the legal admissibility of evidence.
- Ethical and emotional weight of representing marginalized groups.

Key Elements:
• HRC's lobbying efforts and public influence.
• Introduction of petition evidence.
• Courtroom strategy and procedural challenges.

Chapter 54: Cassie Carmichael's Testimony Begins

Main Summary:
Cassie Carmichael testifies about Joey's death. A misstatement triggers courtroom tension, highlighting the emotional intensity of testimony and the fine line between grief and legal procedure.

Discussion Questions:
• How does courtroom procedure manage emotional testimonies?
• What role does careful phrasing play in legal testimony?
• How do the characters respond to grief while maintaining composure?

Emotional Observations:
• Grief and tension permeate the courtroom.
• Anger, frustration, and sympathy are intermingled in reactions.
• Emotional restraint is constantly tested.

Key Elements:
• Testimony regarding Joey's death.
• Courtroom management of emotional witnesses.
• Legal versus emotional accuracy.

Chapter 55: Sympathy and Legal Boundaries

Main Summary:

Zach expresses personal empathy toward Cassie, testing courtroom boundaries. Martinez's frustration highlights the delicate balance between emotional engagement and professional restraint.

Discussion Questions:

• How do lawyers balance empathy with legal strategy?
• What ethical questions arise when defense counsel expresses sympathy?
• How does personal experience shape courtroom interactions?

Emotional Observations:

• Deep empathy and sorrow are present.
• Tension between personal sentiment and procedural rules.
• Frustration and anxiety manifest in Martinez's reactions.

Key Elements:

• Defense counsel empathy.
• Courtroom objections and boundaries.
• Emotional vs. legal narratives.

Chapter 56: Family Support and Emotional Strain

Main Summary:

Lucinda reunites with the children while the extended group, including Zach, Toni, Lindsey, Rich, Steve, Morgan, LJ, and Father John, prepares for the next stage of the trial. The chapter highlights the tension between personal life and the high-stakes courtroom drama.

Discussion Questions:
- How does family presence influence the characters' emotional resilience?
- What role does Lucinda play as an emotional anchor for the children?
- How do the characters balance personal feelings with professional responsibilities?

Emotional Observations:
- A somber, reflective mood pervades the gathering.
- Subtle anxiety about trial outcomes.
- Comfort and reassurance are found in family connections.

Key Elements:
- Family dynamics amid crisis.
- Emotional preparedness for trial proceedings.
- Contrast between personal life and professional demands.

Chapter 57: Morgan's Frontline Presence

Main Summary:
Morgan asserts her desire to sit close in court to be noticed by Dr. Turner, reflecting her unique intuition and foresight. Zach and the others observe her unusual, almost mystical awareness in the courtroom setting.

Discussion Questions:
- How does Morgan's presence influence courtroom dynamics?
- What does this reveal about her character and psychic abilities?
- How does intuition intersect with legal strategy in the story?

Emotional Observations:
- Curiosity and intrigue at Morgan's foresight.
- Subtle tension as characters anticipate the courtroom proceedings.
- Admiration for Morgan's perceptiveness.

Key Elements:
- Strategic seating in court.
- Morgan's psychic insight.
- Observational nuances impacting courtroom perception.

Chapter 58: Medical Experts and Background Checks

Main Summary:
Lea and Samuel Sugarman insist on testifying. Their medical expertise and professional relationship with Kate and Steve provide credibility and context, reflecting the importance of trustworthy witnesses.

Discussion Questions:
- How do medical credentials affect courtroom persuasion?
- How do relationships outside the courtroom influence testimony?
- What ethical considerations arise from personal connections between witnesses and subjects?

Emotional Observations:
- Respect and camaraderie emerge in professional relationships.
- Subtle excitement over the potential relocation to Texas.
- Anticipation of the testimony's impact on the jury.

Key Elements:
• Use of expert witnesses.
• Interplay of personal and professional credibility.
• Preparations for strategic courtroom testimony.

Chapter 59: Detective Cindy Ralston Testifies

Main Summary:
Detective Ralston details the investigation into Joey
Carmichael's collapse and death. Her testimony establishes
the accidental nature of the death and provides clarity for
the jury on procedural and factual matters.

Discussion Questions:
• How does a detective's testimony lend credibility to case
  facts?
• How is the accidental nature of Joey's death emphasized?
• What does this testimony reveal about investigative
  thoroughness?

Emotional Observations:
• Authority and confidence in Ralston's presentation.
• Tension as the jury evaluates complex evidence.
• Relief as clarity emerges about the circumstances of Joey's
  death.

Key Elements:
• Investigation summary.
• Presentation of evidence in an understandable format.
• Role of law enforcement in courtroom proceedings.

Chapter 60: Martinez Reflects on Case Strategy

Main Summary:
Martinez faces internal conflict and external pressure as he contemplates losing the case. He reflects on interactions with colleagues and the impact on his personal life, highlighting professional vulnerability.

Discussion Questions:
- How does reflection on strategy reveal character depth?
- What does the interplay between professional reputation and personal consequences tell us?
- How do colleagues' expectations affect decision-making?

Emotional Observations:
- Frustration and anxiety pervade Martinez's thoughts.
- Subtle remorse and self-doubt emerge.
- Tension between personal and professional stakes.

Key Elements:
- Strategic reflection.
- Impact of colleagues and social networks on legal decision-making.
- Professional vulnerability and ethics.

Chapter 61: Dr. McCall and Professional Boundaries

Main Summary:
Zach questions Dr. McCall about her involvement in Kate's investigative series and professional decisions, highlighting nuances in personal communication, career obligations, and religious choices.

Discussion Questions:
- How does professional discretion affect relationships?
- What insights emerge about the balance between career and personal beliefs?
- How does prior knowledge or lack thereof impact trust between colleagues?

Emotional Observations:
- Respectful curiosity in dialogue.
- Subtle humor and camaraderie.
- Reflection on personal versus professional priorities.

Key Elements:
- Professional boundaries in investigations.
- Intersections of faith and career.
- Nuanced character interactions.

Chapter 62: Lucinda Seeks Reassurance

Main Summary:
Lucinda consults Father John about her fears regarding Kate's potential conviction, reflecting her anxiety about justice, truth, and personal responsibility.

Discussion Questions:
- How does mentorship and guidance provide emotional stability?
- What fears are most prominent for Lucinda, and how are they addressed?
- How does personal anxiety affect the perception of legal outcomes?

Emotional Observations:
- Heightened worry and vulnerability.

- Seeking comfort and insight from trusted advisors.
- Balance of fear and hope for justice.

Key Elements:
- Mentorship and counsel.
- Anxiety and personal stakes.
- Anticipation of legal outcomes.

Chapter 63: Rich Jansen's Closing Argument

Main Summary:
Rich delivers a closing argument, emphasizing the full story of Dr. Lindsey McCall's incarceration and challenging the prosecution's narrative.

Discussion Questions:
- How does firsthand experience enhance the persuasiveness of a closing argument?
- What rhetorical strategies does Rich employ to influence the jury?
- How is the contrast between the defense and prosecution narratives highlighted?

Emotional Observations:
- Determination and confidence in Rich's delivery.
- Courtroom tension as arguments unfold.
- Engagement and curiosity from the jury.

Key Elements:
- Defense closing argument.
- Strategic storytelling for legal persuasion.
- Ethical and factual emphasis in courtroom rhetoric.

Chapter 64: Sam Eldridge's Closing Argument

Main Summary:

Sam Eldridge presents the closing argument, framing the case for justice and highlighting the consequences of misrepresentation.

Discussion Questions:

- How does Eldridge reinforce the defense's narrative?
- What strategies are used to appeal to the jury's sense of fairness?
- How is legal and moral reasoning intertwined in the argument?

Emotional Observations:

- Poised and professional delivery.
- Emotional resonance through moral reasoning.
- Jury attention and reflection encouraged.

Key Elements:

- Final defense presentation.
- Moral and ethical framing.
- Jury-focused persuasion.

Chapter 65: Jury Deliberations Begin

Main Summary:

Jurors convene to discuss the case, weighing evidence and testimony to determine guilt or innocence. The chapter explores group dynamics, decision-making, and moral reasoning.

Discussion Questions:

- How do juror backgrounds influence deliberation?

- What dynamics emerge during group decision-making?
- How is the burden of proof internalized by jurors?

Emotional Observations:
- Tension and focus among jurors.
- Conflicting opinions and debate.
- Responsibility and seriousness in deliberation.

Key Elements:
- Jury deliberation process.
- Interpersonal dynamics and decision-making.
- Ethical considerations in weighing evidence.

Chapter 66: Zach and Martinez Reflect Post-Trial

Main Summary:
Zach and Martinez share a meal, reflecting on the trial, personal growth, and the influences that shaped them. Themes of mentorship, law, and personal memory emerge.

Discussion Questions:
- How does reflection outside the courtroom influence personal understanding?
- What role do mentors play in shaping professional and personal identity?
- How do small moments of reflection provide insight into character development?

Emotional Observations:
- Nostalgia and introspection.
- Gratitude for personal and professional influences.
- Calm after high-stress events.

Key Elements:
- Post-trial reflection.
- Mentorship and influence.
- Character growth and perspective.

Chapter 67: Jury Considers a Hung Verdict

Main Summary:
The jury debates the possibility of a hung verdict, with tension between expediency and moral obligation. Deliberation showcases varied approaches to justice and fairness.

Discussion Questions:
- How do jurors negotiate conflicting perspectives?
- What ethical considerations are highlighted in discussing a hung jury?
- How does peer pressure influence juror decisions?

Emotional Observations:
- Frustration and indecision among jurors.
- Tension regarding responsibility and fairness.
- Awareness of the gravity of their decision.

Key Elements:
- Internal jury debate.
- Ethical and practical implications.
- Conflicting moral reasoning.

Chapter 68: Not Guilty Verdict

Main Summary:
The jury returns a "Not guilty" verdict, reflecting careful

deliberation and justice served. The news impacts multiple characters professionally and personally.

Discussion Questions:
- How does the verdict affect each key character?
- What does this resolution say about the legal system and societal perception?
- How do individuals process relief and closure?

Emotional Observations:
- Joy, relief, and vindication.
- Reflection on personal and professional stakes.
- Emotional release after an intense trial.

Key Elements:
- Verdict announcement.
- Resolution of legal conflict.
- Emotional aftermath for all involved.

Chapter 69: Miracles and Departures

Main Summary:
The group departs San Francisco, reflecting on the miraculous outcomes of the trial and acknowledging the emotional journey they experienced.

Discussion Questions:
- How do characters interpret the outcome as miraculous?
- What is the role of faith and intuition in the story's resolution?
- How does travel and physical movement symbolize transition?

Emotional Observations:
• Gratitude and awe.
• Emotional reconciliation and relief.
• Subtle reflection on divine or extraordinary intervention.

Key Elements:
• Post-trial reflection and travel.
• Faith, intuition, and emotional closure.
• Symbolic journey and transition.

Chapter 70: Arrival in San Antonio

Main Summary:
Kate wakes up dazed after sleeping through the flight from San Francisco to San Antonio, processing the recent trial outcome and the "Not guilty" verdict. She reconnects with her family, particularly her young son Nicholas, and shares a tender moment with Steve, highlighting relief, love, and the grounding presence of family after a highly stressful legal ordeal.

Discussion Questions:
• How does Kate's reaction to waking up reflect her emotional state post-trial?
• What role do family connections play in helping her process relief and recovery?
• How does this moment underscore the personal stakes of the trial?

Emotional Observations:
• Dazed relief and disbelief at the trial's resolution.
• Warmth and tenderness in reconnecting with family.
• Subtle anxiety mixed with joy about regained freedom.

Key Elements:
• Transition from stress to post-trial relief.
• Family as emotional anchor.
• Reflection on freedom, safety, and love.

Chapter 71: Moving to a New Home

Main Summary:
Steve experiences disorientation at the new house, coping with the stress of a move immediately following the trial. Themes of change and personal adaptation emerge.

Discussion Questions:
• How does disorientation reflect the psychological aftermath of high-stress events?
• What role does the environment play in processing recent experiences?
• How do characters navigate sudden life transitions?

Emotional Observations:
• Fatigue and bewilderment dominate Steve's perspective.
• Subtle humor in coping with unexpected change.
• Anticipation of settling into a new environment.

Key Elements:
• Adjusting to a new home.
• Psychological impact of change.
• Physical environment as a reflection of internal state.

Chapter 72: Architectural Appreciation

Main Summary:
Steve tours his new home, absorbing the design details and

elegance. Appreciation of aesthetics reflects personal taste and the significance of thoughtful living spaces.

Discussion Questions:
- How does architecture influence emotional state?
- What does Steve's reaction reveal about his character?
- How do physical surroundings reinforce thematic elements of stability and comfort?

Emotional Observations:
- Awe and admiration.
- Calm curiosity and engagement with surroundings.
- Appreciation for craftsmanship and design.

Key Elements:
- Architectural and interior details.
- Symbolism of home and personal space.
- Emotional impact of the environment.

Chapter 73: Receiving Line for Kate

Main Summary:
Kate is greeted by family, colleagues, and supporters in an orchestrated receiving line, highlighting the personal impact of professional achievements and recognition.

Discussion Questions:
- How does ceremonial recognition affect characters emotionally?
- What role do social rituals play in acknowledging accomplishments?
- How does this moment serve as a narrative resolution?

Emotional Observations:
- Joy and pride in recognition.
- Warmth and communal support.
- Emotional complexity of personal versus public acknowledgment.

Key Elements:
- Receiving line and social acknowledgment.
- Emotional closure for key characters.
- Celebration of achievement and resilience.

Chapter 74: College Station and Home Life

Main Summary:

Morgan and LJ arrive at College Station, acclimating to a new climate, exploring their new home, and preparing meals. The chapter emphasizes friendship, domesticity, and adjustment after a stressful period.

Discussion Questions:
- How does adapting to a new environment reflect personal growth?
- How do friendship and collaboration support emotional well-being?
- How are mundane tasks (like cooking) used to reinforce narrative resolution?

Emotional Observations:
- Relief and contentment after stress.
- Bonding and playful interaction between friends.
- Reflective calm amid routine activities.

Key Elements:
- Domestic routines and friendship.

• Adjustment to the new climate and home.
• Reflection on recent events and personal growth.

6. Reader Discussion Questions

Use these to guide meaningful conversation:

1. Who were the "plausible liars" in this story?

2. How does the title reflect the behavior of the characters?

3. Did Lindsey make the right decisions, even when they put her in danger?

4. Where would you have made different choices?

5. Which part of the medical mystery felt most believable and why?

6. Did the book change the way you think about medical accountability or government secrecy?

7. How did the author balance emotional storytelling with scientific/medical detail?

8. Were you surprised by the final revelations?

9. What did you suspect earlier?

10. What role did fear, pressure, or loyalty play in the characters' decisions?

11. If this were adapted into a film or series, which scenes stand out as the most cinematic?

7. Book Trailer

Trailer Link:
https://tinyurl.com/PlausibleBookTrailer

CUSTOMIZED READER DISCUSSION GUIDE PREPARED BY:
SCOTT ANDERSON, ORGANIZER, CHICAGO LGBTQ BOOK CLUB
MEETUP, CHICAGO, IL, USA

SNEAK PREVIEW OF LIN WILDER'S NEXT NOVEL

One Smooth Stone

PROLOGUE

Save me, O G-d, for the waters threaten to engulf me …

I am wearied by my calling out, and my throat is dry. I've lost hope in waiting …

More numerous than the hairs on my head are those who hate me without reason …

Must I then repay what I have not stolen?

Mighty are those who would cut me down, who are my enemies without cause …

O G-d, You know my folly, and my unintended wrongs are not hidden from You …

It is for Your sake that I have borne disgrace, that humiliation covers my face

I have become a stranger to my brothers, an alien to my mother's sons.

Out of envy for Your House, they ravaged me; the disgraces of those who revile You have fallen upon me …

Those who sit by the gate talk about me. I am the taunt of drunkards …

Disgrace breaks my heart, and I am left deathly sick.

I hope for solace, but there is none; and for someone to comfort me, but I find no one.

They put gall into my meal, and give me vinegar to quench my thirst.

My son. My son.

My heart breaks for you.

And yet, I am in awe of the gifts Our God has so liberally showered upon David, this eighth son of Jesse. Never have you murmured against your father or siblings. Nor have you lamented the isolation and danger you faced daily as a shepherd for Jesse's flocks. Instead, my son, you have gloried in the solitude and meanness of your surroundings, using your beautiful voice and handmade lyre to praise the Lord, Creator of all.

"Hear, O Israel: G-d is our L-rd, G-d is one."

I am called Nitzevet, wife of Jesse and mother of seven sons. My husband and your brothers deny you, my eighth son, and my sons consider me an adultress. In fact, only by the gracious mercy of the God of Abraham, Isaac, and Jacob were you and I allowed to live.

Your father Jesse is head of the Sanhedrin. A position that, at first, he wore lightly. But each time I gave birth to another son, doubts about his ancestry's legitimacy simmered and finally came to a boil.

You see, your great-grandmother is Ruth, the Moabite, wife of Boaz, and mother of your grandfather, Obed. Because the Moabites forbade our purchasing food or drink while traveling through their land during the exodus, the Torah forbids marriage to Moabites. Boaz, known as a prince among the people, sought and was granted permission from the elders to marry Ruth because it was understood the Law forbade male converts, but not female. Women were exempted. But Boaz died the day after the wedding was consummated, and Ruth conceived Obed. To some of the sages, this indicates the illegitimacy of the marriage.

Finally, after the birth of our seventh son Odem, Jesse quietly divorced me. And planned to lie with our maidservant, a Cannanite, whom he hoped would bear him a son with unquestionably Jewish blood. But Donitaya, knowing of my great misery, refused. Instead, she helped me prepare myself with her clothing and fragrance so that Jesse would believe it was she he lay with.

Jesse's rage was almost without bounds when he learned of my deception. But the Lord took mercy on us, my son, and we were permitted to live. Only in your twenty-eighth year has your father learned of your grace, nobility, and greatness. And now, so will the world.